CRIMINAL CITIES

CULTURAL FRAMES, FRAMING CULTURE
Robert Newman, Editor
Justin Neuman, Associate Editor

CRIMINAL CITIES

THE POSTCOLONIAL NOVEL AND CATHARTIC CRIME

MOLLY SLAVIN

UNIVERSITY OF VIRGINIA PRESS
Charlottesville and London

University of Virginia Press
© 2023 by the Rector and Visitors of the University of Virginia
All rights reserved
Printed in the United States of America on acid-free paper

First published 2023

ISBN 978-0-8139-4956-7 (cloth)
ISBN 978-0-8139-4957-4 (paper)
ISBN 978-0-8139-4958-1 (ebook)

1 3 5 7 9 8 6 4 2

Library of Congress Cataloging-in-Publication Data is available for this title.

Cover art: Gremlin/istock.com

CONTENTS

Preface: Atlanta as Postcolonial Criminal City | *vii*

Introduction: Toward a Theory of Cathartic Crime … 1

1. "The Phenomenon of Walking": Mapping Postcolonial Criminal London … 19
2. "Crime Is Crime Is Crime": Belfast and Universalizing Narratives … 48
3. Whiteness, Historical Fiction, and Australian Cities … 73
4. "Shot through with Crime": Bombay after Mumbai … 98
5. Neoliberal Criminality: Post-Apartheid Johannesburg … 124
6. "This Line Created a Country": Nairobi, Father and Son … 151
7. "His Memory Resists Ordering": The Difficulty of Catharsis in Palestine … 177

Coda: *Exit West*, Brexit, and Migration … 199

Notes | *211*
Bibliography | *225*
Index | *241*

PREFACE
—
Atlanta as Postcolonial Criminal City

"Despite the growing reach of Atlanta's rapid transit network, the system's trains and buses do not cross the county line into the booming suburbs north of the city—because the governments there have not wanted them," William E. Schmidt writes in the *New York Times*. "Now, the top transit official here has ignited a controversy by saying that the refusal of the two northern counties [Cobb and Gwinnett] to join the Atlanta system was the direct result of racial fear and animosity." Schmidt's feature on the limitations of MARTA—the Metropolitan Atlanta Rapid Transit Authority—goes on to track how racist attitudes and white flight have stymied the growth of public transportation in Atlanta, and how opponents of increased service often rely on the barely coded and lightly dog-whistled rhetoric of crime. "A bumper sticker sometimes seen on Cobb County cars reads: 'Share Atlanta Crime—Support Marta,'" Schmidt notes, and he quotes the chairman of MARTA, J. David Chestnut, as saying that "whites in the prosperous suburbs of Cobb and Gwinnett Counties fear that Marta's sleek trains and buses will bring blacks and crime from the inner city into their communities." Schmidt's article was written in 1987.

Twenty-five years later, I moved to Atlanta, Georgia, the city I now call home, to attend graduate school at Emory University. One day before I moved into my new apartment near the campus, metro Atlanta voters rejected a proposal (the T-SPLOST) to build an expansive new public transportation system in a city planned for cars and well known for its traffic gridlock. Atlanta was (and still is) changing very rapidly from its "Old South" image to a multiethnic city of transplants and young people, and many long-term citizens and newcomers wanted an updated and modern infrastructure to reflect these changes. As a graduate student who lacked much disposable income, I did not have a car, and the T-SPLOST would have benefited my life enormously. Because it was voted down, however, I soon became well acquainted with MARTA, which remained Atlanta's notoriously limited and unreliable public transportation system.

People (white people, to be specific) were often aghast when they heard I took MARTA to my destination. "But aren't you *scared?*" I would hear, over and over. "Is it *safe?*" Of course, they were not asking if the bus drivers were obeying traffic laws or if the rail system was up to code: just like the suburban white voters of twenty-five years prior, they were expressing anxieties about crime, and pointedly, racially coded crime. I began meeting more and more native Atlantans as I settled into my new city, who told me that in the run-up to the T-SPLOST vote, the anti-referendum side relied heavily on rhetorics of crime to dissuade people from voting for a measure that would have substantially improved the city in which they lived. A poll commissioned by the *Atlanta Journal-Constitution* revealed that 42 percent of respondents believed increased public transportation would lead to increased crime, and, anecdotally, one resident told me that when he tried to convince several of his neighbors to vote for the proposal, he was informed that people "from southwest Atlanta" would use the trains to come to his neighborhood of Buckhead to "steal TVs"—he remembers very specifically that his neighbors were afraid of their televisions in particular being stolen. In what should come as no surprise, "southwest Atlanta" is majority Black, while Buckhead is overwhelmingly white.[1]

Atlanta is, as all cities are, unique and shaped by its particular historical, social, economic, and cultural forces. In particular, some of the major forces shaping Atlanta are the legacies of slavery and how those contribute to the past and present situation of African Americans in the city, which W. E. B. Du Bois, bell hooks, and Henry Louis Gates (among others) have situated as a kind of internal colonialism. Atlanta carries a direct link to many other "post"-colonial cities around the world in its treatment of subaltern populations, and specifically the ways in which ghosts of past racist and imperial structures, attitudes, and institutions continue to influence the contemporary city. In the case of Atlanta, and its public transportation woes specifically, we see issues that link back to slavery, integration, Jim Crow, and even Georgia's status as a penal colony during the era of the British Empire. In the case of 2012 in particular, we may even see burgeoning anxieties surrounding Atlanta's growing place as a center for refugee resettlement, as many of those who are resettled from postcolonial African and Asian nations live in suburban peripheries where rent is cheap but public transportation is not always readily available.

Robert Young has written that one of the key goals of the field of postcolonialism has always been "to locate the hidden rhizomes of colonialism's historical reach, of what remains invisible, unseen, silent, or unspoken. In a sense, postcolonialism has always been about the ongoing life of residues, living remains, lingering legacies" (21). In a microcosmic, Atlanta-specific context, we can see here rhizomes and dynamics of crime, racism, colonialism, and cities playing out in real time, and in a way that is ostensibly silent or unspoken but that is clearly understood by all those in reach of its rhetoric.

Edward W. Soja has written in *Seeking Spatial Justice* (2010) of phenomena like these that it is "fear of potential invasion and violence by what the more powerful perceive as threatening 'others' [that] drives all these processes of spatial control" (44); this democratic T-SPLOST referendum was, essentially, a very effective method of ostensibly democratic spatial control over what many deemed to be "their" territory, "their" public space, "their" city. The referendum failing was a ghostly reminder of the history of Atlanta cropping up in the present, following the logic of racial capitalism: reminders of slavery and Jim Crow, of the need to keep colonial structures in place and the races apart, with crime acting as an explanation for this supposed need. I offer this initial vignette of a postcolonial Atlanta as one example of the many ways crime, cities, colonialism, and changing cultures can work together to produce a narrative that is so instantly recognizable to so many in the twenty-first century. Much as the worry about stolen televisions was fiction (obviously no one is going to steal a television and escape on a train), it is often fiction where we can see these kinds of anxieties most clearly expressed and most creatively rebutted. In the pages that follow, I use my particular placement in the postcolonial city of Atlanta to inform my readings of global postcolonial urban novels and arrive at a theory of why crime (and by extension, mobility) is so centric to these novels and what we, as contemporary readers of fiction and literature, can do with our reading experiences.

I've now lived in Atlanta for over a decade, and the city has seen a lot of changes in the time I have been here. I wrote the initial draft of this preface in the lead-up to the 2019 Super Bowl, which came accompanied by increased MARTA service and a renewed conversation on the importance of public transportation for a twenty-first-century city. Some tangible improvements have been made in Atlanta; there is a growing urbanism movement in the city that is focused on combating gentrification and improving transportation in historically underserved neighborhoods, and in March 2018 the metro area passed a referendum that will allegedly provide for increased regional public transportation.[2] There might be some hope—however faint—that a new consensus about whom Atlanta is for might be emerging, and we may see that consensus continue to grow in power and volume in the months and years ahead. Let us hope that is true not just for Atlanta, but for all postcolonial global cities.

I owe a great debt to so many people for helping me see literature, theory, culture, crime, and cities in new and fascinating lights. My husband, John Larsen, has been the most important figure in my life through graduate school, postdoctoral fellowship, and now assistant professorship, gently urging me to love Atlanta the whole way. (He's finally succeeded.) Our son, Jack, and our dog, Mimz, have been endless sources of joy, love, and meandering walks through the Old Fourth Ward. Jack, I love spending time with you and can't wait to see the person you grow to become and how you choose to inhabit the city of your birth. (Mimz, we have a pretty good idea of who you are and how you use space at this point.)

I would like to thank my parents, Ann and Tim Slavin, for their love and support through all my academic endeavors, and for their many visits to Atlanta where we were able to discuss art, historic preservation, and that all-important municipal urban issue, garbage pickup. My sister, Maggie Slavin, and her boundless passion for and knowledge of Arabic and Western Asian culture have helped shaped my readings on Palestinian literature.

Thank you to my dissertation readers and mentors, Drs. Deepika Bahri, Geraldine Higgins, and Nathan Suhr-Sytsma, for reading what were assuredly terrible drafts of these chapters when I had absolutely no idea what I was doing, and for shaping them into something passable and legible. Thank you to my graduate school cohort, especially Drs. Corey Goergen and Sumita Chakraborty, and my extra-cohort friends, Drs. Josh Cohen, Maggie Greaves, Lindsey Grubbs, Sarah Harsh, Emily Leithauser, Rebecca McGlynn, Marlo Starr, and Marion Tricoire, for their friendship, kindness, and Manuel's times. (Frankly, also thank you to Manuel's Tavern/the Maloof family in general.) Thank you to the wonderful community of Brittain Fellows, who read drafts of this introduction and helped organize my thoughts on so many occasions, and for all the pints at Cypress Street and the now-closed Canteen. Thank you to the leadership of the Brittain Fellowship and for the School of Literature, Media, and Communication at Georgia Tech for helping to support my work through research grants and awards. Thank you so much to Dr. Kevin Gallin, whom I met either at a dorm party or in a psychoanalysis seminar at Notre Dame (who on earth knows), and who has served as that all-important companion for so many of those "So what are you doing now?" questions from college friends.

And of course, thank you so much to everyone at the University of Virginia Press: Justin Neuman, Angie Hogan, and all the readers and reporters who read drafts of this book and gave such helpful feedback to make it publishable. Along those same lines, thank you to Katie Van Heest of Tweed Academic Editing, who was incredibly helpful in moving this manuscript from "dissertation" to "book."

Thanks to the city of Atlanta, and all the friends and family I have made here, for everything.

CRIMINAL CITIES

INTRODUCTION
TOWARD A THEORY OF CATHARTIC CRIME

In one of the most famous and widely read postcolonial urban novels of all time, 1981's *Midnight's Children* by Salman Rushdie, events of the plot are set into motion when a midwife in Mumbai, Mary Pereira, switches two children of differing social classes at birth. Everything that happens after this event is only made possible by Mary's action, which the narrator of the novel designates a "crime" consistently throughout the novel.[1] Mary's "crime" makes possible events in the narrator's personal life, as well as events of national and international significance like the Bangladesh war of independence in 1971 and India's Emergency of 1975–77. The entire novel, narrative, plot structure, character development, and literary technique of magical realism are only possible due to, and indeed hinge directly on, Mary's crime; the crime is totally central to every element of the text, and creates the conditions that make Rushdie's exploration of postcolonial Mumbai, Delhi, and other South Asian urban spaces possible.

This book examines how postcolonial cities have been defined by what authors and audiences label as crime, and explores how contemporary novels set in postcolonial cities use crime as a central narrative trope and a way to negotiate imperial legacies and continuing structures of violence. By asking how crime is defined, and why it is so central to postcolonial literature and the contemporary urban experience, *Criminal Cities* looks at the contemporary novels set within seven Anglophone postcolonial cities in places as varied as Africa (Kenya and South Africa), India, the West Bank, Australia, Ireland, and the United Kingdom itself through the lens of what I am terming "cathartic crime."

"Cathartic crime" is a way to understand crime, as depicted in literary texts and specifically novels, as a route for literary characters to experience collective social catharsis and to urge readers to participate in social and political life. This form of catharsis shifts according to context—in some cases, it may be expressed as a dominant population's anxieties over crime, while in another, it may look like a subaltern population experiencing oppression due to being labeled as "criminals"—but the common structural theme that translates across all cities and sites is the idea of crime as a receptacle for larger cultural and structural attitudes and formations, like racial capitalism, ongoing segregation, colonial urban planning, and rhetorics over violence. Essentially, all stories are crime stories; in much literary fiction, crime features as a central topic or a hinge on which everything else rests, and *Criminal Cities* explores why this is so. In other words, I argue for the necessity of reading depictions of crimes *in* literature—not necessarily crime literature—as receptive sites for anxieties and fears surrounding literary, philosophical, material, and political changes in urban environments.

The way we talk about, construct, and depict crime tends to reflect what society in general is feeling. Fredric Jameson has argued for "the priority of the political interpretation of literary texts" (*Political Unconscious*, 17) and has written that literature may be read as a "symbolic meditation on the destiny of a community" (70); I am generally borrowing from this idea to argue that crime is a form of collective or political unconscious, especially for postcolonial novels set in cities. As Jameson says, "We never really confront a text immediately, in all its freshness as a thing-in-itself. Rather, texts come before us as the always-already-read; we apprehend them through sedimented layers of previous interpretations, or—if the text is brand-new—through the sedimented reading habits and categories developed by those inherited interpretive traditions" (9). The often "brand-new" contemporary texts studied in *Criminal Cities* are approached by readers, then, through "sedimented layers" of ideas surrounding crime, cities, race, gender, and other imperial formations and residues.

Correspondingly, literary depictions of crimes often reflect back the tensions, nostalgias, or disquiet felt, consciously or unconsciously, among larger populations, both dominant and subaltern. These populations will experience crime in vastly different ways; privileged classes will often place a high emphasis on property crime or other crimes against capital, out of fear of losing their position in society, while subaltern populations will have to deal more often with their behaviors being coded as crimes by a colonialist society, as at the same time they are confronted by crimes of violence, hate crimes, and targeted crimes against identity. The common denominator, however, is that crime is used in the postcolonial city-centric novel as a way to work through and negotiate legacies of empire: to achieve a kind of emotional catharsis, whatever that means for the relevant population. By seeing how characters in novels experience cathartic crime, we as readers in the body politic can become more attuned to reflect and act upon how we see similar patterns in the "real world."

Thinking of narrative catharsis as a general outlet for real-world collective anger and unease goes back as far as Aristotle. In *Poetics*, he writes that tragedy, as "an imitation of an action that is serious, complete, and of a certain magnitude," can, "through pity and fear," allow the audience to experience a "proper purgation of these emotions." In other words, if social tensions are ratcheting up to the point where a political assassination seems imminent, staging a play where characters kill the king will allow the audience to undergo catharsis and not actually kill the king in real life. Under this definition, catharsis is a top-down tool meant to keep the crowd's violent tensions at bay. Though I am not writing about tragedy or drama in a classical sense, I note this because literature still often acts as an imaginative site for reflecting social tensions, though it may not have the same directive or charge as the Aristotelian formation; in fact, I argue in many cases that cathartic crime has the exact *reverse* effect, as it can, instead of purging emotions, play the role of alerting readers and the larger body politic to systemic injustices and colonial oppressions in hopes of leading to societal change.

Georg Lukács writes of the development of the novel that "our" modern world—the world constitutive of and created by the novel—"has become infinitely large and each of its corners is richer in gifts and dangerous than the world of the Greeks, but such wealth cancels out the positive meaning—the totality—upon which their life was based" (34). While I do not know if we can quantify how "large" or "rich" or "dangerous" our lives are compared to those of the ancient Greeks, Lukács's corollary point underscores how conceptions of catharsis have changed since Aristotle, and how the idea might be adapted for the contemporary world and the novel in particular.

"For totality," Lukács writes, "as the formative reality of every individual phenomenon implies that something closed within itself can be completed; completed because everything occurs within it, nothing is excluded from it and nothing points at a higher reality outside it; completed because everything within it ripens to its own perfect and, by attaining itself, submits to limitation" (34). The type of "totality" available to the ancient Greeks, who, Lukács argues, experienced the world through epic, is not available to modern and contemporary people in the same way; as such, conceptions of catharsis available to the ancient Greeks, including Aristotle's "proper purgation of... emotions," are not as readily available in the modern world[2] and to modern readers.

And this, according to Lukács, is where the novel comes in. "The beginning and the end of the world of a novel," writes Lukács, "which are determined by the beginning and end of the process which supplies the content of the novel, thus become significant landmarks along a clearly mapped road" (81). The novel maps onto the world, provides it a kind of structure and totality and narrative drive that Lukács argues is missing from the world outside the text. This is why "that totality—the novel—[is] the representative art-form of our age: because the structural categories of the novel constitutively coincide with the world as it is today" (Lukács 93).[3] The novel, then, is an attempt to impose totality and structure on the world; I argue that it is through the form that the possibility for catharsis becomes available once again, especially for a postcolonial urban world.

If it is true, as Frantz Fanon writes, that "the colonized subject discovers reality and transforms it through his praxis, his deployment of violence and his agenda for liberation" (21), it seems logical to conclude that cathartic crime in the novel provides the kind of violent purgative or reparative function Fanon and other anticolonial theorists were seeking. Though Fanon also argues "it is obvious that in colonial countries only the peasantry is revolutionary" (23), I seek to move the conversation to the city, the quintessential space of modernity and colonialism. It is in the city where, of course, the most people live, but it is also where discourses of imperialism, crime, race, economics, and history are also the most densely packed and thus the most ripe for exploration. According to Jameson, "The political, [which is] no longer visible in the high modernist texts, any more than in the everyday world of appearance of bourgeois life, and relentlessly driven underground by accumulated reification, has at last become a genuine Unconscious" (*Political*

Unconscious, 280). This "genuine Unconscious," especially in the city, is, I argue, now experienced largely through discourses of crime; crime is the lens through which many urban dwellers view their environments and attempt to make some kind of sense of the world around them. This is especially true in postcolonial cities, places that are still trying to make sense of the crime of colonialism and negotiate its lingering effects; reading literary cathartic crime provides a way to translate how the crimes of colonialism have affected the city into a novelistic, narrative form.

Fictional narratives such as novels offer that kind of world-making and capability, by imposing a structure on the city and presenting a teleology or trajectory to track. The closure of a narrative by solving a crime has the potential to give the reader satisfaction, to feel as though boxes have been checked and order has been restored to the city. But, as Jameson says in *Raymond Chandler and the Detections of Totality*, "closure—the achievement of a sense of narrative totality—must not be confused with the merely formal ending or conclusion of a work" (52). He goes on: "Although it is nowhere very explicitly argued (Barthes comes closest in various passing remarks), the suggestion is that a work or a narrative is felt to be completed when it has been able to touch all the bases in some underlying semiotic system; that unconscious cognitive acknowledgement of systematicity is then transferred to the surface of the work of art, which can be pronounced in one way or another a full form, a completed thing" (73). This sense of "completion" or "closure" might be, as Jameson says, visible on "the surface of the work," but in the postcolonial novel, collective histories are consistently lurking under the surface and threatening to undo any sense of closure or completion accomplished by the logic or order imposed by the narrative tracking of a crime. Paul K. Saint-Amour writes, "In part because of its insistently literal return, the traumatic past remains transgressively present as revenant, haunting, or possession, dominating the present rather than receding as it should into the past" (14). In the postcolonial urban novel, crime is resonant of "the traumatic past" of the crimes of colonialism, and catharsis depends on confronting what remains "transgressively present." Whereas for Aristotle, catharsis works to focus drama away from "its social meanings" and turn the lens instead on "its effect on individual persons" (duBois 305), cathartic crime looks towards the polis, the city, rather than the individual. Page duBois charges Aristotle's form of catharsis with "a turn away from the collective" and "toward internalization" (305); the postcolonial urban novel attempts to speak to the collective through a structure around cathartic crime, and invites its readers in to create meaning and change in their worlds as well.

The societal change we seek can only come about by squarely confronting colonial legacies and imperial presents still at work in our cities, and catharsis is one of the most powerful ways to take on this challenge. Richard Kearney holds that catharsis, as "one of the most enduring functions of narrative" (51), is utilized in fiction as a way to uncover painful truths, and I use this idea as another foundation for the concept of cathartic crime. Colonial and postcolonial cities often act as palimpsest, where layers of history act simultaneously with each other to produce urban sites that are bewildering, joyful, maddening, and exasperating all at once. By reading representations of crime in the city, we can reveal these imperial legacies, as well as the continuing imperial and racial capitalism that still structures and maps these urban sites. Crime, and a reader's attention to it, can help the characters in novels (consciously or unconsciously) map and negotiate the city, as well as assist readers in making sense of complex and variegated texts. For example, thinking about Salman Rushdie's *Midnight's Children* and *The Moor's Last Sigh* by considering the Bombay/Mumbai criminal "underworld" turns up interesting meditations on continuing British impact in the city, and reading Jean Rhys's *Wide Sargasso Sea* through the lens of violent crime like murder and rape brings up interesting questions of complicity in slavery and colonial trafficking, as well as all of these crimes' ramifications for today. More completely understanding crime in novels as readers helps us as citizens to understand crime and colonialism in real life and in our real cities.

This reading strategy, of course, brings up questions of audience, reception, and privilege. Marian Eide, writing of what she calls "the violent aesthetic," notes that such an aesthetic "engages me in an imaginative response to existing political conditions that challenge my complacent sense of justice. But it is in my peculiar belief that my *particular* reaction could be the *universal* response that the communal work of witnessing begins to take hold, that the private aesthetic response becomes a political (in the widest sense) process" (19). She asks, "Is this bourgeois optimism? Maybe" (20), but argues that this transmutation from the individual to the political can lend itself to wider political work and material societal transformation. Jameson muses on something similar when he writes in *The Political Unconscious*, "The need to transcend individualistic categories and modes of interpretation is in many ways the fundamental issue for any doctrine of the political unconscious, of interpretation in terms of the collective or associative" (68). I hold that, through reading, internalizing, and acting on cathartic crime in the postcolonial urban novel, we can in fact do the kind of collective political work Eide and Jameson write about.

Cathartic crime can present fantasy outcomes for a city worried about its future (a superhero story where Batman or Superman catches and punishes the criminals), or it can be weaponized to whip up fear of vulnerable populations (such as the reprehensible Jean Raspail novel *The Camp of the Saints,* which has recently come into conversation again, given the text's popularity among a variety of Western fascists). I do not describe the various forms cathartic crime can take to claim that it always works for the benefit of justice; rather, I am identifying cathartic crime as a common theme of the postcolonial novel, and when done well, it urges action that will benefit subaltern populations. Even when the novel stops short of this, however (as it often does), cathartic crime still does *something;* the shortcoming can be strategic, or it can have harmful political tendencies, but both evoke thought and concern in the attentive and careful reader. Regardless of intent or outcome, however, cathartic crime in literature usually carries a teleological charge—there is a sense that when the crime is solved, the novel will be over and tension will abate—and is often tied up with logics of mobility and transportation, all while being framed as a search for social cohesion and narrative closure.[4] Because "the novel is concerned, above all, with carving shapes out of history, with imposing a beginning, a middle and an end on the flux of experience" (Bergonzi 13), novels intimately concerned with crime map onto this need to make sense of history and, in so doing, guide us through movement and mobility throughout the city: novels, like physical journeys, help frame experiences as having "a beginning, a middle and an end" in search of catharsis and consistency.[5] Whether this cathartic social cohesion leads to a reactionary mob mentality or a more generous form of cosmopolitanism differs from novel to novel and city to city (crime is understood and processed differently in London than in the West Bank), but theoretical similarities resonate among urban sites and literatures. It is comforting to understand narrative, as well as physical journeys, as having a clear trajectory that culminates in a satisfying conclusion: crime offers an excellent narrative arc onto which readers and members of the body politic can map anxieties, histories, fears, hopes, and understandings of urban environments.

"Crime" in the way we currently talk about it—as a social construction meant to regulate and punish offenses against laws that are enforced by some governmental body—transitioned away from "sin" in early modern England

and was spread, as a concept, along with the British Empire throughout its colonies.[6] Crime in the modern sense began, as Andrew Pepper points out, with "the establishment of the modern state system" or "the publication of Thomas Hobbes's *Leviathan* (1653)" (4), both modern-era-defining events that situated ideas of authority and crime firmly in the secular and with social-contract-agreed-upon authorities like the state and police forces. Conceptions of crime have shifted and changed in the centuries since, but, like the novel and imperialism, rhetorics and concerns about crime are part of the general stew of modernity and Enlightenment discourses, especially as they relate to other notions of individualism born out of this time period, such as the sanctification of private property.[7] Discourses over crime typically reach their height when that other quintessential site of modernity, cities or large urban spaces, is concerned: there is a long-standing tradition of understanding the city as particularly dangerous, as riddled with criminals, in all literary and cultural traditions that I look at in *Criminal Cities*. Particularly relevant to this study on postcolonialism and its afterlives are the myriad stereotypes that ascribe virulent and special criminality to people of color, oppressed populations, or those who lack financial, social, or political capital. The data doesn't bear any of these anxieties out—there is no evidence that either cities or the structurally disadvantaged are more criminal than anyone else (in fact, data usually actually points the exact opposite way)—but that particular bit of cultural imagination is strong enough that many readers will instinctively understand the narrative, and, indeed, it is both endorsed and rebuffed in many of the novels looked at in this text.[8]

What exactly do I mean by crime? For the terms of this project, I use "crime" to mean any action that violates law in the particular place where a character is operating. In postcolonial societies "law" is, of course, colonially mandated and constructed, meaning that actions understood to be crimes are part and parcel of the construction of the colonial capitalist state. Marx has noted that "the criminal not only produces crime but also the criminal law. . . . The criminal moreover produces the whole apparatus of the police and of criminal justice, constables, judges, executioners, juries, etc.; and all these different lines of business, which form equally many of the categories of the social division of labor" (52). Essentially, Marx is arguing that crime is necessary for the capitalist state, and in turn becomes integral to political, economic, and cultural life; this central role that socially constructed visions of crime and the associated "criminal justice" apparatus plays in the "real world" is negotiated through knotty and complex literary texts. This Marxist understanding of the production and experience of crime underlies *Criminal Cities*'s understanding of crime; this book is also, correspondingly, indebted to Fredric Jameson's insistence on the "political interpretation of literary texts" (*Political Unconscious*, 17) and "doctrine of a political unconscious" (20), as well as Michel Foucault's construction of the criminal as a "scapegoat" (259) or "pathologized subject" (277) who, forced into a corner by macro power machinations, serves a necessary (deemed so by the dominant population) social role. Crime—from how it gets defined to who gets punished to how we talk about it—is political, and often points to ideas and fears and hopes society alludes to but does not speak aloud.

Émile Durkheim notes that crime "consists of an action which offends certain collective feelings which are especially strong and clear-cut" (99). With respect to Durkheim, I argue something different here: that "crime" provokes very different reactions based on individual subject positions. In a neoliberal and postcolonial context, there is no bank of "certain collective feelings," but rather a constellation of splintered and differentiated feelings about the same subject that the novel attempts to gather together into a unified social narrative.[9] Given that crime crosses social boundaries, it is an especially intriguing way to explore literature, and specifically, the postcolonial novel, as a way to understand the literary, cultural, and political underpinnings that are contained inside the finished product. Jean and John L. Comaroff build on this notion of the collectivity or the social construction of crime by arguing that crime, in the twenty-first century, "has become *the* metaphysical optic by means of which people across the planet understand and act upon their worlds" (*Truth about Crime*, 8, italics original). This notion of the central importance of crime in helping to structure or shape the way individuals view and act in society is integral to my point that crime acts as a kind of collective social negotiation of the city. By asking not only "Why are crimes so prominently featured in these literary novels?" but also "What is the meaning of the crimes that are written?," I hold that we can better understand novels that rely heavily on depictions of crime, as well as unlock new insights into the cities from which they emerge.

The city is one of the key focal points for the study of imperialism and postcolonialism. In *Edge of Empire: Postcolonialism and the City*, Jane M. Jacobs writes of the postcolonial city that it is "an important component in the spatiality of imperialism. It was in outpost cities that the spatial order of imperial imaginings was rapidly and deftly realized" (4). This "spatial order of imperial imaginings" was first fleshed out by Frantz Fanon in *The Wretched of the Earth*, when he famously drew a Manichean picture of a generic colonial city as divided into the "'native' sector" and the colonizer's section of the city. The latter, according to Fanon, "is a sector built to last, all stone and steel. It's a sector of lights and paved roads, where the trash cans constantly overflow with strange and wonderful garbage, undreamed-of leftovers" (4). It is "a white folks' sector, a sector of foreigners" (4). By contrast, the "native" quarters, or the section of the city where the colonized live, "is a disreputable place inhabited by disreputable people.... It's a world with no space, people are piled on top of each other, the shacks squeezed tightly together" (4). This depiction of imperial spatial organization affirms Edward Said's point in *Culture and Imperialism*, that "imperialism and the culture associated with it affirm both the primacy of geography and an ideology about control of territory" (78). It's very clear, in a dense and packed city, where social control lies, and where it does not. The city, and specifically the city scarred by colonialism, is a site packed full of layers of history and anxiety, and writing that imagines crime provides an outlet for the types of tensions nurtured in such a space. The postcolonial city is full of potential for revisionary and revolutionary activity, or it can be a space that re-creates colonial oppression: Claire Chambers and Graham Huggan point out that "the postcolonial city can alternately be seen as a dynamic site of social and cultural interaction in which colonial legacies have effectively been superseded, or as a riven site of social and cultural conflict in which colonial ways of thinking and acting are either deliberately or inadvertently reinvented and rehearsed" (786). Cathartic crime is capable of doing either of these things in the contemporary postcolonial city. I will define "criminal city" slightly differently in each chapter, but each postcolonial criminal city shares similar characteristics, namely that they act as repositories of the unreparated crimes of colonialism, crimes that must be resolved before reaching catharsis. A criminal city, therefore, is generally one that retains and bears the scars of colonialism into the twenty-first century.

Attention to crime in the city is a particularly essential task in the twenty-first century, as more and more people move into cities and neoliberal capitalism, state-instituted violence, and gentrification continue apace.[10] It is clear to many observers that we are entering some kind of new age of cities—the

United Nations projects that 68 percent of the world's population will be living in cities by 2050—which is why it is especially necessary to turn our attention to these urban sites now. In *Postmodern Geographies: The Reassertion of Space in Critical Social Theory,* Soja writes of the theory of "restructuring," which he holds is "a shift towards a significantly different order and configuration of social, economic, and political life" (159). Restructuring, he explains, "falls between piecemeal reform and revolutionary transformation, between business-as-usual and something completely different" (159). I am not making the claim that the world's cities are about to completely reorganize themselves and we are soon to be living in a completely new world: rather, this is a time of "restructuring," of significant shifts in our daily urban lives, and negotiating narratives of crime is one important way to make sense of all of that, especially as right-wing and reactionary rhetorics seize upon the idea of crime to shore up their own apocalyptic visions for the world.

The idea that cities are changing, and changing fast, is closely linked to imperial and colonial histories and presents. Mimi Sheller notes, "Colonial legacies of fragmented sovereignty and borders have left a highly variegated terrain of social protection and vulnerability" (xi). The cities examined in this study carry some of the highest wealth and power imbalances in the world, from London's ludicrously high rents to the disparity between high-powered Indian businesspeople and those living in the slums of Mumbai. Most people can agree that these imbalances can be traced back to imperial and immediately postcolonial political and economic structures like the deliberate divide-and-conquer strategies of imperialism, the exploitation of natural and economic resources, and the instituting of handpicked successors to European colonial rule. But while it seems obvious that colonialism and its histories continue to shape contemporary cities, there is significantly less agreement on what exactly is meant by "postcolonial."

In his article "In the Gaudy Supermarket," Terry Eagleton, with characteristic dryness, observes, "There must exist somewhere a secret handbook for post-colonial critics, the first rule of which reads: 'Begin by rejecting the whole notion of post-colonialism.' It is remarkable how hard it is to find an unabashed enthusiast for the concept among those who promote it." Gayatri Chakravorty Spivak takes care to differentiate among the terms "*colonialism*—in the European formation stretching from the mid-eighteenth to the mid-twentieth centuries—*neocolonialism*—dominant economic, political, and culturalist maneuvers emerging in our century after the uneven dissolution of the territorial empires—and *postcoloniality*—the contemporary global condition, since the first term is supposed to have passed or be passing into the second" (172). Using the Spivakian definitions, it makes sense to me to situate this analysis in terms of both "neocolonialism" and "postcoloniality"—the cities in question are still subject to "dominant economic, political, and culturalist maneuvers," and all cities (and the world in total) are operating under the "global condition" of "postcoloniality," a general sense of colonialisms lingering on into and influencing the present.[11] As Shashi Tharoor has written, "Those who follow world affairs would not be entirely wise to consign colonialism to the proverbial dustbin of history" (276–77). With this in mind, *Criminal Cities* investigates Robert Young's "living remains, lingering legacies" (21)[12] and examines how they are articulated and processed either positively or negatively through literary depictions of crime.

Many of the imbalances and injustices that I look at in this work are rooted in structures and formations that began in empire and are still with us: racial capitalism, unjust city design, ecological devastation, and inequalities both among and within cities that are the result of colonial policies and ideas. The Enlightenment roots of such legacies lend all of them a particularly teleological feel: the goal of capitalism is to attain more capital; the goal of city design is to continue to "progress" and be "modern" as more and more people come to occupy urban spaces; the inequalities of contemporary life are often the result of ideas of overreliance on "scientific" and "rational" means to an end. These underlying structures may or may not lead to an increase in crime—unpacking that is not the particular goal of this project—but their ends-driven nature works particularly well for an analysis of crime in literature. Stories that feature crime typically have an end goal: to solve the crime and find the criminal. This structure or search for narrative closure maps well onto various Enlightenment ideologies, but also lends itself well to looking at the novel in general, not just the crime novel in particular.

The novel is the quintessential text of modernity. Whether looking at Ian Watt's early study that situated the rise of the novel firmly in the encroachment of modernity to more recent work like that of Srinivas Aravamudan that points to earlier premodern and non-Western models, it seems fair to say that no literary genre has defined modernity more closely than the novel, no matter when and where it springs up. And all of the trappings that come along with modernity, from colonialism to capitalism to increased urbanization to the installation of surveillance systems that have helped to solidify approaches to and attitudes about crime, come together clearly in the novel. Edward Said has written about the novel that it, "as a cultural artifact of bourgeois society, and imperialism, are unthinkable without each other" (*Culture and Imperialism*, 71). This cultural artifact and its understandings of capitalism and imperialism have been well documented, but I insist we must also understand how crime works in this overlapping matrix.

The crime novel as a genre is unapologetically cathartic, especially in its more reactionary forms: think of Tom Clancy's *Patriot Games*, which offers a kind of catharsis for conservative Irish Americans who want to read about the IRA and experience American hegemony and a sense of Irish victimhood concurrently, or Wilkie Collins's *The Moonstone*, which allowed Victorians to experience imperial domination by osmosis. However, by looking at crime *in* literature, we can experience a more complicated form of catharsis: authors of literary fiction that features crime or of less-formulaic crime fiction are not uncritically replicating imperial or colonial structures. Instead, in a deliberate postmodern move, they are achieving catharsis in unorthodox ways or deliberately falling short of a kind of "purgation of emotion." *Criminal Cities*, then, is adjacent to existing studies of crime fiction, but offers a different kind of argument by asking a different kind of question: Why is it that ostensibly "literary fiction," especially in a postcolonial context, so often hinges on depictions of crime? There is no such thing as the novel without the concept of crime, I argue; due to its similarity to the novel form, and how the concept has grown in tandem with the novel in modernity, crime is as constitutive to the novel form as other long-established social constructions such as capitalism, individualism, and imperialism, as pointed out by Ian Watt, Edward Said, and others. It is very difficult to come up with an example of a novel that does not hinge on some example of crime, from *Robinson Crusoe* to twenty-first-century work. *Criminal Cities* explores why that is, and how these representations connect to larger structures of imperialism, capitalism, and mobility.

Indeed, there is an established field of exploring Victorian or colonial-era British crime fiction and thinking through how that genre might be tied to larger imperial and economic systems. Jon Thompson's *Fiction, Crime, and Empire: Clues to Modernity and Postmodernism* (1993) was an early entry into this field, and his work has been followed up by Caroline Reitz's *Detecting the Nation: Fictions of Detection and the Imperial Venture* (2004), as well as

Stephen Arata's *Fictions of Loss in the Victorian Fin de Siècle: Identity and Empire* (2010) and Yumna Siddiqi's *Anxieties of Empire and the Fiction of Intrigue* (2007). These works hold that crime fiction and the figure of the detective were integral to the British imperial project, and that the growth of the crime fiction genre and the portrayal of the literary detective was tied in various ways to imperial ventures and anxieties. Similar work has been done from the colonial side as well, with Upamanyu Pablo Mukherjee's 2003 tome *Crime and Empire: The Colony in Nineteenth-Century Fictions of Crime* working through how depictions of colonized spaces and crime were linked in the era of high imperialism. Many of these works do focus specifically on the site of the city, but by no means all of them do; additionally, this well-established field focuses specifically on the genre of crime fiction, rather than my work on crime *in* fiction, and how that genre contributed to the imperial project, rather than to its legacies.

With regard to the contemporary era, some work has been done on the figure of the postcolonial detective in a way that takes its cues from the texts I have cited above, with *The Post-Colonial Detective* (2001), edited by Ed Christian, looking specifically at the figure of the detective who operates in formerly colonized lands. There is also a growing field on the subject of postcolonial crime fiction, with Christine Matzke and Susanne Muhleisen's (eds.) *Postcolonial Postmortems: Crime Fiction from a Transcultural Perspective* (2006) being a notable contribution to this field. Bran Nicol, Patricia Pullham, and Eugene McNulty have edited a volume, *Crime Culture: Figuring Criminality in Fiction and Film* (2010), that, like my project, focuses on crime *in* fiction, rather than crime fiction, but there is still no existing volume that ties together the imperially inflected subjects of the city and crime and works through how these topics are negotiated through literature.

Criminal Cities builds off of this research, as well as the work of thinkers like Michelle Alexander (*The New Jim Crow*, 2010), who points to racial disparities in crime and sentencing and how this builds on earlier oppressive structures like slavery and Jim Crow, as well as Naomi Klein, specifically her book *The Shock Doctrine* (2007), which argues that neoliberal capitalism deliberately encroaches on vulnerable places as a form of "shock therapy." I will adapt some of Alexander's vital insights about the American penal system to discussions of international dimensions of colonialism and imperialism and how those link to crime, as well as Klein's thoughts on "disaster capitalism" to think through how fearmongering about crime often accompanies larger capitalist projects.[13] With regard to the broader literary and political stakes of my argument, Matthew Levay's *Violent Minds: Modernism and the Criminal* (2019) considers how early twentieth-century British and American novelists understood criminal psychology in their fiction and argues that "criminality served a crucial purpose for modernist literature" (3); though this book does not look at "criminal psychology" per se, and both my geographic and chronological periods are different from Levay's, his understanding of how crime constitutes an essential and under-discussed core of fiction is invaluable to my own work. The sociologist Vincenzo Ruggiero has written a book on crime, literature, and sociology, *Crime in Literature: Sociology of Deviance and Fiction* (2003), that approaches the subject from a social-sciences standpoint, and Andrew Pepper's *Unwilling Executioner: Crime Fiction and the State* (2016) has helped me shape my ideas about how crime in fiction can function as a form of social and political critique. I plan to arrange these critiques somewhat chronologically, in that the chapters are organized roughly by the time the British Empire made its impact on each particular city: as such, London is the first city, Belfast the second, Australian cities the third, and so on. Concentrating on the British Empire specifically allows me to focus on one global system's commonalities and differences, though of course there are many similarities to be traced within the Francophone, Lusophone, and other worlds as well.

Criminal Cities begins by looking at London, the former center of the British Empire, and considering how empire has marked this city into the twenty-first century. I read Ian McEwan's *Saturday* (2005) and Zadie Smith's *NW* (2012) through the lens of cathartic crime, focusing on a home invasion in *Saturday* as a metonym for the invasion of Iraq and white fears of immigration to Britain, and a murder in *NW* as symbolic of larger concerns working-class people of (mostly) color harbor regarding their place in the city. From London, we move across the Irish Sea to Belfast, one of the British Empire's first colonies and site of the long-running colonial conflict known as the Troubles. By looking at Stuart Neville's *The Twelve* (2009), David Park's *The Truth Commissioner* (2008), and Anna Burns's *Milkman* (2018), I consider what (at times forced) catharsis might look like in a site of still-ongoing, though significantly decreased, colonial crime and violence.

We next turn our attention to Australia, which is especially resonant for this project because it began its colonial life as a penal colony for British and Irish petty criminals. This chapter will focus on Sydney and Albany,

Western Australia, by reading Joan Lindsay's *Picnic at Hanging Rock* (1967) and Mudrooroo's *Wild Cat Falling* (1965) as foundational texts and expanding to Kate Grenville's *The Secret River* (2005) and Kim Scott's *That Deadman Dance* (2010) to think through questions of whiteness from the colonial era to the present day. A chapter on Bombay/Mumbai begins with a meditation on the neo-Orientalism of Gregory David Roberts's *Shantaram* (2003), and then asks how the city's name change spurred a literary focus on crime and the gang underworld, looking in particular at questions of religious affiliation and mob violence through Thrity Umrigar's *The World We Found* (2012), as well as Vikram Chandra's *Sacred Games* (2007), paying special attention to caste, economics, and religion.

The fifth chapter will take the literature of post-apartheid Johannesburg into consideration and look at crime through a neoliberal, post-apartheid lens via readings of Lauren Beukes's *Zoo City* (2010) and Phaswane Mpe's *Welcome to Our Hillbrow* (2001). We then move north and east to Nairobi, where I read a father-son duo—Ngũgĩ wa Thiong'o and Mukoma Wa Ngugi—in order to pick apart how depictions of crime have changed from the anti- to the postcolonial eras. The final full chapter considers cities in the Palestinian West Bank and interrogates several layers of colonialism—Ottoman, British, and Israeli—under the lens of mobility justice. By reading Isabella Hammad's *The Parisian* (2019), which takes on the transition from Ottoman to British control; Mourid Barghouti's *I Saw Ramallah* (1997, English translation 2000), on Palestinian refugees and exiles; and Hala Alyan's *Salt Houses* (2017), which covers Palestinian displacement and migration, this chapter will think about contemporary models of colonialism and injustice and how they link to historic formations. *Criminal Cities* concludes with a short coda on the contemporary refugee crisis and uses Mohsin Hamid's *Exit West* (2017) as a way to explore how cathartic crime is wielded in contemporary political and rhetorical spaces. In each chapter, I consider depictions of crime from several angles, keeping in mind Henri Lefebvre's question: "How many maps, in the descriptive or geographical sense, might be needed to deal exhaustively with a given space, to code and decode all its meanings and contexts? It is doubtful whether a finite number can ever be given in answer to this sort of question" (85). Crime is mapped across the world in infinitely variable ways, and these chapters represent the barest slice of case studies. There are more maps to ponder, more spaces to consider, more narratives with many more meanings.

In 1994 feminist geographer Doreen Massey wrote that love of or affection for place, and specifically, a desire for a sense of "coherence" within that space, can too often be "part of what has given rise to defensive and reactionary responses—certain forms of nationalism, sentimentalized recovering of sanitized 'heritages,' and outright antagonism to newcomers and 'outsiders.' One of the efforts of such responses is that place itself, the seeking after a sense of place, has come to be seen by some as necessarily reactionary" (147). It's true that indeed, sometimes attachment to a place and desire for social cohesion can lead to a regressive outlook: this is *my* city, not yours; *they'll* just bring in crime and violence; keep *my* city the way it is forever. It's true, too, that these grassroots emotions are often matched by top-down "planned violence," or what Elleke Boehmer and Dominic Davies say is the use of "urban planning as a violent materialization of colonialism's exploitative project" (3): the deliberate planning of a city for expensive and individualistic cars and not the social good of public transportation, for example. But, as Boehmer and Davies continue, "literature and culture *can*, even if only sporadically and with occasional complicity, conjure urban spaces resistant to the coercive measures of post/colonial planned violence" (9). If "the novel seeks, by giving form, to uncover and construct the concealed totality of life" (Lukács 60), the postcolonial urban novel can use cathartic crime to give shape and meaning to the world, to the "concealed totality of life." It is my hope that *Criminal Cities,* by charting the ways literature negotiates crime and colonialism in the city, can lead to imaginings of a kind of catharsis that allows for urban spaces that resist these types of harmful legacies.

ONE

"THE PHENOMENON OF WALKING"

Mapping Postcolonial Criminal London

In Zadie Smith's novel *NW* (2012), one of the main characters, Leah, is attending a party for Notting Hill Carnival when she overhears a television newscast about a young man's murder. Readers are told she only takes note of it because "it names a local road, one street from her own" (104)—the Albert Road in Kilburn. The television newscaster says: "The young man, named locally as Felix Cooper, was 32 years old. He grew up in the notorious Garvey House project in Holloway, but had moved with his family to this relatively quiet corner of Kilburn, in search of a better life. Yet it was here, in Kilburn, that he was accosted by two youths early Saturday evening, moments from his own front door. It is not known if the victim knew—" Leah, in frustration, shouts at the television set, "He was murdered! Why does it matter where he grew up?" (104). This crime of a young man's murder in a northwest corner of London provides the center around which the rest of the novel swirls. Although none of the other main characters in the text know Felix, it is his death that provides the catalyst for understanding how crime structures the twenty-first-century city of London, and it is how the crime is solved—or perhaps left unsolved—that shapes and challenges various narratives of the city. Above all, it is the emphasis on place and movement from place to place—Felix is not just named, but named locally; his life story is given in the context of mobility and locality; we are clearly to understand him in relation to the two neighborhoods named—that drives home what crime does in the city, and how it opens up or forecloses possibilities for catharsis in this urban space.

Ian McEwan's *Saturday* (2005) also centers around a violent crime, and is also deeply concerned with a specific area of London. Like *NW*, *Saturday* is a story of mobility, of moving from place to place, and it is the crimes that occur along the way that open up the text for analysis and comprehension. This sense of mobility, of teleology, of "what happens next," clearly maps onto traditional crime stories that end in a more complete understanding of who committed a crime and why, as well as onto directions, onto transportation, onto cartographies that point the reader or traveler in the direction that they must go next. Throughout both these novels, characters think about how to physically move through the city; how to metaphorically "move up" in the world; what their country's movement through the globe has meant for their own city; how to understand and solve both the crimes they encounter and the city in which they live. They do this in a space marked by the violences and oppressions of empire. As Jane M. Jacobs points out, in London "the idea of empire is not confined to the past" (40), and its logics remain determining factors in both novels. The London of both *Saturday* and *NW* thinks of transportation and movement, both physical and metaphorical, as a way to inhabit and negotiate this imperially inflected urban space's crimes. By looking at these two novels in tandem, I demonstrate how crime undergirds Britain's colonial and racist adventures both at home and abroad by using characters' experiences of transportation and mobility to map London as a spatial expression of a neo-imperial, neoliberal criminal city.

"THERE IS NO ALTERNATIVE": CREATING THE CRIMINAL CITY OF LONDON

In 1978 Margaret Thatcher gave a speech to the Conservative Women's Conference in which she said, "All over the country, particularly in our large urban areas, old people do go in fear and trembling as never before during either the lifetime of their parents and grandparents." Why are these city residents going in "fear and trembling," you might ask? Well, Thatcher continues, due to rising levels of crime. Some people might believe those levels are rising "due to things like higher unemployment, poor housing, poor pay," but Thatcher, and the Conservative Women, know better. "Rising crime," of course, "is not due to 'society,' but to the steady undermining of personal responsibility and self-discipline—all things which are taught within the family."

This remarkable sound bite manages to contain so much within a few short sentences. Cities are places to fear; recent changes (most likely demographic and racial) are making the world less safe; social welfare is to be disregarded in favor of the nuclear family; the important things are within each individual's control. It is this general neoliberalizing and privatizing ethos, combined with the lightly coded fearmongering about race wrapped up in rhetoric about "large urban areas," that has played such a large role in creating what we will analyze as the contemporary criminal city of London. Thatcherite legacies still structure the city, forty years later, even after eras of "Cool Britannia" and "Third Way" economics. Postwar and postcolonial London, no longer the metropolitan imperial center, is now a place where "the urban and human geography . . . has been irreversibly altered as a consequence of patterns of migration from countries with a history of colonialism" (McLeod 4), so that "London," in certain circles, functions as a code for nonwhite and somehow dangerous or criminal inhabitants. In 1973, Raymond Williams identified a common British attitude toward London as perceiving the city to be a "source of social danger" (217) and a place of "darkness and poverty" (221); these negative associations have only become sharpened in an age of imperially derived racism and neoliberal economic policy.

It is generally agreed that, with Margaret Thatcher at the helm, the United Kingdom actively rolled back the postwar Keynesian consensus that had endorsed strong social programs, a mixed economy rather than pure free marketism, and vigorous government action. This "welfare capitalist" economic structure, spurred to creation by the 1942 Beveridge Report, had created the socialized National Health Service, invested in community projects and development, and implemented massive educational reforms, among other socially oriented schemes. These economic and social reforms occurred in tandem with the severe contraction of the British Empire and significant immigration to the former imperial center from the former colonies; both of these developments had a hand in tremendously re-envisioning the British social landscape. Thatcher's dismantling of this welfare state in the late 1970s and 1980s, moreover, coincided with a rising sense of dissatisfaction from the postcolonial immigrants and their first-generation British offspring, as well as an uptick in the rates of crime (especially violent crime). As Stuart Hall, Chas Critcher, Tony Jefferson, John Clarke, and Brian Roberts have pointed out in Policing the Crisis: Mugging, the State, and Law and Order, however, concern over the "'steadily rising rate of violent crime' which has been growing through the 1960s" is "about other things than crime, *per se*" (vii). Crime, they assert, "has been cut adrift from its social roots" (ix), and, in the Thatcher era, coincided with "cuts in public expenditure and in the Welfare State" (331), leading to "the synchronisation of the race and the class aspects of the crisis" (332); in other words, ideas about "crime" became and have stayed enmeshed with ideas about race, immigration, imperialism, and class. Crime functions in London as ways to whip up panic about the Other, to justify cutting the social safety net ("Why would we help a bunch of criminals?"), and to further construct a city that is clearly divided between valuable people and disposable people. As the former imperial center (and home to one of the world's first formalized police services, the Met) and current postcolonial diaspora magnet, London is still one of the biggest and most powerful cities in the world; the experience of crime takes on special resonance in this city, a nexus where colonialism, diaspora, and narratives of crime meet.

The interplay between racist anxieties, a decaying social net, and a sense of and subsequent panic over rising crime is key to understanding how these forces worked together to create the grid that underlies the city that we see today, even (especially) after the Blairite/New Labour changes of the 1990s. As the historian Frederick Cooper notes, "We can probe the continued traces today of colonial histories while still acknowledging that these histories are not reducible to a colonial effect" (32); London is largely shaped due to traceable colonial histories, but that is not the entire story. In this chapter, I will take these traces and treat them alongside the crumbling of the postwar economic consensus and the rise in acts of and anxiety over crime to consider how postcolonialism, crime, and neoliberalism work as a generative matrix in the contemporary city of London.

By referencing the "criminal city" of London, I am pointing not only to a fear of the unknown, particularly a racialized fear, that often expresses itself in fears about "crime," but also to the disruptive actions Margaret Thatcher and others undertook in order to create a fractured city that can be understood through instances of crime. As we shall see, these fears and fractures are often caught up in discourses about transportation—the main crimes of both *Saturday* and *NW* take place after travel throughout the streets of London, one due to a car crash and the other due to an incident on the Tube. Moreover, both novels are dependent on histories of imperialism—*Saturday* with regard to colonial histories creating the foundation for understanding the invasion of Iraq, and *NW* in terms of postcolonial migration and structures of racism that derive from the empire—and imperialism can be viewed, in part, as a catalog of (mostly forced and unwanted) mobilities. As Mimi Sheller has pointed out, "How, when, and where people, goods, and capital move is, in all respects, a political question" (xii). The politics of this are tied up in the Thatcherite neoliberal turn—fear of crime often expresses itself in a desire for privatized travel, like personal automobiles, while cuts in funding instituted by conservative governments lead to underserved public transportation—but there is also something to be said about what movement has to say about the need for catharsis, the sense of journeying somewhere and reaching some kind of ending.

Attempts at resolving cathartic crime in London's criminal city often leave readers and fictional characters frustrated. Those on the left side of the political system might point to the need to see Thatcher and her legacies, as well as lingering effects of the empire, vanquished in a tidy story about conservatism and white supremacy's crimes. The attempt at catharsis often carried out by figures like Thatcher, on the other hand—rhetorically taking down "the enemy" in front of a legion of conservative women—can have horrific effects in the world of the text or the real world, in that it can encourage violence against marginalized people. By tracking the role transportation throughout the city of London plays in these crime narratives, we can similarly track what opportunities for catharsis are created or destroyed in the criminal city.

"NO SUCH THING AS SOCIETY": THE WITHDRAWAL FROM THE CITY IN *SATURDAY*

Henry Perowne, the protagonist of Ian McEwan's 2005 novel *Saturday*, is a middle-aged white neurosurgeon, with a loving wife, intelligent and beautiful children, and a successful career. He lives in Fitzrovia, London, runs long-distance races, enjoys cooking, and regularly visits his mother in an elderly care facility. Besides his prowess in the medical field, there is very little to distinguish him from the masses of other upper-class white men who populate posh districts of north and central London. His very lack of distinguishing features is, in itself, remarkable. It is not fair to call him "average"—he is too wealthy and holds too prestigious a job for this—but there is very little to mark him as different from the generic type of white man who holds this kind of job and lives in a wealthy part of a major Western city.

Perowne has no strong stances in his intellectual life, either. We are told, on the very first page, that as he wakes up at 3:40 in the morning, he is not disturbed "even by the state of the world." This general indifference to the world around him continues throughout the novel; though he is living in London on February 15, 2003, the day of a large anti–Iraq War protest (in fact, many British media sources from the *Daily Mail* to the BBC claimed that this protest was the largest protest of any kind in London's history), he has no strong feelings one way or the other on the impending invasion. He does not appear to be interested in, or even aware of, debates surrounding economic and social justice; as we shall see, they simply never seem to occur to him. He seems entirely focused on getting together ingredients for a small family party that evening, as he will be welcoming his daughter for a visit from Paris. This is Henry Perowne: a good and bland neoliberal subject, benefiting from the current economic environment, checked out from his surrounding community and city, and reliant only on himself, his family, and his immediate work associates.

Yet, as seemingly distanced from larger society as Henry Perowne is, his February Saturday is witness to two earth-shattering crimes, one public and one private. Henry encounters both these crimes in one day's time, for *Saturday* takes the form, much like Virginia Woolf's *Mrs. Dalloway*, of the lived experience of twenty-four hours in London.[1] While *Mrs. Dalloway* shifts viewpoints and perspectives throughout the text, *Saturday* does not, excising the strong heteroglossic and multilayered texture present in the earlier novel and bending the experience of the city much more strongly in favor of one individual. Nevertheless, McEwan clearly asks his readers to draw parallels between his own novel and Woolf's; both novels feature a plane as a key plot point, both deal with the trauma of war, both depict characters who commit violent acts, both turn on the preparations for a party later that evening.

But while *Mrs. Dalloway* is often understood, at least in part, as a modernist celebration of the city, *Saturday*'s relationship to the city is not quite so clear-cut, in part due to the massively different city London is in 2003 as compared to the same urban space in 1925. Both temporal Londons are haunted by war, imperialism, and runaway capitalism leading to inequality, but the transition is from imperial to neo-imperial, liberal to neoliberal city. Even Perowne's irresponsible rumination, "As a Londoner, you could grow nostalgic for the IRA. Even as your legs left your body, you might care to remember that the cause was a united Ireland" (34), seems quaint and old-fashioned; neoliberal London is not nearly as concerned with nationalist protest and old-fashioned imperial wars. The 2003 version of London is more neoliberal and neo-imperial in nature, marked by issues from postwar Commonwealth immigration to huge gaps between rich and poor to the war in Iraq. Even the name of the novel suggests imperial connotations; Britain is in the "Saturday" of its empire, attempting one last gasp of imperial glory in the form of the invasion of Iraq and subsequent exploitation of its natural resources in the service of capital. Yet, Perowne's lack of ability to engage with his surroundings and their imperial echoes is a key element of tension in the text.

Saturday begins with Henry Perowne waking "some hours before dawn" and going to stand at his bedroom window. He is unsure what wakes him, but he takes the opportunity to look out over the city in the quiet hush of the early morning.[2] He thinks, looking out "towards a foreshortened jumble of facades, scaffolding and pitched roofs," that "the city is a success, a brilliant invention, a biological masterpiece—millions teaming around the accumulated and layered achievements of the centuries, as though around a coral reef, sleeping, working, entertaining themselves, harmonious for the most part, nearly everyone wanting it to work" (3). This rather utopic vision has been read as Perowne's wholehearted endorsement of the city,[3] and it is fair to say that Perowne's rhapsodic view of the "brilliant invention" smacks of the urbanophile modernists. The next major event of his day—seeing a plane on fire descend to the earth—also calls to mind the sense of community in the city engendered by the spotting of a plane in *Mrs. Dalloway*, though in this case Perowne is alone, and it is so early we can assume very few people have seen the same plane. Perowne's criminal city is a rather more complex depiction of London than a straightforward love, and in order to fully understand how *Saturday* inhabits its narrative of the city, it is necessary to distinguish the relationship between the author McEwan and his literary creation Perowne.

It is surprising how many literary critics have understood Perowne's worldview in *Saturday* as being in lockstep with McEwan's or the novel's own. It is true that Henry Perowne and Ian McEwan share many biographical details in common, from living in Fitzrovia to some of the more specific elements of each family. In a 2005 interview, Laura Miller of *Salon* also notes, "One of the many things they [Perowne and McEwan] share is a complicated attitude toward the invasion of Iraq." Yet, this by no means indicates that Perowne is meant to be read as a one-to-one translation of McEwan, nor that we are to understand *Saturday* as endorsing Perowne's viewpoint; this is a work of fiction, after all. Yet, in his assessment of the novel in the *New York Review of Books,* John Banville seems unwilling to entertain any possibility that Perowne and *Saturday* may have divergent opinions on the world Henry Perowne inhabits. Banville points out, correctly, that "owning things is important to Perowne, an unashamed beneficiary of the fruits of capitalism." He notes, moreover, that "the politics of the book is banal," that "*Saturday* has the feel of a neoliberal polemic gone badly wrong," concluding, straightforwardly, "*Saturday* is a dismayingly bad book." Elizabeth Kowaleski Wallace seems similarly attached to the idea that the viewpoints of Henry Perowne and the book itself can be closely conflated. She notes, "The novel seems to imply that the author endorses Henry's perspective" (466), saying, "McEwan's novel explicitly acknowledges neither an evolving story about Britain's imperial past nor the contested public debate about its multicultural future" (469), regretfully deciding that "as Henry looks out over the city of London, he fails to register the momentous social, political, and cultural changes that have swept across England in the wake of England's imperial greatness" (467). In Kowaleski Wallace's and Banville's views, then, the novel itself, like Henry, is not interested in engaging with questions of empire, neoliberal economics, or the contemporary city.

On the contrary, Perowne's very obliviousness to the political, social, and historical factors that surround him—what Kowaleski Wallace calls his "[failure] to register" events in postwar British history and what Banville calls "a neoliberal polemic gone badly wrong"—is in itself what gives the novel a subtle power to critique the legacies of the empire via its depictions of crime. Sarah Brouillette points to "the intimate links between author, character, and reader" and wonders if these links "may be precisely the point of this mode of narration" (184). The close links are indeed the point; the attentive reader is meant to unpick these seemingly close links in a way that the blinkered Henry cannot or will not. Though Perowne is clearly very good at his job and intelligent enough to become a renowned physician, he seems to lack the critical thinking capabilities that lead to, yes, his failure to fully take in "London's vibrant multicultural scene" (Kowaleski Wallace 465) or to ask, "What does England become in the wake of its imperial greatness?" (Kowaleski Wallace 466). As I will continue to demonstrate, Henry is not a bad man, or even an unintelligent one; he is simply a product of his neoliberal, Thatcherite and Blairite city, which carries with it a certain inability to be able to be critical of his surroundings and his place within them. Though he is "an habitual observer of his own moods" (4), he is constitutionally unable to move outside his assessment of himself to an assessment of the world around him. He is the neoliberal's obsession with the individual taken to its most logical conclusion, and, thus, to the careful reader, McEwan, via his distance from his protagonist, is able to use Henry's experiences of the city and crime to offer up thoughtful critiques of the neoliberal criminal city.

After we read Perowne's thoughts on the city, we learn that he does not enjoy reading—his poet daughter, Daisy, believes him to have "astounding ignorance" and "poor taste and insensitivity" (4)—and that he also has no time for religion or spirituality. We also learn that he works so constantly as to have little room for much else in his life. Yet Perowne does not seem at all inclined to question why he needs to work so hard, or why he has so little time for or interest in reading literature or engaging with questions of a spiritual or theological nature—he simply accepts, as a received and unquestioned notion, that his life is full of work and that even sex with his wife, Rosalind, must be "snatched . . . from the jaws of work" (22–23). Without work, the reader learns, "Henry and Rosalind Perowne are nothing" (23)— a troubling statement, but one Henry does not seem to consider problematic. He lives for work, and its logics dominate his days.

Perowne's method of being in the world is profoundly individualistic, with the only people outside himself he engages with being coworkers or family members. He is Margaret Thatcher's aphorism brought to life: "There is no such thing as society. There are individual men and women, and there are families." Indeed, Perowne tries his hardest to cut himself off from the city at large, living as he does behind front doors that come equipped with "three stout Banham locks, two black iron bolts as old as the house, two tempered steel security chains, a spyhole with a brass cover, the box of electronics that works the Entryphone system, the red panic button, the alarm pad with its softly gleaming digits" (37). Lest the reader miss the point, McEwan continues, "Such defences, such mundane embattlement: beware of the city's poor, the drug-addicted, the downright bad" (37). Such an intense level of security reflects the larger societal anxiety over an increase in crime, but, as we will see later, the existence of such security doesn't make much difference.

After seeing the plane on fire, Perowne turns on the news to learn the event was nothing particularly spectacular: a cargo plane had mechanical failure, everyone survived, and it was not linked to terrorism or anything headline-grabbing—an early indication of a lack of catharsis, of something that fizzles out rather than satisfyingly presents a neat and thematically related ending.[4] As the novel and the day proceed, Perowne heads out to play squash with an American colleague, Jay Strauss. He drives his car to the gym, rather than walking or taking public transportation; this mode of travel further highlights the privatization of Perowne's life. En route, he nearly drives through the antiwar protest, but it is a narrow miss and he is diverted by traffic police. Perowne's frustrated movement throughout the city, brought up short by a protest against the invasion, facilitates the reader's thinking about two crimes: what will ultimately become a massively failed and stalled imperial movement to Iraq—a real-life war crime—and the eventual private, fictional crime that will come of Perowne's diversion.

Soon after crossing the protestors' route, he gets into a minor car accident with three vaguely threatening men, named Baxter, Nark, and Nigel. This brief instance of immobility sets up the core action of the novel. Baxter is clearly the ringleader of the small troupe, and Perowne diagnoses Baxter (correctly) with Huntington's disease after a short interaction. Baxter, distressed at losing face in front of his cronies, leaves the scene of the crime, but the scene has been set for the rest of Perowne's Saturday. This scene neatly melds together the two major crimes that *Saturday* explores: a neoliberal, personalized home break-in Baxter will perform later that evening, and the imperialistic, public crime of the impending invasion of Iraq. Perowne, traveling along in his car, has managed to braid together two strands of contemporary London—he is witness to, though not actively participating in, a public crime in the form of an upcoming imperial action in Iraq, and he is the catalyst for a looming private crime, in the guise of Baxter, who will break into his home later that evening. The two crimes are, of course, dependent upon each other; Baxter enacts the fears of those who, like Perowne, think their safety is likely threatened by the "Other," and the upcoming invasion dramatizes white Britons' anxieties about loss of empire and receding standing on the global stage. A clarifying event is necessary to jolt the reader out of Perowne's blinkered mindset and into an understanding of Perowne as an unreliable and untrustworthy narrator of London and its crimes.

As Perowne drives about the city, he consistently allows himself to revisit personal memories as prompted by his surroundings. The tension between Perowne's and *Saturday*'s understandings of the city is brought to a head as Perowne reminisces about the time he met Prime Minister Tony Blair, at a gala to celebrate the opening of the Tate Modern.[5] He and Rosalind somehow break away from the party and end up in a deserted gallery full of Rothkos. As they move into the next room, it is empty save for an exhibit consisting of a low pile of bricks and, surreally, the prime minister and his entourage. The narrator tells the reader, "The Perownes had come in on an oddly silent moment. Blair and the director smiled and posed for the cameras, whose pictures would also include the famous bricks. The flashes twinkled randomly, but none of the photographers was calling out in the usual way. The calmness of the scene seemed an extension of the Rothko gallery next door" (145). The oddness of the scene is taken further when the museum director, who knows Rosalind, waves the Perownes over to meet the prime minister. To Perowne's surprise, when Blair shakes his hand, "Blair was looking at him with recognition and interest. The gaze was intelligent and intense, and unexpectedly youthful. So much had yet to happen" (145). Blair and Perowne then have this conversation:

> He [Blair] said, "I really admire the work you're doing."
> Perowne said automatically, "Thank you." But he was impressed. It was just conceivable, he supposed, that Blair with his good memory and reputation for absorbing the details of his ministers' briefs, would have heard of the hospital's excellent report last month—all targets met—and even of the special mention of the neurosurgery department's exceptional results. Procedures twenty-three per cent up on last year. Later Henry realized what an absurd notion that was. (145)

Neoliberal rhetoric aside—the care aspect of Henry's profession has been brushed aside in favor of discussion of "targets," "results," and procedures going up—the scene is fascinating in its revelation of the novel's mindset, rather than the ambivalent and oblivious Perowne's. The prime minister goes on to say to Perowne, "In fact, we've got two of your paintings hanging in Downing Street. Cherie and I adore them" (145–46).

> "No, no," Perowne said.
> "Yes, yes," the Prime Minister insisted, pumping his hand. He was in no mood for artistic modesty.
> "No, I think you—"
> "Honestly. They're in the dining room."
> "You're making a mistake," Perowne said, and on that word there passed through the Prime Minister's features for the briefest instant a look of sudden alarm, of fleeting self-doubt. No one else saw his expression freeze and his eyes budge minimally. A hairline fracture had appeared in the assurance of power.
> Then he continued as before, no doubt making the rapid calculation that given all the people pushing in around them trying to listen, there could be no turning back. Not without derisive press tomorrow.
> "Anyway. They truly are marvellous. Congratulations." (146)

And thus the scene ends. Though Perowne does not take that any further than wondering "if such moments, stabs of cold panicky doubt, are an increasing part of the Prime Minister's days, or nights" (146), I read this scene as being full of larger implications. Though Perowne does not recognize the monumental significance in his remark "You're making a mistake," or in Blair's momentary self-doubt, the novel, through this seemingly minor event, is telegraphing to the reader that, in fact, Blair is making a mistake. *Saturday*, at its core (and like its inspirations *Mrs. Dalloway* and *Ulysses*), is a novel about everyday events taking on larger political meaning, and this scene is an excellent example of such. The novel's viewpoint is that his backpacking onto an American neo-imperial war is doomed to failure; his attempt to drag Britain away from Saturday and to the, say, Wednesday of imperial greatness will not succeed (but he can't back out now, "not without derisive press tomorrow"). With subtle moves like this one and others, *Saturday* undermines the criminal city by challenging the neoliberal subject's experience of it: in other words, by calling our attention to Blair's public crimes, the novel invites us to engage in modes of critique against them.

The party scene of *Saturday* provides the setting for the private crime that acts as the "climax," such as it is, for the novel. As Perowne is cooking fish stew for the evening's get-together, various members of his nuclear family start trickling in—first, his daughter, fresh off the train from Paris; followed by his father-in-law, the famous poet John Grammaticus; then his musician son, Theo. His wife, Rosalind, is last to arrive, and she is escorted by none other than Baxter, who has a knife to her ribs, having broken in past the house's multitude of locks against "the city's poor, the drug-addicted, the downright bad" (37). Emily Horton points out that Perowne "implicitly compares Baxter to the terrorist 'other' (also an invader in the Western home)[,] . . . tying the narrative into a defence of Western military imperialism" (141). Baxter, this "terrorist 'other,'" has Nigel with him, and the two force the family members to take out their cell phones and put them on the table, thus severing their even-nominal connections to the outside city.

Baxter begins the violence of the evening by breaking Grammaticus's nose, and follows up by forcing Daisy to strip. When she is naked, it is revealed to everyone in the room that she is pregnant, much to Henry's surprise. Made uncomfortable at the sight of a pregnant woman, Baxter casts about for a new object of ridicule and lands on a proof copy of Daisy's volume of poems, *My Saucy Bark* (the title being an allusion to a Shakespeare sonnet). He tells her to read a poem, and Nigel follows up by saying, "Let's hear your dirtiest one. Something really filthy" (228). Her grandfather calls out to her to "do one you used to say for me" (228) (the reader is aware that Grammaticus would give the child Daisy pocket money for each canonical poem she learned by heart and recited to him), and she understands him immediately, opening her book but reciting from memory Matthew Arnold's "Dover Beach." Here again, McEwan distances himself from Perowne and Perowne from the reader; the astute reader can suss out fairly early that she is reciting "Dover Beach" (especially as the poem is printed as an appendix to the novel), but Henry is none the wiser, thinking the poem is one of Daisy's own. When she finishes, Baxter is elated, charged up by the effects of the poetry, and newly susceptible to persuasive words from Perowne. Perowne tells him he has papers on a promising treatment for Huntington's disease upstairs, and he talks Baxter into following him to his home office. Once there, Perowne and Theo work together to overpower Baxter and throw him down the stairs, knocking him out cold.

This scene has produced almost as many different reactions as there are interested literary critics. Martin Ryle is of the opinion that "we can read this homosocial melodrama as related metaphorically to the novel's theme of war, terrorism, and antiwar protest," with Baxter acting as the terrorist and Perowne positioned as homeland security actor (28); he also says, "The Baxter plot discloses and stages an anxious concern with the question of relative privilege" (29), thus drawing the two strands of neoliberal and neoconservative forms of these crimes together nicely. Michael L. Ross agrees with Ryle's first contention, saying, "*Saturday* reflects the susceptibility of the nation to assaults by predatory forces sited both within and far removed from its increasingly porous borders" (82), reminding us of the novel's (post)colonial themes. Richard Brown sees Baxter as a corollary to *Mrs. Dalloway*'s Septimus Smith, whose violent suicide disrupts Clarissa's party, while Molly Clark Hilliard points to the "genuine resonance" between Arnold's period and our own (183). Sarah Brouillette argues that this scene paints Baxter as an "underclass criminal" who is "softened by his encounter with a canonical poem, thus paving the way for the Perownes' final triumph over him" (198), though she also points to Henry's "[putting] himself in Baxter's position" the second time Daisy recites the poem as one of the few times Henry is able to move outside his immediate self and family (192). Elaine Hadley, in perhaps the most sustained critique of the "Dover Beach" scene and its aftermath, says, "'Dover Beach' is thus genealogically linked to *Saturday* through their representation of a shared faith in the liberal cultivation of the self as in itself a good" (94). I concur with Brouillette's reading of the crime scene as being deeply, almost imperially, concerned with power dynamics, and tend to agree with Hadley's assessment of both texts being focused on the individual. Yet, I disagree with her and Alexander Beaumont's related claims that this individualistic philosophy means that *Saturday* is a liberal, rather than a neoliberal, text (Beaumont 147), and Horton's that it acts as a "defence of Western military imperialism" (141). *Saturday* is, rather, both a neoliberal and neo-imperial text, *and* one invested in working against neoliberalism and neo-imperialism, in that its portrayal of crime in London works against the criminal city.

To further illustrate my point, I turn, again, to Elizabeth Kowaleski Wallace. Taking into account the "Dover Beach" scene, the injury of Baxter, and the follow-up scene where Perowne goes to the hospital to stitch up and heal Baxter, she asks, "Could his point really be to suggest that, when confronted by those who hate us, the West need only resort to its wits, its encyclopedic knowledge of science, and to hold out hope of a 'cure' in order to distract those who would otherwise seek to harm us? That, in the end, we will easily overpower those who invade the sanctity of our homes, and that it will then be our obligation and duty to 'fix' whatever injuries they've received in the process?" (476). Kowaleski Wallace is of the opinion that "as absurd as this line of thinking is, it seems warranted, given the climatic scene of the novel" (476). However, I maintain the answers to these questions are more complicated. Though by "he," Kowaleski Wallace means McEwan, I argue that this is not the novel's point, but rather that of Perowne and the neoliberal system into which he and many other subjects have been interpellated. This is, quite literally, the imperial fantasy—that "they" are out there, "they" hate "us," "they" want to do violence to and commit crimes against "us," but it is all okay, because "we" are smarter than "them," "we" have more than "them," and if "you" just let "us" try to help "you," "we" can swoop in and, after performing necessarily violent crimes of our own, "we" can begin to fix "you." (Often, even, "they" are viewed as genetically deficient from "us.") Perowne is unaware that he thinks like this, but I read the novel's focus on the crimes in his Saturday as being absolutely clear on the fact that he does view the Other with this type of imperial gaze (and, correspondingly, that the reader is meant to find this gaze disquieting and upsetting).

As Perowne and Theo push Baxter down the stairs, Baxter locks eyes with Henry. He has an expression on his face "not so much of terror, as dismay" (236). As he continues to fall, "Henry thinks he sees in the wide brown eyes a sorrowful accusation of betrayal. He, Henry Perowne, possesses so much—the work, money, status, the home, *above all* [italics mine], the family—the handsome healthy son with the strong guitarist's hands come to rescue him, the beautiful poet for a daughter, unattainable even in her nakedness, the famous father-in-law, the gifted, loving wife; and he has done nothing, given nothing to Baxter who has so little that is not wrecked by his defective gene, and who is soon to have even less" (236). This, then, is the crux of the matter and the deep, underlying crime that undergirds the city: the city Perowne inhabits creates such vast gulfs between rich and poor, healthy and sick (especially in a neoliberal age where cuts to the National Health Service on which Baxter surely relies are an ever-more-present reality), privileged and not, that they have become completely insurmountable. Perowne has everything that matters in the criminal city, *above all* the family, and Baxter has nothing.[6]

To Perowne's credit, he seems to have at least a fleeting understanding of this, which is perhaps why he goes to the hospital to operate on Baxter after injuring him. Yet, at the end of the novel, when he has returned home after operating and gone once again to stand on his balcony, thinking about history and the future, he only momentarily acknowledges his complicity in the day's crimes, if not the composition of the city overall. He thinks to himself that "twenty hours ago he drove across a road officially closed to traffic, and set in train a sequence of events" (288), but he follows up by closing his mind off to Baxter's situation and chalking it up to his "dim, fixed fate" (289). There is no acknowledgment of the ways in which the decimated National Health Service has failed an ill man like Baxter, or that a less individualistic, more communitarian society might at least have found a way to ease a dying man's last days. No, thinks Henry, it is only to be fate: no one is at fault, least of all himself. There is no villain, only fate.

The final lines of the novel are heartbreaking in their simplicity. As Henry goes back to bed and draws close to Rosalind, he kisses the nape of her neck. "There's always this, is one of his remaining thoughts. And then: there's only this. And at last, faintly, falling: this day's over" (289). In the final moments of his Saturday, after twenty-four hours whose events should have served to shock Henry out of his neoliberal complacency, he ends his day by concluding, "There's only this." As Christina Root has pointed out, the echo of James Joyce's "The Dead" is clear in the "faintly falling"; yet, while Joyce's final paragraph is often read as a universalizing, communitarian gesture, I read *Saturday*'s "faintly falling" as Perowne's reinscription of individualistic neoliberal ethics. Alexander Beaumont disagrees, pointing to what he sees as communitarian strains in the book. He claims, "The novel attempts to retain its early endorsement of the city right up to its conclusion" (142). The city is, or should be, a place of interdependency, of community, of multiplicities of experience—much as it is in *Mrs. Dalloway*, for example. Henry Perowne's neoliberal London is none of those things. Though Beaumont writes that Perowne wholeheartedly believes "he must attend to his obligation to those with whom he shares urban space" (142), it is not fair to say that Perowne has this understanding of the city. Rather, Perowne has a fleeting sense of what Beaumont terms "civic duty" (142), but only because he feels a personal sense of duty to Baxter—not because Baxter is first and foremost a fellow citizen with whom Perowne is to share urban space. It is, then, *Saturday*'s awareness that a subject like Perowne would not move out of his complacency that constitutes its version of cathartic crime. Perowne's inability, to the very end, to realize his privileged position in the city and complicity in various crimes—and *Saturday*'s knowledge of the fact that its protagonist is fundamentally unreliable—may seem a failure on the part of McEwan, but it is, rather, a larger indictment on the crimes of the neoliberal city of London.

Because we reach a troubling sort of catharsis—the supposed evildoer, Baxter, gets his head bashed in by the noble man just defending what is rightfully his—it is possible to read *Saturday* as a surface-level endorsement of Margaret Thatcher's vision, where families form the primary unit of society, self-discipline is all that is necessary, and there is no communal good or need for a just city or "large urban area." However, by reading *Saturday* as a crime story wherein the actual criminal is not Baxter, but a series of imperially rooted and neoliberal economic and social policies enacted primarily by Thatcher but including many others, we can instead see that the catharsis reached is actually quite horrifying. Though Perowne misses the opportunity to critically examine an instance of crime that may jolt him into a more nuanced understanding of his city, we as readers should not miss the opportunity to examine and critique this instance of cathartic crime.

"TODAY THIS IS BRENT, TOMORROW IT COULD BE BRITAIN": THE FRAGMENTING OF THE CITY IN *NW*

The criminal city Zadie Smith's 2012 novel *NW* portrays would, on the surface, appear to exhibit few to no similarities with the one in *Saturday*. One novel shows glossy central London as experienced and understood by a wealthy white middle-aged man; the other depicts a simultaneously decaying and gentrifying northwest London (NW) via multiple changing perspectives, from an Irish Protestant woman (Leah) to a young Black man (Felix) to the Irish Protestant woman's best friend, a woman of Jamaican ancestry first named Keisha and then Natalie. *Saturday* remains relatively narratively conventional; *NW* consists of five sections, narrated by the three above characters in vastly different styles. Different as their subject matters and forms may be, *Saturday* and *NW* should be understood alongside each other for their understandings of cathartic crime and of London as a criminal city; both continually urge the reader to acknowledge their and our complicity in neoliberal, neo-imperial systems and processes.

NW is deeply, intrinsically concerned with the city and with narrative form. *NW*'s London, far more than *Saturday*'s, is a city where wealth meets poverty at sometimes jarring angles. As Boyd Tonkin of *The Independent* writes, it is in *NW* that "the spectacular collisions and disjunctions of a divided city enact its author's doubts about what kind of novelist she [Smith] is—and how the novel might make sense of these jagged splits and rifts." These "jagged splits and rifts" are visible not only in the content of the novel but in its forms, divided in perspectives and narrative styles as the text is. The first section ("Visitation"), Leah's, is told in a modernist stream-of-consciousness; the second ("Guest"), Felix's, in a straightforward third-person narration (what Alexandra Schwartz of the *Nation* calls "downright retro"); the third ("Host"), Natalie's, in 185 short, numbered vignettes, a kind of fractured bildungsroman; the fourth ("Crossing"), also Natalie's, as a geographically marked chronicle of a nighttime walk through NW; and the fifth ("Visitation"), also Natalie's, in much the same style as Felix's. *NW* can be seen as "a hotchpotch in five parts," as Christian Lorentzen notes in the *London Review of Books*, or, more scathingly, as "[falling] so far short of being a successful novel, though it contains the makings of three or four," in the opinion of Adam Mars-Jones for the *Guardian*. Ruth Franklin of the *New Republic* is so annoyed as to exclaim, "We get it! The form reflects the content.... The story of a fragmented existence must be told in fragments. But there is something that feels a little too pat about it, too literal, too tidy about its untidiness." However, Ron Charles writes in the *Washington Post*, "If *NW* is difficult to enter, it's not more difficult than moving into any new neighborhood: at first, you can't imagine you'll ever learn your way around the winding streets, but soon this strange habitat feels like home." Reading *NW* as both novel and city interpellates the reader into the narrative of the novel's criminal city and its correlating messages about urban life, including how one moves about the city. In short, it allows one to participate in Zadie Smith's London, in all its messiness, crises, and inequalities.

This is a city where opportunity, in the form of two young Black men named Felix and Nathan, is lost, and where neoliberal ideologies coalesce in a space inhabited largely by postcolonial immigrants and their offspring. David Marcus in *Dissent* argues, "*NW* seeks to render not only the cognitive disorder of postmodern experience but also the social and psychological disorders of postmodern—that is, post-welfare state—capitalism" (70). *NW* argues that postmodern capitalism distributes its rewards unequally, based largely on geography and how people can or cannot move about the city and change their locations. Even the titular gesture of *NW* draws attention to the centrality of place to the novel, as well as a particular kind of imperial bureaucracy as established and put in place by the Royal Mail. "NW" stands for the postcode of northwest London; while in most of the rest of the United Kingdom, postcodes can be traced to the city to which they relate ("CF" for Cardiff, "LE" for Leicester), London postcodes relate to the area of the city (the previously mentioned "NW" for northwest London, "SE" for southeast London, and so on). Thus, Smith draws the reader's attention almost immediately to the fact that this novel will focus on London, but a specific area of London—not the center of London, but the northwest portion of the city, a place thought by many to be extra, unimportant, or even criminal; a nowhere (NW) in the context of the capital of the former largest empire in the world. NW, in the eyes of both the neoliberal powers that be and the imperial technologies that shaped London and its colonies, simply does not matter and is not important—a far cry from Henry Perowne's Fitzrovia. Indeed, *NW* is cleanly rooted in the part of the city Zadie Smith most firmly identifies with (Lauren Elkin of the *Daily Beast* calls her "the Bard of Willesden Green"), much as *Saturday* is for Ian McEwan.

Important as well are how Smith's characters inhabit that location, and how they draw cartographies that mediate among the weight of history, myth, and personal lived experience. Unlike in *Saturday*, multiple maps or narratives constitute the novel city of *NW*; Anne Enright notes "though it remains absolutely rooted, stuck to the map, contexts change and narrative styles shift." By narrating (in markedly different styles) the lives of many characters, but most specifically those of two women, Zadie Smith maps her home neighborhood, relying on the central fulcrum of crime to help us understand the space.

Natalie and Leah, as residents of NW, dwell on what many people would consider the periphery of London. It is considered by outsiders to be a "nowhere," violent, impoverished, criminal, but its residents do not see themselves as peripheral. For instance, while traveling on the Tube, Felix "considered the tube map. It did not express his reality. The center was not 'Oxford Circus' but the bright lights of Kilburn High Road. 'Wimbledon' was the countryside, 'Pimlico' pure science fiction. He put his right finger over Pimlico's blue bar. It was nowhere. Who lived there? Who even passed through it?" (190). To the residents of NW, then, central London is nowhere, and Willesden is central. The tension between these conceptions will unfold through the novel, as Leah and Natalie figure out ways to resist the centrally determined myth of the city by incorporating their maps and their travel into the central narrative. It is important to note, as Lauren Elkin does, that in many ways *NW* is "a novel of mobility"; the characters are often moving throughout the city, usually by foot or public transportation (Elkin further notes that "public transport comes to signify a refusal to buy in to the upwardly aspirational values of Thatcherite Britain"; compare this to Henry Perowne's driving). This mobility helps to move the narration forward and more firmly entrench the reader into Zadie Smith's London, while simultaneously ironizing the Thatcherite emphasis on upward mobility by pointing out ways in which some people, like Felix and Nathan, will be constantly rendered immobile by the pressures, crimes, and systems present in neoliberal London. Unlike in *Saturday,* where time ticks forward smoothly throughout the day and Henry Perowne (for the most part) easily navigates the city of London in his car, *NW* presents a city wherein the teleology is jumbled, the inability to move is consistent, and the ability to complete a narrative or a journey is continually frustrated. This is due, Smith suggests, in large part to the legacies of imperialism, which have created a corner of the city for the children of postcolonial immigrants where their moves will be continually frustrated by imperial constructions like racism and neoliberal capitalism.

When readers first meet Leah Hanwell, she is "in a hammock, in the garden of a basement flat. Fenced in, on all sides" (3). She is not doing anything much, just lolling about in the summer heat. Adam Mars-Jones thinks this opening is "reminiscent of *Ulysses,*" and indeed the narrative style echoes the techniques of modernist stream-of-consciousness; however, Leah, unlike Leopold Bloom, is "fenced in," hammocked away from her city. The action in the novel begins with, essentially, a minor crime, when a young woman named Shar rings the doorbell to Leah's flat, startling her out of her lethargy.[7] Shar seems to be controlled by Nathan Bogle, Leah and Natalie's former classmate, in a scheme that involves going around to different houses in the neighborhood and asking for money under the pretext that her mother has been taken to the hospital and she has no cab fare to get there (again a focus on mobility about the city)[8]. Leah's choice to answer the door, let Shar in, and give her money is the catalyst for a scene in which we learn a great deal about Leah's sense of loyalty to her space, as well as her lack of a sense of urgency about time. Smith tells us that Leah lets Shar into her home because "Leah is as faithful in her allegiance to this two-mile square of the city as other people are to their families, or their countries" (6). This early awareness of Leah's relationship to her space colors our impressions of her experience of the city throughout the rest of the novel. She adheres to northwest London, the place in which she grew up, never branching too far away from the Caldwell housing estate in which she first met her childhood friend Natalie (in fact, on page 14, Leah demonstrates she can still point to the flat in which she was born). Except for her stint at university, Leah never has protracted experiences outside NW anywhere in the novel, and a crime that comes to her[9] is the first motor for readers to learn more about Leah and her life.

Our early image of Leah as hammocked and "fenced in" is also a good gateway to explore how Leah experiences time, and what this means for her personal cartography of London. While her mother seems incredibly anxious for Leah to have a baby, referencing Leah's "ticking clock" (20), Leah does not share her mother's concern. Her husband, too, feels a keen sense of urgency, reminding Leah of her age (thirty-five) because he is concerned that they have been trying and failing to get pregnant (23). Leah, on the other hand, flatly "fears the destination," which has "something to do with death and time and age" (27). She thinks to herself, "I am eighteen in my mind I am eighteen and if I do nothing if I stand still nothing will change I will be eighteen always. For always. Time will stop. I'll never die. Very banal, this fear" (27). She has no desire to engage with progress, asking, "Why must love 'move forward'?" (28) and "Why won't everybody stay still?" (85). While clearly a desire to stay young, this desire to live out of time also suggests a refusal to live in her contemporary neoliberal, postmodern age; by checking out of society and withdrawing from forward movement, refusing to undertake the traditionally feminine role of pregnancy, Leah is articulating a desire to live outside the space of traditional Enlightenment teleologies and of the forward progression of London's history.[10] This, in and of itself, is viewed by many as a form of crime against nature or gender.

Her desire to live outside time has a direct effect on her mobility in her space. If Leah's cartography of London were to be viewed on Google Maps, it would be heavily concentrated in the shadows of the Caldwell housing estate tower where she has spent the vast majority of her life. There may be a few juts out into central or south London, but the map would reflect the reality that Leah admits to herself, that she, "born and bred, never goes anywhere" (55). In fact, the text of a Google Map, inserted without context on page 41 (within Leah's narrative section, so logically, readers can assume it applies to her), directs her only from the NW8 postcode to the NW6 postcode. Her geography through both time and space is self-contained, immobile, fenced in, hammocked.

Leah and Natalie, though they have been best friends since childhood, are completely different people. Known as Keisha in childhood (readers never know exactly why she changed her name, but it seems to have something to do with her professional aspirations in a white society), Natalie sets a clear pathway for herself from early childhood. As the two are writing down their future career goals, Leah writes down "manager," while Keisha opts for "doctor or missionary" (205). Natalie's intensely upwardly mobile mindset contrasts sharply with Leah's complacency, and the differences between the two mappings of the city become more and more obvious as the two grow up, apart, and back together.[11] As adults, their various experiences and reactions to the crimes they are presented with also mark their personal divergences.

Natalie's experience of space is, fittingly, an almost 180-degree turn from Leah's. Like Leah, she spends some time away at university and returns to London soon after. However, unlike Leah, Natalie lives in many different areas in the city before eventually returning home to NW. When she finally does return, with her husband in tow and a family soon on the way, she buys a flat that is "twice the size of a Caldwell double," a far geographic and imaginative cry from Leah living still so near to the towers where the two grew up. While Leah "passes the old estate every day on the walk to the corner shop" and "can see it from her backyard," Natalie "lives just far enough to avoid it" (70). If there is a gentrified section of Kilburn, this is where Natalie lives; this is Natalie's map of living in the city, as opposed to Leah's. Natalie adheres to the neoliberal dream of what should be done to postcolonial places like Kilburn; they should be homogenized, gentrified, monetized, with the poverty and crime that also occupies the neighborhood out of sight and out of mind.

With regard to time, Natalie's cognitive map is also vastly different from Leah's. Natalie's narrative section is peppered with the phrase "That was the year . . ." followed by various popular culture references, like "It was the year people began to say 'living the dream'" (301). This gives readers a sense that Natalie is always highly clued into the passage of time, especially as it relates to the individual's experience; this would make sense for someone keyed into a neoliberal logic that favors individualism, progression, and accumulation over time. Readers watch Natalie develop in her narrative section over a span of many years, while all of Leah's section takes place while she is thirty-four, almost thirty-five. As Bill Schwarz says, "Cartographies are not innocent" (157); there is a reason people, and these women, map their spaces and experience their cities in the way they do.

And the reasons for these cartographies, these methods of travel, have to do with the central feature of the novel, the crime of Felix's murder. Indeed, these cartographies are not innocent, if we want to understand "innocence" in the sense of "lack of implication in a larger crime." This larger crime is both Felix's murder and the series of decisions that have structured London in such a way that Felix's murder seems almost inevitable. The death of Felix, a character no one else in the narrative really knows, ruptures the narrative of the novel, and provides a juncture for understanding the imperial and postcolonial crimes that have structured the city, as well as what Natalie and Leah have to do with the narrative of NW and the larger city of London.[12] NW is not peripheral to London; indeed, it is central, and it is necessary to understand Willesden and Kilburn and the people who live there and the crimes they negotiate if we wish to understand the larger narrative of the criminal city. The city has been structured deliberately in such a way that all residents, Natalie and Leah included, are implicated in its larger crimes.

Natalie's major cartography of the city comes about in the fourth section of the novel, titled "Crossing." Natalie has a fight with her husband, Frank, because he has just discovered she has been conducting sexual trysts throughout the city via an account she has registered on a website under the email account KeishaNW@gmail.com.[13] She leaves their home, going, in answer to her husband's shouted inquiries, "Nowhere" (355). (Nowhere, as noted earlier, might be interpreted as NW.) In the following narration, Natalie very explicitly maps her space by walking through the streets of northwest London. Smith allows readers to track her movements by giving particular sections of the narrative titles like "Willesden Lane to Kilburn High Road," "Shoot Up Hill to Fortune Green," "Hampstead Heath," etc. Natalie, through her wanderings, stays true to the geography of constant mobility she has mapped out throughout the novel, but this time in a fairly non-teleological move, her mobility has no apparent purpose and she confines herself solely to NW.

Through her rambles, Natalie does not move through the city as an intensively driven, individual agent. She becomes part of the city, layering her map on top of the existing city geography, rather than blazing through it unheeded. Readers are told, "Walking was what she did now, walking was what she was. She was nothing more or less than the phenomenon of walking. She had no name, no biography, no characteristics" (360). Natalie creates a text, a map; she is fully a part of the city, of it and making the city her own through the act of walking.

Early in her walking, Natalie is briefly prevented from traveling down a road because of an investigation into Felix's stabbing, causing her to need to reroute. As she turns around, she encounters Nathan Bogle (who insists on reverting to history and calling her Keisha throughout their time together).[14] It seems likely that Nathan has just been involved in the stabbing, though it is not made entirely clear and the evidence never goes beyond the circumstantial.[15] Yet it's this death that provides the fulcrum on which the rest of the novel turns, and why we need to read it to more completely understand NW and its centrality to the criminal city of London.

We as readers don't know a great deal about the actual stabbing; we have the news report from Leah's section, Felix's perception of events as he gets stabbed,[16] and Nathan's vague references: "This is on him. Always taking shit too far. How can I stop Tyler though? Tyler should stop Tyler. . . . This isn't even on me, it's on him" (370). But we do know that Felix was mugged[17] before he was stabbed; we know that it is clear Nathan wants to keep moving to avoid the police roadblock; and we also know that Natalie cannot go home for reasons of her own, and so the stage is set for a nighttime ramble through NW for Natalie and Nathan.

As they walk, they talk about the past and take drugs, which adds to the hallucinogenic feeling of the section. Nathan reminisces that, in their school days, he was good at math and very talented at soccer, but that he doesn't "like to think about them days. . . . At the end of the day I'm just out here on the street, grinding" (366). He tells Natalie, "There's no way to live in this country once you're grown. Not at all. They don't want you, your own people don't want you, no one wants you. Ain't the same for girls, it's a man ting. That's the truth of it right there" (376). Nathan's observations about the racist nature of British society, which itself has been born of imperial adventures, is not a mitigating condition for murder, but it does help the reader to understand what at first seemed to be a random act of violence. It is remarkable that the entire narrative, on the surface about a friendship between two women, finds its center in this crime, this murder; this act is what was needed to confront the material reality of the criminal city. No longer Leah's lazing about or Natalie's willful blinkers; it is only by physically engaging with the city and talking with someone fresh from the crime that it is possible to recognize that this life Natalie lives, the mobility she has been allowed, is not possible for so many of the people she grew up with. Nathan's story is necessary to understand the rest of the novel, just as NW is necessary to understand the rest of London.

But, as with the rest of *NW*, everything remains just a little "off," a little off-kilter, a little too sideways. When Natalie and Nathan reach Hornsey Lane, Natalie tells Nathan to stop, for this was where she wanted to go all along. She admits to herself, "That was true. Although it could be said that it did not really become true until the moment she saw the bridge" (383). Natalie climbs onto a bridge and looks through a barrier of railings. What she sees is narrated as follows:

> The view was cross-hatched. St. Paul's in one box. The Gherkin in another. Half a tree. Half a car. Cupolas, spires. Squares, rectangles, half moons, stars. It was impossible to get any sense of the whole. From up here the bus lane was a red gash through the city. The tower blocks were the only thing she could see that made any sense, separated from each other, yet communicating. From this distance they had a logic, stone posts driven into an ancient field, waiting for something to be laid on top of them, a statue, perhaps, or a platform. A man and a woman walked over and stood next to Natalie at the railing. Beautiful view, said the woman. She had a French accent. She didn't sound at all convinced by what she'd said. After a minute the couple walked back down the hill. (384)

Natalie's map of London certainly does not match neatly with the central, dominant myth of London. For one, it is broken up and incomplete: "cross-hatched" and "impossible to get any sense of the whole." She *observes* what is commonly thought of as the center of the city,[18] rather than *being* a part of it, and the bus lane, a symbol of the spatial mobility on which Natalie prides herself, is "a red gash through the city." Her center is the tower blocks, "the only thing she could see that made any sense." They have "a logic," and she likens them to the image of "stone posts driven into an ancient field," another instance of layering in the city geography. Marcus notes that "in the puzzle-piece streets of Northwest London, we realize that there is very little that provides coherence but the estates themselves" (71). It is these estates (and, to some extent, the values of the bygone era of welfare capitalism that they represent) that provide the logic for organizing Smith's novel and city; they are, in Lorentzen's words, the "hooks on which Smith can hang her portrait of North-West London." It is a crime that has spurred Natalie to get here and complete her map, to make NW the center of the narrative. At the same time, Felix's death is rapidly becoming the center of the narrative as well. But what is the import of having this violent crime and this criminal city central to this world Smith is writing? The answer comes in the failed catharsis of the crime, which takes place in the final section of the novel, again titled, like Leah's section, "Visitation."

"Visitation" opens sometime after Natalie's fight with her husband and subsequent late-night journey through the streets of London. Frank, clearly still very angry with her, leaves her for the day with the children. Natalie takes them shopping but receives a phone call from Leah's husband, who is upset because he has discovered Leah's birth control pills, which she has stolen from Natalie. Leah, in response to his anger, goes outside and drops herself into her hammock, where she refuses to move or speak. Leah's husband asks Natalie to come over and talk to Leah for him, and Natalie obliges.

In the scene, Leah tells Natalie she doesn't understand why she leads the life she leads, why Shar is addicted to drugs and Leah is not, why that "poor bastard on Albert Road [Felix]" (400) was stabbed and she was not. Natalie gives her the following reasons: "'Because we worked harder,' she said, laying her head on the back of the bench to consider the wide-open sky. 'We were smarter and we knew we didn't want to end up begging on other people's doorsteps. We wanted to get out. People like Bogle—they didn't want it enough. I'm sorry if you find that answer ugly, Lee, but it's the truth. This is one of the things you learn in a courtroom: people generally get what they deserve'" (401). This answer is patently untrue—what James Arnett classifies as evidence of Natalie's "false consciousness" (4)—but it fits with Natalie's map of the city and the way crime is treated in postcolonial London: people generally get what they "deserve," as it corresponds to racial and colonial logics.[19] Natalie, however, chooses to ignore that and pays lip service to an idea of justice as being "colorblind"—she, and the criminal city, pay no mind to the determinacy of geography. To return to the start of the chapter, it is much like Leah's exclamation when she finds out about Felix's death via the television news. Place, and where one is from, matters deeply, and Leah should know that better than anyone. People don't get what they "deserve," and Natalie should know *that* better than anyone. Place and the crimes interlocked into those places work together to create the city Smith inhabits and shapes. Felix has been central to the entire story, not an elsewhere; he, his neighborhood, and the crime that ends his life are the hinge on which everything turns, much like NW's relationship to the greater city of London.

The ending of *NW*, in which Leah and Natalie report Nathan to the police on suspicion of Felix's murder, has received a tremendous amount of critical attention, much like the climactic scene of home invasion in *Saturday*. Lauren Elkin writes that "Smith runs out of steam toward the end; the scene between Natalie and Leah seems curiously staged and plotted in a novel that prefers to meander." Rachel Cooke, while using the same "running out of steam" metaphor, additionally notes that "Leah and Natalie retreat shufflingly to a position previously held up by the novel for our disapproval (the idea that people get what they deserve)." But perhaps the staging and plotting and retreating are all for a purpose; the reporting of this crime is the catalyst in the part of the novel where Leah and Natalie refuse to undergo or give the reader any kind of catharsis, where they fully buy into neoliberal notions and see it as their duty to be caught up in networks of surveillance and complicity and blame. David Marcus notes, "There is nothing pleasing or satisfying about the end, even if some kind of justice is served." I think it is clear that Smith knows her end is not pleasing or satisfying or cathartic; she has not "run out of steam." Rather, I argue that, like *Saturday*, *NW* is arguing "strenuously," to borrow a word from Ruth Franklin, against its own conclusion. It does this, I believe, in order to refuse the reader the cathartic satisfaction of a neatly solved crime.

After Natalie gives her unsatisfying answer to Leah's query, the two women sit silently in the yard and grope for something to talk about. Natalie tells her she thinks she knows what happened "in Albert Road" (400)—in other words, what happened with Felix's murder. The two women send an email, but find this "not very satisfying" and feel "disappointed" (401). They decide instead to call the police, telling themselves that at the very least, Nathan Bogle is a "person of interest" and that "it's just the right thing to do" (401). The final scene reads as follows: "Leah found the number online. Natalie dialed it. It was Keisha who did the talking. Apart from the fact she drew the phone from her own pocket, the whole process reminded her of nothing so much as those calls the two good friends used to make to boys they liked, back in the day, and always in a slightly hysterical state of mind, two heads pressed together over a handset. 'I got something to tell you,' said Keisha Blake, disguising her voice with her voice" (401).

Does it seem likely Nathan had something to do with Felix's death? Perhaps, but the evidence never leaves the realm of the circumstantial, and it would hardly pass a good-faith test of reasonable doubt. That's not to say, of course, that a jury would not convict; we know far too well the racial disparities in conviction and sentencing, in the United Kingdom as well as in the United States. By making this phone call, Leah and Natalie become complicit in whatever happens to Nathan; his earlier observations about the fate of Black men in London have been proven correct. Catharsis is not possible in the story of this crime, for there are too many layers—was Nathan controlling Shar? Did he, in fact, kill Felix?—and too much history to fully reach a satisfactory answer. As John Berger writes, "It is scarcely any longer possible to tell a straight story sequentially unfolding in time. And this is because we are too aware of what is continually traversing the storyline *laterally*" (22). There is too much history, too many heavy social and political factors, affecting the space of NW to be able to tell a "straight story sequentially unfolding in time" that might allow the reader a kind of catharsis.

In *Raymond Chandler and the Detections of Totality*, Fredric Jameson writes of crime fiction that "the moment of violence, apparently central, is nothing but a diversion" (5). The "moment of violence" in NW ultimately acts as a kind of diversion as well, a way to ask the reader to think more deeply about the criminal city of London. Though the entire novel of NW has centered around the murder of Felix, the lack of catharsis in this crime narrative means that the novel is unable to offer us any kind of clear direction or program for going forward. The reader finishes the novel feeling deeply unsatisfied and a little confused and disoriented—so did he do it or didn't he? Do we sympathize with Leah and Natalie, or with Nathan? Why did this book end not with a bang, but with a whimper?

Both *Saturday* and *NW* lull us into thinking London is a city with a clear teleology, and that these narratives will similarly follow a clearly plotted trajectory that will end with a satisfying conclusion. We follow Perowne as he moves logically through his day and logically through the city in his car; we follow the characters of *NW* as they take orderly bus routes and follow the carefully organized train stops; everyone seems to physically move throughout the city in a way that makes the reader believe the narrative will move in a similar way and reach a logical conclusion, even if the narrative seems disjoined as in *NW*.

But neither of these novels leaves us with an identifiable catharsis or a clear-cut sense of morality or ethics, and that is largely the point. Henry Perowne never reaches any kind of political understanding (even though he might believe that he does), and, seemingly, neither do Natalie or Leah. But, as Richard Kearney writes, catharsis "is a matter of retrieving painful truths . . . rather than some alchemical potion" (63). These truths have been retrieved, and they are available for the careful reader even as they may not be for the main narrators, and that's the point. By having access to the distance between the characters and the text itself, we can unpack racialized panics over crime, discourses over immigration, fears of invasion by the Other, and understand that the denial of catharsis is a way to remind us that empire is not over, and that we need to be pushed into awareness and action, especially in the center of the former empire. This is a lesson that transitions well to Belfast, a remaining outpost of a much-shrunken British Empire.

TWO

"CRIME IS CRIME IS CRIME"

Belfast and Universalizing Narratives

Robert McLiam Wilson's 1996 novel *Eureka Street* is often held up as one of the quintessential novels of the Troubles, the violent conflict in Northern Ireland that consumed the region from (give or take) 1968 to 1998. Alternately narrated by best friends Jake Jackson, a Catholic, and Chuckie Lurgan, a Protestant,[1] the novel follows their lives around Belfast in the years immediately preceding the 1998 Good Friday Agreement, which brought a measure of peace to the city and to Northern Ireland in general. Though the two young men often engage tangentially with the Troubles—Jake is constantly ready to argue about any political points, and Chuckie uses the violence to turn a profit by developing a complicated entrepreneurial scheme revolving around the selling of dildos—the most concrete example of the type of violence associated with the ongoing British occupation of the city occurs with a break from either Jake or Chuckie's narration. About halfway through the novel, the narration moves to an omniscient point of view to give the reader a depiction of an explosion in a sandwich shop in the Belfast city center. After the violence, Wilson writes,

> So, thus, in short, an intricate, say some, mix of history, politics, circumstance and ordnance resulted in the detonation of a one-hundred-pound

bomb in the enclosed space of the front part of a small sandwich shop measuring twenty-two feet by twelve. The confined space and the size of the device created a blast of such magnitude that much of the second floor of the front part of the building collapsed into it and out onto the street. There were fourteen people in the sandwich bar. There were five people in the beauty parlor upstairs when it collapsed and twelve on the street in the immediate vicinity of the flying shrapnel and collapsing beauty parlor. Thirty-one people in all, of whom seventeen stopped existing then or later and of whom eleven were so seriously injured as to lose a limb or an organ. (225)

The clinical detachment with which Wilson describes the violent event, the crime, is underscored by the later assessment of the root causes of the violence. "For the men who planted the bomb knew it wasn't their fault," Wilson writes sarcastically. "It was the fault of their enemies, the oppressors who would not do what they wanted them to do. They had reasonably asked to have their own way. They had not succeeded. They had then threatened to do violent things if they did not get their way" (228). The impersonality of this summation of an extraordinarily complex historical reality continues as Wilson writes, "When this had not succeeded, they were forced to proceed with extreme reluctance to do those violent things. Obviously it was not their fault" (228). In answer to the question "What had happened?" Wilson's narrator answers, "A simple event. The traffic of history and politics had bottlenecked" (231). It's inexplicable, the narrator says. It's just a confluence of incomprehensible people carrying out incomprehensible violence: only "some say" the situation is "intricate." This is nothing but a universal story about why violence is bad and murder is to be condemned. It's a simple event. In the telling, Wilson's narrator denies and forgets the knotted history of imperialism that has led his characters to this point in this city.

But this explosion, of course, was in 1996. Today in the Belfast city center, one could easily be forgiven for thinking the city's rough and violent past is behind it. Stunning, well-kept Victorian and Edwardian architecture lines the grand streets, people flit in and out of shops, and as if in direct challenge to the temperamental Irish weather, Parisianesque sidewalk cafés offering deals on carafes of wine abound. Campaigners urge pedestrians to take pamphlets on the dangers of gentrification, an issue that would have been unthinkable even twenty years ago in the city of *Eureka Street,* and gleaming tourist attractions like the *Titanic* exhibition are seemingly everywhere you look. Walking around for just twenty minutes in 2016, I heard, in addition to English, at least four different languages from people who could have been either tourists or residents. After a few minutes of perambulation, one is left with an image of a bustling, happening city, one that has rebounded from the religious and political violence of the past with a vengeance.

Scratch a little deeper under the surface, though, and one begins to realize that ostensible rebounding is a little forced, slightly contrived. Take, for instance, the rebranding of Belfast's neighborhoods into "quarters"—Cathedral Quarter, Queen's Quarter, Titanic Quarter, Gaeltacht Quarter, and North Belfast. When asked if it bothers anyone that there are five, rather than four, quarters to the city (and that one is not given a formal "quarter" name), my tour guide rolled his eyes. "It drives me absolutely fecking *mad*," he said through gritted teeth. Though it irritates him that no one can count, he continued, what annoys him even more is the artificial way in which the city has been divided and labeled. "These have nothing to do with neighborhoods or districts," he explained. "These quarters have no bearing on the actual areas of the city; the lines are just drawn arbitrarily. Sure, it's just for the tourists—Belfast itself is not this city."

Belfast revealed its "actual" self when I pulled out my phone to Google Map my way to the Divis Tower, a housing estate located at the bottom of the Falls Road, a famous Catholic and republican area of the city. (The Falls Road and its parallel, the Protestant and unionist Shankill Road, are notably not branded as being included in any of the quarters of the city.) I typed "Divis Tower" into the destination box, changed my settings to "walking," and hit the button, expecting to be given straightforward walking directions to the tower. I did, indeed, receive directions, but I also received a shock, for Google Maps had automatically corrected the "Divis Tower" I had typed in to "Patrick Rooney, August 14, 1969."

Patrick Rooney was a nine-year-old child who was the first child to die in the Troubles when he was shot dead by the Royal Ulster Constabulary in the Divis Tower on August 14, 1969. It's unclear why typing "Divis Tower" into Google Maps automatically corrects to his name and death date[2]—a rogue Sinn Feiner coder at Google? Hackers? A glitch in the matrix?—but the message is clear: Belfast may have been divided into these new shiny quarters, but the need for a resolution to past crimes hovers just barely below the surface in this criminal city. Glossy and universalized narratives of the city, like the ones that drive my tour guide "absolutely fecking *mad*," do not allow for any kind of catharsis: what is needed is attention to particularity, to Belfast's specific situation, and to what the crimes in this city mean.

The opening line of *Eureka Street* tells its readers, "All stories are love stories." I argue that this ethos represents a flattening of the history of Belfast that is all too present in contemporary Belfast literature; what is needed, instead, is an understanding that "all stories are crime stories," and that these crimes must be picked apart and reparated before a more just city can be imagined. Anna Burns's *Milkman* (2018), Stuart Neville's *The Twelve* (2010), and David Park's *The Truth Commissioner* (2008) all present aesthetic responses to the need for catharsis in Belfast through various temporal understandings of imperially and Troubles-created crimes. No matter the time period—past, present, or future—none of these novels presents a possibility for catharsis or closure, instead (either strategically or un-self-consciously) portraying the nature of the Troubles as senseless violence, essentially nonpolitical in its nature and unable to be navigated or brought to a close. By rendering Belfast as just inherently violent and as inhabited by parochial people with petty grievances who cannot be sympathized with or understood, it is impossible, these novels seem to argue, to use crimes or portrayals of crimes to bring about any kind of narrative or real-life catharsis.

"A CONTEMPORARY COLONIALISM": THE SITUATION OF BELFAST

Belfast's growth as a city occurred after the British plantation of what we would today call Northern Ireland, when the British Empire encouraged the migration and settlement of English and Scottish Protestants into the heavily Gaelic and Catholic northeast of Ireland. In the nineteenth century, Belfast established itself as a site of industry and manufacturing, primarily known for its linen mills and shipbuilding (both industries indelibly linked to the wider British imperial project). Tensions promulgated by the original plantation of the land were exacerbated in the urban space of Belfast, as Protestants were favored in the industrial labor market and Catholics largely left out. With the partition of Ireland into the Republic and the North in 1921, Belfast, despite its relatively large Catholic population, was made the capital of the new statelet of Northern Ireland. Partition also established a parliament at Stormont, "a Protestant Parliament for Protestant people," in the potentially apocryphal words of Lord Craigavon, the first prime minister of Northern Ireland. In this "Protestant state," ongoing colonialism alongside capitalism and continuing structural discrimination were wielded as tools for privileging Protestants and leaving Catholics at a disadvantage.

Even after southern Ireland gained its independence from Britain, first via Home Rule and later by full severance from the rapidly shrinking British Empire, the North and Belfast remained part of the United Kingdom. The colonial roots of such a political arrangement manifested themselves in the violence of the Troubles, which raged in varying forms of intensity from the 1920s (with the periods of most protracted violence beginning in the 1960s) up to 1998 with the signing of the Good Friday Agreement. Though the Good Friday Agreement is far from perfect, its democratic nature (it was voted on through a series of referendums) and its power-sharing and devolution models have allowed for an overwhelming amount of "buy-in" from the population of Northern Ireland, leading to a sharp decrease in paramilitary and extralegal, as well as police and British, violence.[3] Despite some sporadic flare-ups since 1998, the Good Friday Agreement is typically taken to be the "formal" end of the Troubles, leading to investments of European Union money in the country and the rebranding of Belfast into the tourist destination depicted at the start of this chapter. The Agreement's "neoliberal agenda" (Heidemann 7) has gone a long way toward a cosmetic erasing of the Troubles past and a papering over of Belfast's troubled history in the interest of putting forth a gentrified and sanitized version of the city. However, the Agreement has left the city in an uneasy state of limbo: without a clear and firm transition away from the injustices of the past, without a hard catharsis reached, remnants of sectarian violence still linger and divisions still remain. Belfast, then, remains a "criminal city" in the sense that the ongoing crimes of imperialism have never been fully reparated, and tensions (and sporadic violences) born of the ongoing British occupation persist despite late twentieth- and twenty-first-century attempts to wish them away.

These divisions and violences, often talked about in the language of crime and violence, can be traced back to imperial arrangements. Though it is true, as Deepika Bahri says, that "if the Irish case evinces symptoms of postcoloniality at all, it is still grudgingly conceded to be only arguably, anomalously, or putatively so" (55), meaning that the situation of Ireland in larger postcolonial discourses is shaky or tenuous, I hold that Ireland, due to its centuries of British governance and continuing British occupation of the North, can be firmly situated in a colonial and postcolonial context. As Maureen E. Ruprecht Fadem writes, "The roots of the contemporary Troubles are not found, as widely believed, in protracted tribal mentalities or cultural hostilities. They are located in the ways colonial discourse came to be enunciated and reified" (17). For this reason, Seamus Deane of the Field Day group of writers and intellectuals writes, "We are not witnessing in Northern Ireland some outmoded battle between religious sects that properly belong to the seventeenth century. We are witnessing rather the effects of a contemporary colonialism that has retained and developed an ideology of dominance and subservience within the readily available idiom of religious division" (8). Others disagree with this framework—Justin Quinn, for instance, writes of Northern Ireland that "there is no clear and consistent line between colonized and colonizer" (99), and Edna Longley directly contradicts Deane by saying of the work cited above, "Field Day understandably favours theorists who might help to insert Northern Ireland/Ireland into the colonial/post-colonial frame (especially its simpler models)" (28), while noting that "uneven civic development in the British Isles [and] European contexts" (28) might trouble the strict binary Deane has set up. However, even if the paradigm may not be as clean-cut as Deane would lead the reader to believe, it is true that the divisions first enunciated by empire remain, at least, in the cultural and literary imagination of the city, even if the reality on the ground is more complicated after the power sharing of the Good Friday Agreement. Regardless of these reforms, Protestants retain most of the economic and social power in Northern Ireland, and the country was forced to Brexit along with the rest of the United Kingdom, even though a majority of the Northern Irish population voted against the measure, given that they must follow what the more populous England votes to do. This "contemporary colonialism" entrenches and thrives upon divisions initially created by empire. It is necessary to take this colonial history into account in order to present a full and appropriately complex novelistic treatment of Belfast, especially when it comes to crime.

In 1981, in the midst of the bloodiest times of the Troubles, Margaret Thatcher gave two speeches on Northern Ireland, and specifically on republican hunger strikers in the Maze Prison, who were asking to be given political status within the prison walls. In one March speech, she declared, "There is no such thing as political murder, political bombing, or political violence. There is only criminal murder, criminal bombing, and criminal violence. We will not compromise on this. There will be no political status." In April, she reiterated, "There can be no question of political status for someone who is serving a sentence for crime. Crime is crime is crime: it is not political, it is crime, and there can be no question of granting political status." This understanding of the world is, of course, impossibly and performatively naïve—of course crime is always political, especially in a colonial situation—but it also mirrors closely the narrative of Belfast in *Eureka Street*, that violence in Belfast is just a "simple event," an instance of incomprehensible violence. It is impossible for a city to reach a kind of catharsis if the story is presented in such a simplistic way: indeed, if crime is "not political," what's the point of getting to the root of it, if those carrying it out are simply madmen bent on "criminal murder, criminal bombing, and criminal violence"?

This chapter, by looking at three novels, will hold that crime and the city of Belfast itself are too often flattened in novelistic treatments of the Troubles; failure to attend to the realities of the criminal city forecloses any possibility for cathartic effects of crime. I draw here on Peter Mahon, who writes of what he calls a "rhetoric of sameness" or a "recurrent and enduring agnosticism" that "threads its way through over thirty years of commentary (academic, journalistic, and anecdotal) on the Troubles" (3). "The notion," he continues, "that both sides of the political divide in Northern Ireland are essentially the 'same' is also often found in Northern Irish literary and cinematic texts that deal with the Troubles" (3), citing *Eureka Street* in particular. Mahon contends that these types of texts "view the political violence in Northern Ireland as something that is visited upon 'ordinary people' who, regardless of their background, spend most of their time trying not to get caught up in it" (3).

This may seem positive or even progressive on the surface; indeed, even Mahon acknowledges that the rhetoric of sameness is "borne of a well-meaning desire that seeks to find what the two conflicting communities in Northern Ireland have in common" (3). However, Mahon argues, "the rhetoric of sameness not only reduces the possibility of seeing politics at work in how Troubles texts stage intersubjective relationships; it also prevents the reader from engaging with the ways such texts set about reinscribing the subject" (7). According to Mahon, the rhetoric of sameness strips agency from the reader and makes it less possible for them to "think and act politically outside of [the rhetoric of sameness's] apparently apolitical frame" (7).

This rhetoric of sameness also prevents the reader from reaching any kind of catharsis at the conclusion of each crime story.

This is all despite Northern Ireland's reputation as a hotbed of crime fiction. Northern Irish fiction in recent years has made a substantial name for itself via the subgenre of what Val McDermid, among others, has termed "Emerald Noir": William Meier and Ian Campbell Ross note that "the subject of crime in Ireland since 1921 also reveals ways in which twentieth-century Irish crime continues to be marked by its colonial past" (15). Even as it engages with a colonial past, however, novels concerned with crime (crime literature or crime in literature) in Belfast tend to present the Troubles as a nonspecific, universal act of violence that is to be condemned and depoliticized. I argue that the tendency to universalize in literary and political discourses about Belfast—to argue that "crime is crime is crime" or that the situation in Belfast is a "simple event" not worthy of getting to the bottom of—prevents the city from fully reconciling its past and moving to the future. By portraying sectarian violence as just straightforward, depoliticized crime, Belfast novels will never come to a catharsis: in fact, the lack of reconciliation at the ends of these texts points specifically to the need to take history and colonialism seriously.

"DO NOT GET IN HIS VEHICLES": ANNA BURNS'S *MILKMAN*

Anna Burns's *Milkman*, winner of the 2018 Man Booker Prize, is the tale of an insular community engaged in sectarian warfare with another community "over the road" that is loyal to a country "over the water." The city is not named, though it bears strong resemblances to the Belfast of Burns's birth, specifically during the 1980s, the bloodiest times of the Troubles. Nor are the characters named: the story is told from the point of view of "middle sister," and everyone is defined in relationship to her: "little sister," "brother-in-law," "maybe-boyfriend," etc. The only named character is Milkman, a shadowy and dangerous paramilitary who becomes fixated on middle sister, following her on her runs and showing up to give her rides from place to place. Middle sister, who has a sort of vaguely defined relationship with someone she calls "maybe-boyfriend," is actively uninterested in pursuing a relationship with

Milkman (he does not deliver milk, "Milkman" is his last name), and yet the community seems to believe she is romantically engaged with him, treating her with a mixture of suspicion, fear, and respect. The novel, though never specifically naming the events of the Troubles or specifics about the city of Belfast (or even names of individual characters), is recognizably about Northern Ireland's colonized situation, and even more specifically about a type of gender-based violence men rarely have to deal with: stalking and unwanted sexual interest. It is this lack of geographical, personal, and chronological specifics that prevents the novel from reaching a satisfying conclusion: without details on which we can peg our reading, *Milkman* remains simmeringly violent, never coming to a full boil.

Though intimately concerned with transportation and mobility throughout the city—one of Milkman's key seduction techniques involves trying to get middle sister to get into his car, she goes on runs throughout the city, her maybe-boyfriend works in a car repair shop—*Milkman* never engages with teleology in a way that such focus on mobility and movement might suggest. Merritt Moseley calls it a "hypnotic read" (153), and *Milkman* is undoubtedly such: the city the novel depicts seems permanently locked in a sort of odd stasis, as though people are waiting with bated breath for some kind of resolution or event that never really happens. Middle sister's family has been deeply and indelibly scarred by the unnamed conflict, with family members murdered by paramilitaries or the state, emigrating to escape the violence, and becoming involved in the violence locally. Yet even with the personal nature of the fighting, middle sister seems remarkably disengaged from the roots of the violence and disinterested in interrogating why particular things and events happen the way they do: she doesn't even really seem to have an opinion on the conflict, preferring instead to focus on the judgmental and insular nature of her own community. Dwight Garner observes that the novel "circles and circles its subject matter, like a dog about to sit, while rarely seizing upon any sort of clarity of emotional resonance." Middle sister muses of her upbringing in such an environment, "At the time, age eighteen, having been brought up in a hair-trigger society where the ground rules were—if no physically violent touch was being laid upon you, and no outright verbal insults were being levelled at you, and no taunting looks in the vicinity either, then nothing was happening, so how could you be under attack from something that wasn't there?" (6). The presence of a background menace that no one wants to talk about keeps the novel in a kind of suspended animation:

nothing's there, even though clearly something *is* there, and the lack of discourse keeps the community circling around the heart of the matter. This, of course, is the point; by refusing to engage with specifics, Burns's novel mirrors well the state of ongoing violence and colonialism in the criminal city of Belfast.

Peter Mahon has written of Troubles texts that they "foster a human essentialism" (5), which can certainly be seen in *Milkman*. Claire Kilroy writes of the novel that "although [it] is set in Northern Ireland during the 1970s, it prompts thoughts of other regimes and their impact: Stalinist Russia, the Taliban." Middle sister herself alludes to her lack of desire to be weighed down by the specifics of her community and her city's historical situation: speaking of her habit of reading books while walking around, she says of her chosen reading material, "This would be a nineteenth-century book because I did not like twentieth-century books because I did not like the twentieth century" (5). Fair enough—as elucidated above, the twentieth century has not been kind to middle sister, her family, or her community. She later notes, "I myself spent most of my time with my back turned in the nineteenth century, even the eighteenth century, sometimes the seventeenth and sixteenth centuries, yet even then, I couldn't stop having a view" (112). The consistency of middle sister's back-turning to the present makes it difficult for the reader to get a firm grasp on the city, which is, of course, the point.

Unspecified though it is, the city in *Milkman* is riddled with crime and violence. Murders, both by paramilitaries and state police officers, happen on a regular basis, carbombs (stylized as one word through the novel) consistently explode, and a menacing figure known as "tablets girl" goes around trying to poison people. Because most of these crimes have a political valence—Milkman is a paramilitary for, we can assume, one of the Catholic/republican groups in the area, and the carbombs are a recognizable IRA tactic from this time period—middle sister understands intimately the partisan nature of her community, even if she is not particularly interested in engaging with it. As Milkman's stalking grows more and more intense, she begins to realize that he intends to get rid of maybe-boyfriend: "Maybe-boyfriend," middle sister muses, "was to be billed under the catch-all of the political problems even if, in reality, the milkman was going to kill him out of disguised sexual jealousy over me" (115). Her realization causes her to begin to drift away from maybe-boyfriend, without telling him the specifics of why in fear that will put him in danger, and she becomes even more aloof from the community, heightening her lack of belonging and disengagement from the specifics of history.

Aaron Kelly has written of crime fiction that it has the potential to "[provide] resolutions to history" (7). *Milkman*, though not typically classified as crime fiction, certainly is deeply and inextricably concerned with figurations of crime—both crimes committed by paramilitaries and those committed by state actors—and with what those figurations mean for a family, a community, a city, a nation, a world. However, it cannot provide a resolution to history in the way Kelly indicates crime fiction typically can, largely due to the aforementioned lack of specifics that preclude climax, catharsis, or resolution. But the potential for catharsis is also largely predicated on the possibility of teleology: we've progressed far enough, we're at a breaking point, we need something to take us over the edge to feel some kind of relief. Besides the lack of specifics about history and geography, *Milkman* cannot (and steadfastly refuses to) reach this point due in large part to its understanding of urban space and geography, and what possibilities are inherent for moving around and mapping said space.

As previously mentioned, middle sister enjoys going for runs in her city, and she spends a significant amount of time walking or running around, either for exercise, for transportation purposes, or to get some reading done. One of the first things we learn about her is the way she moves throughout her city: "Cars were not in abundance then," she tells us, "and public transport, because of bombscares and hijackings, was intermittently withdrawn.... I liked walking" (3).[4] Her thinking, she says "was at its best, its most flowering, whenever I was walking" (80). This, of course, puts her on display for the neighborhood, and is potentially one of the reasons why Milkman is drawn to her to begin with; she is seemingly available, and he can observe her movements in a way he could not someone who travels less or who uses different routes or transportation methods. One of the main areas where he accosts her, repeatedly, is while she is running for exercise through the local parks and reservoirs. She has to run an odd route, "owing to religious geography, which meant repeatedly going round a much smaller area in order to get a comparable effect" (11). This compacted space makes middle sister easier to track down and follow, and much of Milkman's pursuance of her relies on transportation and mobility as well.

One of the first things Milkman tries to do is curtail middle sister's mobility, and get her to rely on him for these kinds of needs. He pressures her to accept rides from him, telling her that she would "be spared the bother of bus-jackings, of those public vehicles getting caught up in every riot and crossfire, plus I'd be spared all other irritations of daily public transport as well" (136). The campaign to accept a ride from Milkman intensifies, and middle sister's oldest friend takes her out for a drink, warning her, "*Whatever you do, no matter what, friend, do not get in his vehicles*" (298). It is clear that relying on Milkman for transportation and mobility represents crossing some line that can never be uncrossed.

It's notable here the way power is spatialized, not only in terms of religious geography but also in terms of gender. It is a common trope of literature dealing with the Troubles to represent the city of Belfast as cross-hatched by borders, some visible and some invisible, that cannot be crossed by those belonging to the "wrong" religious community: these borders may be represented by tangible entities such as "peace walls" that divide Catholics and Protestants, or they may be understood as silent shibboleths that are intuitively understood by all who inhabit this particular urban space. Eamonn Hughes has noted that Northern Irish, and particularly Belfast, writers tend to share "an interest in geography" (8), which is closely linked to a concurrent focus on how the city is mapped via literature, and particularly the novel. However, typically this interest in geography and mapping manifests itself through the male gaze: Bernard MacLaverty, Glenn Paterson, and Robert McLiam Wilson (of *Eureka Street*) are all the writers that come most immediately to mind.

But it is rare for a novel to deal with issues of how the city is mapped and how people move throughout it in terms of gender and sexual violence in the context of the Troubles. Catherine Toal has written of *Milkman*'s "attention to the still underplayed dynamics of gender inequality during the Troubles, in particular women's vulnerability to a predatory violence at once psychological and physical," which is a consistent theme of the novel: middle sister refers to Milkman as being "much more frightening, much more dangerous" than even a brother-in-law who made sexual passes at her when she was twelve and he thirty-five. Because middle sister has an extra layer of sexual violence and gender-based crimes to deal with, the novel naturally gravitates toward a more universalizing tone: in addition to Kilroy's citation of Stalinist Russia and the Taliban, middle sister's travails with regard to sexual harassment would be familiar to virtually any woman or femme who has ever lived in a community of any size. The unwanted sexual attention is also what limits her geography, movement, and mobility to an extent that surpasses the traditionally male-dominated category of Troubles fiction.

These limitations are what might prevent the community, and middle sister in general, from reaching a boiling point, though they live in a world of ever-present and constant crime. Catharsis, according to Aristotle, is closely linked to the importance of a building plot, and it necessitates a sense of teleology: things get worse and worse and worse until they are unbearable, and an act must come about that brings the audience to catharsis. Middle sister is never allowed to run until she is naturally out of space; she must continually do loops to avoid sectarian geographies. She cannot move about her city in a straightforward manner, and this mobility and mapping links in with the novel's sense of circling around the drain but never quite getting to the heart or the specifics of what is going on in this city.

Bertolt Brecht writes that the crime novel affords us the pleasure of "specifying the causality of human actions" (93). Because *Milkman* never gets particularly specific about the cause of the violence and crime in the unnamed criminal city (that is clearly Belfast), the reader cannot drill down into the root of why people are behaving the way they are. Brecht also writes that "catastrophes" in the crime novel allow us to "infer the manner in which our social formation functions" (94). However, in *Milkman,* because there never is a catastrophe, just consistent, low-level threats—what Mark O'Connell calls "a pulsating menace"—readers never reach enlightenment or catharsis or an understanding of how "our social formation functions." There is no catastrophe to get us there. This city, though about middle sister's particular experience, could be anywhere that young girls face violence, anywhere divided by religious or ethnic tensions.

Milkman was published in 2018, twenty years after the Good Friday Agreement and somewhere around thirty years after the worst bloodshed of the Troubles in the 1980s, which seems roughly the time period in which the novel itself is set. The characters living in the city of Burns's making never reach any kind of resolution. Though Milkman is eventually shot and killed by state forces, the conflict continues unabated and Milkman is even turned into a hero. Little boys in the neighborhood begin "taking turns at being good guy in their new play of the latest martyr killed recently in the political problems: Renouncer Hero Milkman, shadowed, set upon, then gunned down in their usual cowardly fashion by that murder squad spawned by a terrorist state" (341). Middle sister must continue living in a world of gendered violence and expectations as the political battle rages on and her community continues to be oppressed by the state: even through all this crime, nothing is enough to bring the community any kind of resolution. And for an audience reading in the supposed safety of the twenty-first century, it seems an ominous warning that things have never really changed since the days of *Milkman*: after all, with renewed sectarian violence in the North and gendered violence continuing, the universalizing tale of the novel seems still applicable almost anywhere and anytime.

"TIMES CHANGE, EVEN IF PEOPLE DON'T": STUART NEVILLE'S *THE TWELVE*

Gerry Fegan, the protagonist of Stuart Neville's 2010 thriller *The Twelve* (also published as *The Ghosts of Belfast*), is a former IRA man who has recently been released back onto the streets of twenty-first-century Belfast after serving time in the Maze prison for the murder of twelve individuals, carried out at the behest of various IRA commanders. He is haunted by the ghosts of those he has killed—three British soldiers, two each of Ulster Defense Regiment and Ulster Freedom Fighter paramilitaries; a policeman; and four civilians unfortunate enough to have been in the way when Fegan set out to kill his targeted victims. The twelve ghosts follow Fegan around, demanding retribution in the form of killing those who ordered or otherwise orchestrated their murders. Fegan becomes convinced that the only way to rid himself of these ghosts is to enact justice in the way his victims are asking, and so he takes off on an avenging tour of Belfast, murdering those—politicians, lawyers, clergymen, and others—who had ordered the murders of the original twelve. The revenge Fegan engages in on behalf of his victims functions as an explicit example of cathartic crime, demonstrating in the meantime how imperial legacies have mapped Belfast and the limitations of seeking catharsis through further violence.

As Fegan carries out his crimes, we encounter former IRA paramilitaries who, in a post-Agreement era, have turned into capitalist investors wrangling London money earmarked for development and tourist attraction schemes. Fegan's first present-day victim, the IRA-man-turned-developer/politician Michael McKenna, observes, "The Brits are throwing so much money at this that I almost feel bad taking it off them. Almost" (8), indicating how money from London, intended as a form of reparations for the Troubles, instead has merged with the leftovers of the Troubles-era purveyors of violent crime. The ghosts that haunt Fegan and whom he must destroy, then, act as spectral reminders of colonialism and the Troubles—entities once thought dead that are back in less tangible, more ethereal, shiftier form, constantly present and reminiscent of the physical violence of the late twentieth century.

Aaron Kelly has written of the Northern Irish thriller that, despite what preconceptions readers may hold, in Northern Ireland and Belfast, "the putatively ungraspable and penumbral conspiracy, which ultimately foreshadows and obsessively stalks these texts is none other than the seemingly vast inscrutable logic of the global conspiracy of global capitalism itself" (164). This emphasis on the "global conspiracy of global capitalism" can also be seen in the work of Joe Cleary, who has written that in some newer thrillers "the North is now to be redeemed not by the British security forces but by the energies and excitements of global capital" (141)—for Cleary, it is no longer British security forces controlling the North, but global capitalism. The neoliberal capital investments made in Belfast—in the form of money earmarked for tourist attractions, or community arts schemes, or street beautification plans—are universalizing gestures, in that they erase the specificities of Belfast's history and specific struggles in an effort to present a face of a "normal" city, a place where people would like to visit and live and work and play, something like a northern Barcelona, seemingly (though not realistically) free of the colonial and sectarian baggage of the past. By placing Gerry Fegan at the center of *The Twelve*, Neville allows his readers to occupy both the gritty Belfast of old and the contemporary neoliberal Belfast with the shining new face. We see how Fegan's crimes expose the colonial sectarian rifts that underlay his original murders, as well as the continuing imperialism and neocolonialism—in the form of normalized foreign capital investment—that persist in structuring his city, and how they make any form of catharsis untenable and unsatisfying. Readers, in short, see how Belfast can simultaneously be mapped as the city of the five gleaming quarters and as the criminal city of Patrick Rooney, a confluence that goes unnoticed by many.

When we first meet Gerry Fegan, he is exceedingly drunk in a shabby Belfast pub and in the company of the ghosts of his twelve murder victims. We are told the ghosts follow Fegan everywhere, that he knows tonight they will follow him "through the streets of Belfast, in his house, up his stairs, and into his bedroom" (3). We seem to have a protagonist tortured by his actions, stuck in a rut and attempting to move forward against the tide by engaging in vigilante criminality, a fairly standard revenge story. If he can kill those who made him kill in the first place, the logic goes, the crimes will be put to bed and Fegan will have some sense of closure. But *The Twelve* also presents a novel of a depoliticized Belfast, where Fegan's crimes are shorn of their historical baggage and understood instead as simply irredeemable violence. Fegan thinks of his time in prison: "They called people like him political prisoners. Not murderers or thieves, not extortionists or blackmailers. Not criminals of any kind, just victims of circumstance" (9). This categorization, thirty years after Margaret Thatcher railed against such classifications, bothers him greatly, for Fegan concludes while in the Maze prison that there is no difference between him and an "Ordinary Decent Criminal," the slang term for someone who commits a non-paramilitary crime; he tells the politician Michael McKenna darkly, "There's no respecting what I've done" (11). The novel presents Fegan's crimes as simply "criminal murder, criminal violence"; he thinks to himself of his past and present crimes, "Times change, even if people don't" (6), indicating he sees himself as an inherently violent man, shorn of political context.

The same night we readers meet Fegan, he takes McKenna to the docks to commit his first post-Agreement murder. After a few reminiscences on how the city is changed and is getting substantially wealthier, McKenna realizes why the two are there and tries to wheedle his way out of his impending death by appealing to his and Fegan's shared past. He calls up a specific memory, "that time the Brits got us for bricking them" (21), and reminds Gerry, "You were never scared. Not of anybody. You stood your ground. You waited til you saw the whites of their eyes before you chucked yours" (22). Though Fegan tells him to stop, dreading the memories as they "cursed him" (22), McKenna senses an opening and keeps going, bringing up when the soldiers "got hold of wee Patsy, and he pissed himself all over one of them" (22). This brings a smile to Fegan's face, but the moment is ruined when McKenna reminds him that they joined the IRA the next day. The reminder of the IRA, and the crimes he committed for the organization, strengthens Gerry's resolve, and he once again tells McKenna, "That's enough" (23).

That tactic proving unsuccessful, McKenna tries guilt instead. "It was me got you in, Gerry," he says. "They'd have never taken you without me.

Don't you forget that. You'd have been nothing without me, just another Catholic boy on the dole" (23). Far from this working to shame Gerry away from murder, this makes him double down: Gerry places the blame on McKenna, retorting, "That's right . . . I'd have been nothing. I'd have *done* nothing. And those people would be alive. That boy would be alive. He'd have a wife, children, a home, all of that. We took that away from him. You and me" (23). Fegan, no longer interested in memories of a boyhood spent acting out against British soldiers or reminiscences of the big man he became within the paramilitary organization, wipes away the specifics of the crime he committed and all hint of imperial or political context: to McKenna, Gerry's victim was "a fucking tout" who betrayed the anticolonial cause and "squealed to the cops" and "was dead the second he opened his mouth" (23), but to Fegan, he is a blank slate of a human who should have had a family and a home. Just before he pulls the trigger on McKenna, Fegan mutters to himself, "Jesus, I promised myself I'd never do this again" (23), right before he does.

This instance of "criminal murder" is quickly divorced from its political and historical context; Edward Hargreaves MP, Minister of State for Northern Ireland, says when told of the murder, "So, it's not political. Let's try and keep it that way, shall we?" (50). Though the Troubles are always present in the background, serving to highlight and give context for character development and the map of the city, twenty-first-century Gerry Fegan is not a man with any political convictions or acting on behalf of any kind of political or military group. He has wiped out any specificities about the twelve murders that landed him in jail. Gerry Fegan, republican nationalist, no longer exists; the crimes of imperialism have been seemingly rinsed away by prison time and the Good Friday Agreement. In their place, supposedly, are universalized Ordinary Decent Murders, committed against a backdrop of a gentrifying city. Because Gerry is deeply uneasy with the new city in which he finds himself, and lacks knowledge of how to adapt himself to this new world, he resorts to actions that he has performed in the past, but he removes all notions of what might be specific to Belfast or to Northern Irish colonial history from them, mirroring the city's developments that have taken place while he has been in prison.

In the twenty-first century, foreign and imperial investment has taken on a new intensity in Belfast; the Good Friday Agreement, with its focus on ending the conflict, works to drive home the "key ideological message" from "both the Irish and British states" that "peace dividends are to be achieved through conventional economics. A dropping unemployment rate, additional and religiously mixed middle-income employment, and a vibrant city-centre nightlife are meant to show that Belfast is 'booming' in a different way" (Shirlow 101). Economics are held to be the panacea, the accompanying fundamentalist narrative to the idea "only neoliberalism can fix it." There is, to crib another line from Margaret Thatcher, essentially no alternative.

We see the effects of such gentrification in *The Twelve*, shortly after Fegan has been released from police custody for the shooting of Michael McKenna (charges are ultimately dropped), and he is being driven home by his "human rights" lawyer, another former IRA man named Patsy Toner who has, like McKenna, reinvented himself for an era of "peace." (It is unclear if this Patsy is the same one who "pissed himself.") They drive along the Lisburn Road, and "designer boutiques, restaurants and wine bars passed on either side. Students and young professionals crossed at the lights. *They think the city belongs to them now*, Fegan thought" (36). He sees a young woman cross the street, and Fegan "wondered if she was even born when they scraped the body parts off the streets with shovels" (36). Fegan, not part of this twenty-first-century scene, is "angered at his own bitterness. The quiet after weeks of clamour unsettled him . . . he found the clarity disorienting" (36). Released into a city he does not recognize, Fegan still lives in a space the young professionals cannot see, a place in which "the eleven [remaining ghosts] were there somewhere, just beyond his vision, waiting" (36), where he finds the lack of Troubles violence "disorienting" rather than calming or soothing. Fegan's unease at the sleek Belfast of wine bars is not just the disquiet of a man so recently incarcerated attempting to find his way back into modern urban life; it is a gesture to the reader that crime and violence, even if depoliticized, still snake under the surface of the city, and that these crimes are invisible to those who live in a gentrified Belfast and think the city belongs to them and is just like any other city in Europe. Fegan no longer believes his crimes had any political meaning, but still believes that he is still a violent man; just as his crimes are universalized in the twenty-first century, so is the narrative of Belfast the city. Times change, even if people don't.

By killing all the people who ordered his Troubles murders in order to, in turn, rid himself of the ghosts that remind him of his Troubles and colonial past, Fegan is participating in that erasure of community memory. To be clear, I do not wish to sound nostalgic for the times "when they scraped the body parts off the streets with shovels" (36); however, Fegan's actions in ridding himself of anyone who reminds him of the Troubles participates in globalized capital's project of minimizing the effects of Belfast's imperial and colonial violence in favor of a projection of a city that has safely shuttered its past and achieved closure to become just like any other city. After he has killed everybody that "needs" killing, the final ghost leaves him, granting him "mercy" on the way (460); the implication is that all Fegan's crimes are individualized acts of violence against individual people who can grant him individual mercy, not that the crimes are part of a larger matrix of colonialism and layers upon layers of history. Instead, one person's ghost can wave a magic wand and grant Fegan mercy.

And in so doing, Fegan's participation in the project to universalize Belfast, to absolve it of its sins and make it into a city just like any other, has a twofold effect. By looking for a kind of closure or catharsis from the Troubles era, but by doing so in ways that are strongly reminiscent of the Troubles and the colonial past, Fegan simultaneously tries to erase community memory and works to reinforce it. He participates in "the history of capitalist imperialism" (Lazarus 15) while trying to put to bed "the ongoing life of [empire's] residues" (Young 21), trying to map a city divorced from his and its past crimes but not engaging in a nuanced way with the issues that marked this past. In this way, Fegan participates in ideologies similar to those of the narrator of *Eureka Street*, the novel which, for Heidemann, is a "transition text" that "anticipates certain political developments" like neoliberal "global capitalism, consumerism, or proto-cosmopolitanism" (64). *Eureka Street*'s status as a "transitional," or bridge, text, and its foreshadowing of future neoliberal developments, contributes to that same text's casting of the Troubles and colonial struggle in Belfast as just a simple humanitarian issue; the message is that it is deplorable that both sides are killing each other, a message seemingly unaccompanied by political analysis or further deconstruction. Peter Mahon writes that *Eureka Street* endorses a "rhetoric of sameness" (4), a philosophy that "both sides of the political divide in Northern Ireland are essentially the same" (3). Cleary writes of that novel that "there is little attempt imaginatively to explore why the communities should be so divided in the first instance, why the cycle of violence should be so sustained, or why so concentrated in working-class districts" (141). Both analyses translate well to Neville's novel. *The Twelve*, by its main character's lack of attention to colonial and historical root causes of crime and its wish instead for the divisions and violence to be over and shelved (while simultaneously being vaguely annoyed at those too young to remember the Troubles), demonstrates neoliberalism and neocolonialism's potentials to gloss over, forget, push aside, and universalize the specificities of local spaces, making *The Twelve* a fascinating case study for the post–Good Friday Agreement city of Belfast.

"A PATHETIC AND PRIMITIVE TRIBAL WAR": DAVID PARK'S *THE TRUTH COMMISSIONER*

Anna Burns's *Milkman* focuses on Belfast at the height of the Troubles; Stuart Neville's *The Twelve* is a realistic (except for the ghosts) take on the city in the immediate aftermath of the Good Friday Agreement; David Park's *The Truth Commissioner* is a projected, imaginary future for a Belfast that eventually undergoes a South African–style Truth and Reconciliation Commission. The novel focuses on four men—head Truth Commissioner Henry Stanfield, former IRA man and current Minister for Children and Culture Francis Gilroy, retired RUC detective James Fenton, and ex-IRA man and current resident of Florida Michael Madden (who goes by the name Danny now)—as they navigate the realities of post-Troubles Belfast and, in particular, the disappearance years earlier of a young man named Connor Walshe. Stanfield is charged with overseeing this, as well as many other, cases, and Gilroy, Fenton, and Madden are reluctantly drawn back into a history they had hoped to leave behind many years earlier.

The Truth Commissioner meditates a great deal on the nature of truth: Is there such a thing as objective truth? Is it helpful to hear it? Can the truth bring some kind of closure, catharsis, climax? In the process of mulling over these kinds of questions, the novel suggests that there is something precious about the conflict in Northern Ireland, that the people involved are uniquely wrapped up in their own nonsense and that they refuse to join the rest of us here in the civilized twenty-first century. The novel does not see the Troubles as a colonial or postcolonial conflict, choosing instead to portray the violence and associated crimes as incomprehensible and thus never able to be sorted out or brought to anything resembling justice.

The opening scene of the novel covers the murder of Connor Walshe, but the identities of the men involved are deliberately left obscure. The novel then jumps decades into the future, where we meet Henry Stanfield, who is in South Africa on a training trip for his own upcoming mission as a truth commissioner in Northern Ireland. The trip is coming to an end, and he is out with many younger lawyers who have convinced him to go shark diving off the coast. He does not want to be there, but is afraid of losing face before his subordinates; he reluctantly joins them on the boat, ruefully thinking to himself, "At the end of a three-week fact-finding trip to South Africa, to see what lessons could be gleaned from their experience of a Truth and Reconciliation process, this is not the perfect climax he envisaged" (9). This sense—that there will not a be a perfect climax, no catharsis—pervades the rest of *The Truth Commissioner*, as Park provides the reader with plenty of crime, bloodshed, and violence, but with no sense of a closure coming anywhere near the proceedings.

Stephen O'Neill writes of the conflict in Northern Ireland that "the interpretation of the Troubles as rooted in a widespread mentality or inherited characteristic rather than the neglect of the state has been particularly influential" (177). Stanfield seems to subscribe to this ideal, chalking up the Troubles as a sort of immature playground fight among violent people who can't be trusted to do anything differently, rather than as a conflict born of colonialism and oppression. He thinks of the conflict:

> And after all, what was it really, except some rather pathetic and primitive tribal war where only the replacement of traditional weapons by Semtex and the rest succeeded in bringing it to temporary attention on a bigger stage? Now the world doesn't care any more because there are bigger wars and better terrors and all that remains is this final tidying up, this drawing a line, this putting to bed—the euphemisms he has had to endure are potentially endless—but as he takes one final look at the sealed tightness of the sky and then tells Beckett to drive him to the office, there is only one image that he nurtures and it's of an old manged, flea-infested dog returning to inspect its own sick. (25)

Though Stanfield's words are harsher than those entertained by middle sister in *Milkman* or Gerry Fegan in *The Twelve*—"pathetic and primitive tribal war" strikes me as especially condescending, patronizing, and dismissive—they help to situate the novel in a similar genre of Troubles fiction. Like middle sister's vague, unnamed, and nonspecific city and Fegan's insistence that he's not a political prisoner and that his crimes are ordinary and decent, Stanfield's musings on the Troubles—a conflict he is both dismissive of and paid to help shepherd to a narrative close!—indicate that this is just a pesky little flare-up, that the uncivilized people up there in Belfast have no business complaining about their weird little sectarian conflict that no one can be bothered to understand. Whereas middle sister is dealing with layers of trauma, augmented by the sexual violence she has to undergo, and Fegan might need a comforting narrative to make himself comfortable with his own actions, Stanfield is actively trivializing, superior, and disdainful. Even though he was born and spent his first twelve years in Belfast, the son of an Irish Catholic mother and an English Protestant father, he tacks onto centuries of dehumanizing British stereotypes about the Irish. He thinks, looking at the city, that "something primitive . . . still lurks just below the surface" (39). This charming attitude—he uses "primitive" twice in fourteen pages!—is an early indication to the reader that this truth and reconciliation commission, thought experiment though it may be, will not be a particularly productive use of anyone's time.

Stanfield, the either imported Brit or the West Brit (depending on your perspective), is not alone in thinking of the commission as being useless. Francis Gilroy, the former IRA man and, in the time of the novel, Minister for Children and Culture, is similarly suspicious. "This was always a bloody stupid idea," he mutters to his deputy, Sweeney. "Don't know why we ever signed up to it," Sweeney agrees. "Because we had to," Gilroy sighs. "Because we sang so loud about having the truth on everything they ever did that we stumbled blindly into the net and then it was too late to get ourselves out when they turned round and asked for our truth. Maybe it's time to let the dead stay dead, move on instead of digging them back up every day. It's like having a ghost permanently on your shoulder. You've heard of *Hamlet*, haven't you?" (97). The dig about Gilroy thinking *Hamlet* a somewhat obscure cultural reference aside—Park seems to get a kind of pleasure out of portraying Gilroy as an uncultured oaf, holding him up for reader ridicule and snarkily ironizing his current job—Gilroy's thoughts on the aftermath of the *Troubles* fall closely in line with those of Gerry Fegan. Both former IRA men want the dead to "stay dead," both wish to no longer be haunted by the ghosts (either literal or metaphorical) of the past. Both are skeptical of the idea of any kind of communal reckoning and simply want for themselves, as individuals, to be left in peace.

Fenton, the retired RUC detective, feels much the same. His former coworker Alec tells Fenton he must testify at the commission, telling Fenton that Connor Walshe's family "[wants] some form of closure." "We all know what happened to him," Fenton retorts. "The IRA said he was a tout and shot him, then disposed of his body somewhere. How will that help them find closure? And what about my closure? When am I allowed to walk away and put it all behind me?" (134). Danny, or Michael Madden, feels the need to "walk away" even more strongly, having escaped to Florida and having lived there under an assumed name for several years. But he, too, is drawn back to Ireland, and to Belfast, to reckon for his past crimes, when he is also called back to testify in the case of Connor Walshe.

And what good does this truth and reconciliation commission do? Not much, according to Stanfield. He notes that when he concludes a trial, all of a sudden the victims' families understand "that this is all they are to be given and they realize it's not enough" (246). The truth and reconciliation commission cannot achieve any kind of resolution for Belfast; these people are, the novel suggests, too locked into their petty prejudices to ever change. They are thought to be unreasonable and incomprehensible: Walters, an employee of the British prime minister, mutters that "they will give up anything—their wives, their money, their self-respect—before they'll give up their past. And that makes constructing the future a little difficult, as you can imagine" (256).

The idea that the past is constantly cropping up in Belfast and making a future untenable is a common one; after all, I experienced it myself when just trying to Google Map my way to the Divis Tower. But the way many Belfast novels—*The Truth Commissioner* included, but far from exclusively—seem to dismiss the concerns of people imbricated in decades, even centuries, of violence as being just unthinkingly attached to the past, unwilling to break out of their parochial concerns and prejudices, belittles the specifics and the facts of the nature of the Troubles. It makes the future hard to imagine—not because of how silly and narrow-minded the people involved are, but because the past that is never reckoned with, that is actively dismissed as trivial, cannot be taken seriously.

The Truth Commissioner ends with the building the commission has been held in burning down, with all the relevant and important documents conflagrating in the process. With the destruction of the archive, of the past, of history, the truth and reconciliation commission comes to a halt as well. Stanfield thinks to himself, "There'll be an inquiry of course and for the rest of their bitter, corrosive history each side will blame the other and each year a new and blossoming conspiracy theory will apportion blame . . . Who is to know? Who will ever know the truth?" (369). At the end, Northern Ireland is still imagined inexplicable, populated by petty people with petty concerns and petty grievances. Even in the throes of a truth and reconciliation process, no one suggests actually attempting to understand the roots of the crimes and the violence: this is all brushed aside, and the narrative made universal, just another violent place with violent people. We made a half-hearted attempt at catharsis, Stanfield thinks, and we failed, so obviously this was all just pointless, because these primitive people are just going to fall back into their primitive ways. Nothing to be done about it.

Stephanie Lehner writes that "a detailed engagement with how to deal with the issues of human rights violations, sufferings, and inequities—of both past and present—has been also conspicuously missing from the negotiations that led to the Good Friday Agreement" (66). This lack of engagement, in turn, has foreclosed "the possibility of truly radical and/or meaningful change" (66). In the novel, she argues, "truth-telling . . . has not the aspired cathartic effect" but instead focuses on "the private redemption of these masculine figures" (74). Lisa Propst agrees, saying that the novel "seems to take a pessimistic view of Northern Ireland suspended in hostility" (297), and Joseph O'Connor says that "it is not a novel about politics at all. Its preoccupation is the private."

Perhaps this is the key issue with all of these novels: the experiences described in each are so private, so individualistic, that no communal kind of climax or catharsis is ever possible, reflecting (intentionally or not) some of the failings of the Good Friday Agreement and peace process more generally. This might be an inherent limitation of the novel form—as Bernard Bergonzi writes, "The novel is the characteristic literary form of an age of bourgeois individualism" (41)—but the fact remains that no reckoning with the past, no understanding of root causes, is brought to bear on the private experiences each main character has. Middle sister is left to navigate layers of violence on her own without support from her community; Gerry Fegan has to negotiate his crimes and his personal history without the understanding of his actions as being linked to a larger cause; and the men of *The Truth Commissioner* see the murder of Connor Walshe, and all related Troubles crime, as simply resonant of a primitive people in a primitive place stuck in a primitive time in history.

In a 2018 episode of the Irish sitcom *Derry Girls,* a young Ukrainian girl who has been sent to Derry to recover from the disaster at Chernobyl says dismissively to her host, "You people like to fight each other, and to be honest, no person really understands why. . . . You're not two different religions here, you're different flavors of same religion, no?" This flattened understanding, what Peter Mahon calls "a sort of clichéd lip-service" (5), of the Troubles can be played for laughs, certainly, but it also makes any serious weighing up of the past very difficult, foreclosing any opportunities for communal catharsis. Cathal Goan writes of the Troubles, "There is no closure, it seems to me; at best, and with considerable effort, there is critical assessment and reassessment conducted with sufficient humility to recognize differing perspectives and truths, and generosity enough to concede the validity of others' memories and the fallibility of our own" (179). Even the best Goan hopes for—"critical assessment"—is not accomplished in this series of Troubles novels, because the peace process itself never fully reckoned with the full weight of colonialism in Northern Ireland. Without a serious engagement with the political and colonial roots of the Troubles (an opportunity that does not seem particularly forthcoming), Belfast as a city will never reach narrative catharsis.

THREE

WHITENESS, HISTORICAL FICTION, AND AUSTRALIAN CITIES

In 1979, a song about outsize punishment for a petty crime during Ireland's Great Famine shot up the Irish pop charts. "The Fields of Athenry," an Irish folk ballad written by Pete St. John, tells the story of a young man named Michael who committed the crime of stealing corn to feed his family (as well as doing some possible anticolonial sabotage). As a result, Michael has been sentenced to transportation to the British penal colony at Botany Bay (now part of Sydney), Australia. After introducing Michael, his story, and his love, Mary, the song ends this way:

> Against the famine and the crown,
> I rebelled, they brought me down
> Now it's lonely round the Fields of Athenry
> By a lonely harbour wall
> She watched the last star falling
> As the prison ship sailed out against the sky
> Sure she'll live in hope and pray
> For her love in Botany Bay
> It's so lonely round the Fields of Athenry

About a decade later, the Irish megaband U2 put out a track that tells of a man who "fought for justice and not for gain," but who was still sent away to Van Diemen's Land (now Tasmania), another British penal colony in Australia. Like "The Fields of Athenry," "Van Diemen's Land" understands the transported Irish criminal as a victim of British imperialism; both songs feature sympathetic protagonists who committed sympathetic crimes, implicitly anticolonial resistance against the Empire.

Both songs are set during the nineteenth-century Famine, but both were written in the late twentieth century: "The Fields of Athenry" in 1979 and "Van Diemen's Land" in 1988. These songs provide a rich launching pad for a transition from Northern Ireland, a situation of contemporary colonialism (where texts are often reliant on Peter Mahon's "rhetoric of sameness"), to Australia, currently a wealthy majority-white nation with its own history of convict-led settler colonialism (where the understanding of Irish and poor British people in the context of empire takes on substantially different valences). In this chapter, I will focus on two Australian criminal cities—Sydney in the east, and Albany in the west—that were either founded as or have layered pasts as penal colonies, and historical fiction published in the twenty-first century that looks at that past through a contemporary lens.

Historical fiction says much more about the times during which it is written than the times in which it is set. "The Fields of Athenry" cannot tell us much about the Famine, but it can tell us a great deal about how Irish people in 1979 understood the Famine and related convict transportation to Australia.[1] As Fredric Jameson says, "Neither the reader's reception of a particular narrative, nor the actantial representation of human figures or agents, can be taken to be constants of narrative analysis but must themselves be ruthlessly historicized" (152); we must historicize the contemporary reader's understanding of these narrative tropes that are familiar to Australian audiences. In order to understand how today's Australian readers and writers do—or do not—find catharsis from past criminality, this chapter will therefore not look at "classic" convict novels like Marcus Clarke's *For the Term of His Natural Life* (1874),[2] but rather contemporary fiction that covers the same topics. And so Kate Grenville's *The Secret River* (2005) and Kim Scott's *That Deadman Dance* (2010) tell us far less about the European foundings of Australian cities than about how contemporary white and indigenous Australians interpret, translate, and work through that history for twenty-first-century readers.

In a simplified narrative of Australia's late eighteenth-century foundation as a penal colony, crime is committed in the imperial center (either England,

Scotland, Wales, or Ireland)—often out of material need due to unjust societal structures and dispossession—the convicted are transported to Australia, and then the formerly dispossessed become the colonizers themselves, murdering and displacing indigenous Australian peoples. Bill Ashcroft, Gareth Griffiths, and Helen Tiffin write of this series of events, "White European settlers in the Americas, Australia, and New Zealand faced the problem of establishing their 'indigeneity' and distinguishing it from their continuing sense of their European inheritance" (134)—in other words, the settlers fought to be seen both as distinct from their former British home, and as still trying to maintain a claim to whiteness. This, Ashcroft and colleagues write, has created a situation where Aboriginal Australians are "doubly marginalized—pushed to the psychic and political edge of societies which themselves have experienced the dilemma of colonial alienation" (142). Australia is founded on what Bob Hodge and Vijay Mishra call "a double guilt: the dispossession of the Aboriginal people and the excessive punishment of large numbers of British and Irish people, mainly from the poorer classes, for crimes against the property of the ruling class" (116). However, when the "excessively punished" reached this distant outpost of the British Empire, they committed a series of vicious settler colonial crimes against the original inhabitants of that space to found their European criminal cities, which in Australia means cities founded on this "double guilt" of the penal colony and subsequent genocide of indigenous Australians. Though the legal code at the time would not have understood either of these acts as crimes, they are retroactively understood to be so; in keeping with the nature of historical fiction, which reckons *with* the past while not being *of* it, our contemporary legal code is constructed in such a way that we understand both forced transportation and the murder and "dispossession" of human beings to be crimes.

Given its distinctive history as a penal colony for empire, Australia has a literary culture more settler colonial than postcolonial—Ralph J. Crane notes that "much contemporary Australian and New Zealand fiction has more in common with contemporary American fiction than South American or West African fiction" (393). If perhaps an outlier case in the present volume, Australia holds an undoubtedly unique position in the matrix of crime, transportation, and empire that *Criminal Cities* constructs that makes it a necessary inclusion. With the country's strong tradition and market in historical fiction (Pinto 190), Australia's experiments with genre are strong examples of cathartic crime.

There are, of course, several historical novels besides *The Secret River* and *That Deadman Dance* that implicate travel and settler colonialism in crime. *Picnic at Hanging Rock,* Joan Lindsay's 1967 novel about Victorian schoolgirls who mysteriously disappear at Hanging Rock, outside Melbourne, is archetypal of this Australian historical genre. It involves travel from a city to a rural area; it attempts to wrestle with the meaning of whiteness in a settler colony; and most of all, it asks questions about what constitutes a crime in the Australian context. Reg Lumley, the brother of a woman teaching at the school, shouts at the headmistress, Mrs. Appleyard, "It's not right, in my view, that a respectable young woman like Dora should be connected in any way whatsoever with crime and all that sort of thing" (153). Mrs. Appleyard responds coldly, "Be careful how you express yourself, Mr. Lumley. Not crime. Mystery if you like. A very different matter" (154). There is a sense, in the white writing on this topic, that the invocation of "crime" assigns guilt to the white settler, and as such, the topic must be skirted around at all costs.

The tone—and the stakes—are sharper when an unnamed young Aboriginal man is the one caught up in the matrix of crime in Australia. The narrative of Mudrooroo's *Wild Cat Falling,* published in 1965,[3] is focused on a young man's transition out of prison, and includes flashbacks that explain how the man became involved in crime throughout his childhood. Along the way, the text marks several injustices done to the Aboriginal community by white Australians. Though Mudrooroo's claims to indigeneity have been called into question, *Wild Cat Falling* remains a text that uses crime as a mechanism to highlight violences done to the Aboriginal population, rather than as a way to signal white guilt as in *Picnic at Hanging Rock*.[4]

All too often, white Australian writing on the convict past or how crime manifests in the present remains oblivious to white privilege or settler colonial complicity in imperial crimes. Meg Keneally's *Fled* (2019) is a good example. Following the exploits of Jenny Gwyn, a Cornish transportee loosely based on the Australian folk hero Mary Bryant, *Fled* is a novel of remarkable "color-blindness," a novel that holds up an individual, liberal, Enlightenment-era notion of freedom as the highest possible good. Jenny Gwyn, who is arrested for highway robbery, is transported to Australia, and manages to escape before being rearrested and transported back to Britain, is an ideal of white feminism; *Fled* rarely mentions the Aboriginal people who were living in Australia long before Jenny got there, and figures Jenny as a heroine rather than as someone with a relative amount of privilege who was only able to escape due to her position in the colony that dispossessed the original inhabitants. The novel ends back in Britain where it started, because for Keneally and Jenny, freedom is contingent on the metropolitan, imperial center. The narrative loops around colonial logics, and ends up exactly where it started, rather than proposing new and potentially more just ways for living in a world beginning to be shaped by the British Empire. In other words, there is nothing resembling catharsis for either the reader or the historical protagonists; there is only repetition of the same old imperial themes.

The Australian folk hero Ned Kelly receives the historical fiction treatment in Peter Carey's *True History of the Kelly Gang* (2000). Like "The Fields of Athenry" and "Van Diemen's Land," *True History of the Kelly Gang* is largely a story of Irish victimization under the British Empire. While it is true that, in Ireland, Irish Catholics were subject to all manner of indignities (including transportation), upon arrival in Australia, the Irish began to be inscribed into whiteness.[5] In Peter Kelly's narration, Ned Kelly's father "were a quiet and secret man he had been ripped from his home in Tipperary and transported to the prisons of Van Diemen's Land I do not know what was done to him he never spoke of it" (7). Ned Kelly becomes a criminal himself, a bushranger (the Australian equivalent of a highwayman) who robs people in rural Australia and attains mythological status among white Australians due to his anti-authoritarian spirit and common man appeal.

Carey's novel notices that a great deal of Ned Kelly's popularity derived from the understanding that he was rebelling against the British Empire: "The British Empire had supplied me with no shortage of candidates these was men who had had their leases denied for no other crime than being our friends men forced to plant wheat then ruined by the rust men mangled upon the triangle of Van Dieman's Land men with sons in gaol men who witnessed their hard won land taken up by squatters men perjured against and falsely gaoled men weary of constant impounding on & on each day without relent" (342). *True History of the Kelly Gang* recognizes how convict transportees' well-founded sense of victimhood could turn into a kind of self-satisfied whiteness upon Australian shores. Settlers weaponize their colonial victimhood—what Eve Tuck and K. Wayne Yang have termed one of the "settler moves to innocence"—and rather than acknowledge their complicity in the larger imperial project, white settlers continue to understand themselves as victims, even as they commit violence against Aboriginal Australians. In the contemporary historical novels under the microscope here, much of white

Australia remains stuck in this loop begun in eighteenth-century Britain, of expelling convicts from the center of empire as if that would purify society. The Australian carceral project was meant to be a kind of catharsis for imperial Britain, enacted via mobility and transportation and then the foundation of new cities; instead, it created a new type of original sin. In contemporary Australia, it will be impossible to achieve catharsis without breaking free from this history; when apologies are offered, they must be made in the right spirit, and only when the wronged parties are ready and willing to hear them.

"A WORLD IN THEIR CULTURAL IMAGE": AUSTRALIA, CRIME, AND WHITENESS

Within colonial discourses, Australia occupies an extraordinarily vexed place, even more than most settler colonial nations. Australia as a white European space was founded via the forced removal of unwanted people who were thought to be outside the mainstream of the ideal British nation, due to criminal pasts or convictions, in a kind of purging for the metropolitan imperial center.[6] However, once in Australia, the white settlers became the colonizers, murdering entire Aboriginal communities and committing a great deal of violence against the people and the land, with very little self-awareness about what happened in the transition.[7] At first the convict transportees, who were generally poor and who typically committed property crimes we would today classify as "petty" or as "misdemeanors," truly were victims of the British Empire and its expanding systems of capitalism and law. Many (not all) convicts were victims of an overzealous legal system paranoid about crime (Robert Hughes 25), and many never received a fair shake at the hands of the British state.

However, the privilege of their white skin rapidly transmuted the transportees' position in life when they were shipped to the South Pacific. All of a sudden, they were able to possess things in life they hadn't before, and they were able to rule over others in ways others had once ruled over them. This reversal of fortunes is seen in Australian city planning, which laid the groundwork for the criminal cities of the eighteenth century. The desire for "spatial control," Edward W. Soja writes in *Seeking Spatial Justice*, is driven by "fear of potential invasion and violence by what the more powerful perceive as threatening 'others'" (44), an observation that is certainly true of Australia and the establishment of urban centers there. Town centers were established on the grid system: from these cities, or "secure administrative centres," writes Jane M. Jacobs, "settler expansion could move outward into those lands where the fantasy of *terra nullius* was less surely inscribed" (105). Contemporary Australia has "the highest-city-based population in the world" (Knight, *Australian Crime Fiction*, 4), as most white residents live among the outer edges and very few in the Outback, where many Aboriginal communities successfully lived for centuries. Upon arrival in Australia, white Australians began to form a planned community around whiteness, which spiritually extended back to the metropolitan center that had kicked them out with little dignity.

This city-based settlement pattern, an aggressive imposition of British cultural values and spatial understandings onto foreign soil, was a key step in the establishment of a dynamic Charles W. Mills has termed a "racial contract." The racial contract, here defined as implicitly understood among white Australians in Australia and vis-à-vis their relationship to the British imperial center, is a "set of formal or informal agreements or meta-agreements . . . between the members of one subset of humans" to categorize themselves as "white" and "the remaining subset of humans as 'nonwhite' and of a different and inferior moral status" (Mills 11). This is done in order to ensure that the "white" individuals hold positions of power over those deemed "nonwhite," who are forced to inhabit "a subordinate civil standing" within white spaces (Mills 11). White settlers inherently understood that it was better to define themselves as white, and to organize themselves as such, maintaining links with their former white imperial home. A narrative emerged wherein Australia and its cities became "a fragile outpost of the 'white race'" (Affeldt 448). The convicts and the elites had to invent something to bring them together, as neither group, who had previously understood themselves to be enemies, had the capacity to go it alone in a strange new place.[8] Race and racism were leveraged in order to band together against the Aborigines. This continues to happen in the twenty-first century, because, as Patrick Wolfe reminds us, settler colonialism is a structure rather than event; colonialism and its legacies did not end in the eighteenth century, but have persisted into the present.

Whiteness is a complex and changing spectrum that bends to meet the needs of the dominant cultural frame of the times, or the needs of a reader. Literary whiteness in Australia serves the purpose of constructing victimhood and heroism, based on received ideas about crime and punishment at the hands of the British Empire. The Racial Contract legitimates a very flexible definition of crime in Australia, and prevents white communities from investigating further their own complicity in a societal order that is seen as "normatively legitimate" (Mills 30). That inability to see one's complicity—that white fragility, in Robin DiAngelo's famous term—ultimately thwarts the catharsis of Kate Grenville's 2005 novel *The Secret River*, more apologia than apology, and then dooms the Aboriginal protagonist of Kim Scott's *That Deadman Dance*. Australian criminal cities, set up as misbegotten transportation-laden catharsis schemes, became milieus of racial bargains that continue to forestall any efforts at true cathartic crime.

A "DOUBLE APOLOGY": KATE GRENVILLE'S *THE SECRET RIVER*

The idea for *The Secret River* struck Kate Grenville in 2000, when she was demonstrating on the Sydney Harbour Bridge in support of "reconciliation between black and white Australians," although she admits that she would "have been hard pressed to say exactly what I thought reconciliation meant," vaguely referencing "what had gone on in Australia over the last 200 years" (*Searching* 10). Published in 2005, *The Secret River* is the narrative of William Thornhill, a petty criminal from London who is arrested for theft and subsequently transported to Botany Bay, Australia, with his wife, Sal, and their children. The novel is based on Grenville's research into the past of one of her ancestors, a man named Solomon Wiseman who was transported to Australia for a similar crime. In an anecdote published in *Searching for the Secret River* that is often cited in the critical literature on the novel, Grenville is demonstrating in Sydney when she notices "a group of Aboriginal people leaning against the railings watching us" (12); in particular, "a tall handsome woman frankly staring" (12) stands out. After the woman notices their group, Grenville writes, "our eyes met and we shared one of those moments of intensity—a pulse of connectedness. We smiled, held each other's gaze, I think perhaps we gestured with our hands, the beginning of a wave. It should have made me feel even better about what I was doing, but it sent a sudden blade of cold to my warm inner glow" (12). Suddenly, she realizes, "I didn't know much about what had gone on between the Aboriginal people and the settlers in those early days.... Until this moment it had never occurred to me to wonder who might have been living on that land, and how he'd [Solomon Wiseman] persuaded them to leave it" (12–13).

This is a remarkable anecdote, though perhaps not only for the reason Grenville thinks it is. What she seems to view as a moment of self-awareness functions instead as a remarkable admission of a blinkered worldview. She writes, "In that instant of putting my own ancestor together with this woman's ancestor, everything swivelled: the country, the place, my sense of myself in it" (13). She decides she needs to learn more about Solomon Wiseman and "what he might have done when he crossed paths with Aboriginal people" (13). Even in this moment of supposed political and ethical awakening, the moment is focused primarily on Kate Grenville, and not the Aboriginal people her ancestor likely murdered and certainly dispossessed. She treats the Aboriginal woman on the bridge as being there to serve Kate Grenville's own needs, rather than a fully fledged person with beliefs, needs, and a history of her own. Grenville decides to dig into history not to seek justice for the woman on the bridge, but to help reorient herself to the white settler colony in which she feels comfortable. Because her ancestor is safely in the past, this can come across as a bold move rooted in a keen sense of social justice; the actual effect is that by interrogating only the past, Grenville signals to herself and to her readers that they no longer need to wrestle with the complexities of the present. Struck with a newfound sense of guilt, Grenville presents *The Secret River* as an action-oriented project, designed for her own and other white Australians' catharsis. But, as Robin DiAngelo writes, "When we are mired in guilt, we are narcissistic and ineffective: guilt functions as an excuse for inaction" (135). And so the novel allows for a surface-level reckoning with the past without properly negotiating the present. It achieves what Tuck and Yang call the "metaphor of decolonization." As they put it in "Decolonization Is Not a Metaphor," "When metaphor invades decolonization, it kills the very possibility of decolonization; it recenters whiteness, it resettles theory, it extends innocence to the settler, it entertains a settler future" (3). Grenville's novel appears to think of itself as part of a decolonizing project, but without a literal "land back" decolonization, all that happens is that the author manages to put herself and other white Australians at the center of the narrative while paving a path for a continued future in the country.

Susannah Radstone declares, "*The Secret River* isn't history. Its time and its place is contemporary Australia, 'remembered' through the evocation of the past" (295), an assessment with which I wholeheartedly agree. Thornhill (Wiseman)'s arrest transports him to Australia, where he then becomes mired in bloodshed and violence that his descendent feels the need to apologize for centuries later in order to shed a sense of guilt or wrongness. Grenville's novel is an example of the genre of the "sorry novel," or the "peculiarly post-colonial fictional genre . . . whose main feature is to rework, rewrite, or reimagine history in order to make a political point about the present" (Kossew, "Saying Sorry," 172).[9] Whether her attempt is successful, especially in the context of whiteness, is another story.

William Thornhill is born into Dickensian-style poverty in eighteenth-century London. He marries his childhood sweetheart, Sal, and they begin a family in the same poverty-stricken conditions in which they were both raised. While working along the River Thames, Thornhill sees an opportunity to steal some wood and is caught; he is initially sentenced to death, but his sentence is commuted to transportation to New South Wales. Upon arrival in Botany Bay, he and Sal and their family live for a time in the growing city that will one day become Sydney, but they eventually strike out on their own and establish themselves further upriver on their own homestead, driving off the original inhabitants in the process.

There is no doubt William and Sal drew a rough lot and were treated unfairly in London; they were born into an inherently unjust system, and few, if any, opportunities presented themselves to work their way out of it. Thornhill reflects on the limited life chances of men like him when he thinks about the convicts that keep arriving in Australia: "He could hear the great machinery of London, the wheel of justice chewing up felons and spitting them out here, boatload after boatload, spreading out from the Government Wharf in Sydney, acre by acre, slowed but not stopped by rivers, mountains, swamps" (214–15). It is certainly true, as Raymond Williams has pointed out, that "the idea of emigration to the colonies was seized as a solution to the poverty and overcrowding of the cities [in England]" (281), and how that strategy for getting rid of what was viewed as "excess people" only contributed to poor people's sense of victimhood and unbelonging. Indeed, Thornhill's understanding of himself as a casualty of the British Empire is well founded at the start of the novel; however, as Marguerite Nolan and Robert Clarke point out, "the convict protagonist becomes wealthy through perpetuating acts of violence against those he dispossesses" (20), thus turning Thornhill from colonized to colonizer. Though Grenville does seem to be aware of this—she certainly does not wholeheartedly endorse Thornhill's actions—she never engages thoroughly with what this means for anyone besides Thornhill; not the Aboriginal people he encounters, not his family, not his descendants, all of whom used to live on the site that becomes the criminal city of Sydney. As Nolan and Clarke say, the novel soon becomes "a genealogy of contemporary settler subjectivity, which is trapped in its own narcissistic melancholia" (21).

Grenville's analysis of hierarchies and how they relate to Thornhill's understanding of his own subject position initially suggest that *The Secret River* might lead us to a productive sort of cathartic crime. While a young man, Thornhill suddenly begins to understand how his society is structured: "he had a sudden dizzying understanding of the way men were ranged on top of each other, all the way from the Thornhills at the bottom up to the King, or God, at the top, each man higher than one, lower than another" (26). He continues to nurse this understanding of the order of society all the way to Botany Bay, where he encounters an Aboriginal man acting ridiculous in order to attract attention and money from the white convict settlers. "Men came from all the streets around," Thornhill observes, "cheered to watch this black insect of a man capering before them, a person lower in the order of things even than they were" (92). Thornhill is aware of the ways capital and race work together to structure both criminal cities of London and of Sydney, and is adept at noticing even how this works within himself. After several years, he becomes a free man and receives the right to buy his own British convicts, and he decides to acquire an old friend from London who has been sent over on a recent transport ship. He says of the realization he and Sal have that they have moved up in the world, "They had power almost of life and death over Dan Oldfield, and something in them both was enjoying it" (177). This acute and slightly guilty observation is underscored by his noticing "Dan flick[ing] a quick look between the two of them, as if wondering to himself what it was about New South Wales that could bring such a change" (177).

The almost alchemical transformation that New South Wales has brought about—Thornhill from the bottom of life's ladder to nearing the top—is brought about via the additional element of race, which was not a conscious consideration to the Thornhills and their community in late eighteenth- and early nineteenth-century London. Because of the small number of British settlers in Australia at the time, it was important that they band together to create a cohesive society, a London in miniature. William Thornhill, as a now-freed convict, is near the top of the social hierarchy in Sydney. Even Dan Oldfield, a convict who has not yet attained his freedom, ranks above the indigenous inhabitants of the place and is a necessary cog in the society they are building. Even though Sydney, at the time, is described as "a sad scrabbling place[,] . . . a half-formed temporary sort of place" (75), establishing the sorts of hierarchies and social organizations that existed in London helps solidify the city into a more formal outpost of the British Empire. Soon, Sydney begins to grow in size and sophistication; Thornhill thinks to himself a few years in that "Sydney seemed a metropolis, different only in degree from London" (135). The newest criminal city of the British Empire has begun to fully establish itself, continuing to grow thanks to the labor of convicted British men, the slaughter of Aboriginal peoples, and the expansion of capitalism and European urban planning.

The city, however, soon loses its appeal for Thornhill, and he decides that he would rather travel a little further into the interior and establish a homestead of his own, thinking this acquiring of private property will match his newfound social ascendancy. "He let himself imagine it," Grenville writes, "standing on the crest of that slope, looking down over his own place. Thornhill's Point. It was a piercing hunger in his guts: to own it. To say *mine*, in a way he had never been able to say *mine* of anything at all. He had not known until this minute that it was something he wanted so much" (106). The imposition of British capitalist and land ownership norms onto Australian society is never quite fully successful, however; after Thornhill builds his small home and farm, he keeps trying to reassure himself that it really belongs to him. "'My own,' he kept saying to himself. 'My place. Thornhill's place.' But the wind in the leaves up on the ridge was saying something else entirely" (139).

The reason Thornhill never feels fully at home is because the land is, of course, not his. He has a flimsy claim to it, as a freed British convict, but European understandings of capitalism and private property have not penetrated this new land and its inhabitants yet. Laws and maps may exist that deed the land to the British, but these are social constructs at best; what is to be done when the people the British view as their inferiors do not recognize the rights incurred by these documents and lofty ideas?

As the novel proceeds, Thornhill and many of the other settlers grow more and more discomfited with the Aboriginal presence that continues to surround them. They decide to go on a raid to tamp down what they view as unacceptable Aboriginal resistance, which will involve moving across many areas the settlers view as remote. An army captain instructs them to form a human chain so as to avoid getting separated, and draws them a map to demonstrate the movement they will make. Thornhill looks at the map with disgust:

> On the map, Captain McCallum's plan looked childishly simple, and on the map it was easy to imagine it: the human chain, the proceeding, the justice being dispensed. The map was correct enough ... the map was correct, and there was no arguing with the captain's logic, the elegance of the pincer-movement and the human chain.
> But Thornhill had been there and knew that the map was correct only in its generalities. (263)

The disjuncture between European hypothetical plans and Australian lived reality is emphasized when the battle itself takes place. It is far from the neat, teleological advancement that Captain McCallum had envisioned; instead, it is a bloody free-for-all, in which Thornhill and many others act atrociously, commit several violent acts of murder, and generally assert their imagined rights to the land and, by extension, the people.

When it is all over, more space has been cleared for further British settlement, and Thornhill acquires an even larger piece of property and eventually becomes the richest man in the Sydney area. The transition is complete; he can no longer lay claim to being oppressed, but is instead a full-fledged oppressor. Nicholas Blomley writes, "At the outset, Thornhill craves a space that is his own; at the conclusion, it becomes a place that shapes who he is" (214). The power of this kind of space, one that can confer the privileges of whiteness and completely reshape its inhabitants, is an ironic kind of criminal city; it has also managed to transform Thornhill from a small-time and disrespected criminal to a murderer who is revered and honored by his community. Thornhill realizes that he is no longer committing (petty) criminal acts out of desperation; he asks himself, "How had his life funnelled down to this corner, in which he had so little choice? His life had funnelled down once before, in Newgate, into the dead-end of the condemned cell. But the thing that lay ahead of him there had been out of his hands. There was a kind of innocence in waiting for Mr. Executioner. The difference with this was that he was choosing it, of his own free will" (301). Later, when surveying his new and bigger home, Cobham Hall, he thinks to himself, "Cobham Hall was a gentleman's residence. Did that mean he was a gentleman? . . . He knew that feeling now; the feeling that whatever a man wanted, he could have" (316). In other words, Thornhill has discovered his powers and privileges that have been conferred onto him due to his race and due to his colonial power; he's discovered his whiteness, and it's a hell of a drug.

Yet, even with his newfound power, Thornhill never feels quite at ease in Australia, in the criminal city of Sydney he has helped to build. The book closes with Thornhill, now an old man, sitting on his property and musing:

> For all it was what he had chosen, the bench he sat on here felt at times like a punishment. He had never forgotten the narrow bench in the passage of the Watermen's Hall, where William Thornhill had sat with dread in his heart to see whether he could become an apprentice. This bench had been part of the penance a boy paid for the chance at survival. This bench, here, where he could overlook all his wealth and take his ease, should have been the reward.
>
> He could not understand why it did not feel like triumph. (333–34)

Even at this moment, which offers only a shallow reading of Thornhill's complicity, Grenville paints him in a sympathetic light. Thornhill is a tragic figure in this estimation; the reader is reminded of his disadvantaged past and encouraged to think of him in as favorable a light as possible. He may not have the wherewithal to understand *why* his ill-gotten wealth does not "feel like triumph," but we are led to understand that he is suffering, and so, the implication goes, isn't that punishment enough?

Of course it isn't, and of course Thornhill is not a tragic figure but a murderer who became complicit in a racist, capitalist empire, instead of extending sympathy and compassion to those harmed by it as he once was. Kate Grenville, in an interview with Benedicte Page, says, "It was important to me that the reader be completely drawn in and empathise with Thornhill and his family, so that the shock that comes later asks the question: 'If I had been in that situation, what would I have done?' I wanted to put the reader through the experience of what it must have been like, with all the complexities and gray areas" (1–2). Her disclosure says it all. There are no complexities or gray areas. There is no need to empathize with Thornhill. There is a very clear assumption on Grenville's part that the reader will be white, as she does not even pause to consider the impossibility of asking an Aboriginal person or other person of color to go "through the experience of what it must have been like." What Grenville views as a cathartic experience for herself and for other white Australians is, in fact, an exercise in white narcissism that demonstrates the power and reach of the racial contract; she will bend over backward to find nuance in the story of her ancestors from years past without extending grace or humanity to currently living Aboriginal people.[10]

This white narcissism, as I have termed it above, has been better theorized by Tuck and Yang, who classify Grenville's striving for victimhood as one of their signature "settler moves to innocence."[11] "Settler moves to innocence," they say, "are those strategies or positionings that attempt to relieve the settler of feelings of guilt or responsibility without giving up land or power or privilege, without having to change much at all" (10). A settler move to innocence ensures that decolonization remains a metaphor through the attempted purging of white guilt, and that nothing has to change in twenty-first-century Sydney, even through a cosmetic stock-taking of the past.

Grenville's specific "settler move to innocence" would be best categorized under Tuck and Yang's "colonial equivocation," which they explain as "a more nuanced move to innocence [that homogenizes] various experiences of oppression as colonization" (17). In other words, this looks like saying, "I was oppressed, too" (American readers may be familiar with the "the Irish were slaves, too" trope, or the "anti-Italian discrimination" claims). This "equivocation" means Grenville's historical novel is not successful in the way she wants it to be, as the white narrative remains the center of the story. "What Grenville strives to accomplish in her novel," according to Dolores Herrero, "is a kind of impossible task. She tries her hand at offering a double apology: examining her own convict ancestor's implication in acts of Aboriginal genocide and dispossession, while also acknowledging the strength, courage, and determination that made settlement possible" (90). Grenville, through attempting to offer this "double apology," also attempts to speak for the contemporary Aboriginal community of Australia. Of the Aboriginal reception of the novel, she says, "They recognise that the book is my act of acknowledgment, my way of saying: this is how *I'm* sorry" (quoted in Maral). But we must wonder, who is "they"? Why aren't "they" allowed to speak, and why does Grenville feel the need to paraphrase their words for "them"?

Because white readership is assumed, and because whiteness, white privilege, and white fragility are not directly interrogated, nor is the Aboriginal position examined, the novel cannot come close to an ethical sense of catharsis. There is an argument that Grenville behaved ethically by only telling the story of William Thornhill; one might reasonably argue that an attempt to explore the consciousness and subjectivities of Aboriginal individuals might look like cultural appropriation, or an attempt to speak on experiences she herself cannot share. However, as Inga Clendinnen points out, "she felt no such inhibition about claiming to penetrate the minds of British convict-keepers, convicts and settlers of 200 years ago, even to the extent of diagnosing the pathological mental condition she thought she found there" (23). Clendinnen goes on to ask, "How much 'culture' do we really share with British people of 200 years ago? Are we seduced into an illusion of understanding through the accident of a shared language?" (23).

I think Clendinnen is right to point out the cultural and historical distance between contemporary and colonial Australia, and I would go even further than that. The affiliation Grenville seems to share with her ancestor goes deeper than genealogy or a shared language (which is far from an "accident," but rather a carefully plotted and executed expansion of empire), and extends to racial identification and shared colonial history. Like Thornhill/Wiseman, Grenville depicts herself and other white Australians as victimized colonial outsiders who made tough but ultimately understandable decisions in service of their own livelihoods. Because *The Secret River* attempts to find some kind of "reconciliation between opposing stories" (Merli 212), it can never move past its status as a type of both-sides, centrist-apologia for white settler colonialism.

What seems to be a robust apology falls apart at even the slightest pressure. The weaknesses and fallacies in the apology are what prevent *The Secret River* from utilizing its crimes to offer a sincere form of catharsis for all of its readers. Eleanor Collins writes, "Like national myth, the novel is a form of narrative that classically concludes with unity, at least with unity of understanding" (169), and writes of *The Secret River* specifically, "Neither novel nor nation can find unity in this encounter" (170). Kate Mitchell points out, "Since our complicity in colonisation is structural, not simply individual, there can be no resolution" (268). Grenville has focused on the individual, on personal family history and silent interactions with women on bridges, and has hoped that will be enough. By her own admission, she has hoped for a "reconciliation," as noted at the start of this section, but as Tuck and Yang say, "Reconciliation is about rescuing settler normalcy, about rescuing a settler future" (35). It is a shallow move that ensures the settler remains at the center of the Australian narrative.

There is a sense that reading *The Secret River*, especially as a white Australian or white citizen of another settler colony, marks someone as one of the "good ones." It's meant to be a congratulatory act, a pat on the back in novel form, telegraphing to other members of the settler community that one gets it. As Jodi Gallagher writes, *The Secret River* and other sorry novels "provide a comforting view of Australia's settler past for readers at home—superficially acknowledging the violence that characterised the colonial encounter without suggesting that contemporary society needs to institute major changes in ways of thinking about that encounter" (242). It's a performance, not a comprehensive attempt at reparation and catharsis.

Any catharsis effected by *The Secret River* is personal, for Grenville and for some readers. Kate Grenville congratulated herself on her work in a 2005 piece for the *Age*, exclaiming, "But now I feel a great sense of relief I've taken the skeleton out of the cupboard. The kind of paralysis we've been in over what we should do about our Aboriginal heritage can be opened up, and we can move on. There's a chance for something better to happen" (quoted in Merli 214). Grenville may have felt some guilt about her ancestor's, and her own, complicity in white settler colonialism, but inserting herself into the forefront of that conversation and deciding she gets to be the national speaker on a topic is a shockingly insensitive display of white privilege. The guilt exorcised here is the kind Audre Lorde describes: "Guilt is not a response to anger; it is a response to one's own actions or lack of action. If it leads to change then it can be useful, since it becomes no longer guilt but the beginning of knowledge. Yet all too often, guilt is just another name for impotence, for defensiveness destructive of communication; it becomes a device to protect ignorance and the continuation of things the way they are, the ultimate protection for changelessness" (282). This guilt is an excuse to continue "things the way they are," to promote "changelessness" under the guise of liberal attempts at reparation. It is an attempt to recapture the kind of "totality" Lukács writes about when he speaks of the Greeks and completion and catharsis (34); however, as "the novel is the epic of an age in which the extensive totality of life is no longer directly given" (56), that type of totality and catharsis is not possible. This is why *The Secret River* cannot work as a thoroughly cathartic effort, because it cannot be anything but a contemporary gloss over the bloody reality of the past. In lieu of reckoning with Australia's racist, bloody, colonial past, we are instead just given an image of an old white man bemusedly rocking himself on the porch of his palatial estate, wondering vaguely why things are wrong. The necessary work to figure it out and change it is neither described nor attempted.

Though I do not think this was Grenville's intent in writing the novel, this lack of catharsis actually mirrors fairly well the larger question of ongoing colonialism. The settler colonial project in Australia is not over, of course; Australians live the effects of colonialism every single day in the ongoing structure. Grenville's portrayal of Thornhill has an effect beyond that of her desired or stated one; it demonstrates to us as readers that the failure of closure demonstrates complicated and unfinished colonial projects at work in contemporary Sydney. Sydney as a criminal city remains a sign of ongoing negotiation, where even the "liberal" settlers very often get it wrong.

That's not to say, of course, that the current situation is exactly the same as it was in the era of *The Secret River.* Eventually, convict transportation to Sydney of the type William Thornhill endured did cease, but the foundations for the criminal city that Solomon Wiseman and others helped to build had already been laid. Botany Bay became Sydney, which grew from the hardscrabble collection of huts William Thornhill lived on the fringes of to one of the largest and most prosperous cities in the twenty-first-century world, built on the spoils of capitalism, empire, and genocide. But the ending of convict transportation to Sydney was not the end of the story on how crime founded modern Australia, as when transportation ended on the eastern part of the continent, it began on the west coast. Kim Scott's *That Deadman Dance,* set in the city of Albany, explores a different region of Australia from a different perspective, leading to a textured and layered exploration of cathartic crime and how imperialism built yet another criminal city.

"THIS OTHER STUFF": KIM SCOTT'S *THAT DEADMAN DANCE*

That Deadman Dance focuses on a transgression *against* settler colonialism, and brings in Aboriginal and indigenous voices to an extent not seen in the typical sorry novel. The novel demonstrates how settler colonialism rejects any sincere attempts at bringing people together via criminalizing indiscretions against the burgeoning racial contract. Scott's novel is set in the early decades of the nineteenth century, in a European settlement called King George's Town (later Albany, Western Australia, the oldest colonial settlement in the west of the country). The narrative follows the founding and early years of the colony, and outlines how a combination of convict labor and the implementation of European laws and penal codes stressed the indigenous Noongar community to the point of breaking and fragmentation. With a keen eye for how urban planning and crime work together to both create and destroy societies, Kim Scott's novel mourns the past, as well as the lost promise of what might have been, for the Aboriginal community to whom he can trace his own ancestry.

In the world of the novel, Dr. Cross, an Englishman, is the founder of the original European settlement. Early on in his time in Australia, he writes home to urge for more English immigrants to come join the burgeoning city, which is suffering for lack of labor as transported convicts, who have been vital to the establishment of the settlement, are arriving in fewer and fewer numbers. He presses the need for more people to travel, people "who are willing to explore the surrounding country and able to rise above torpor and timidity so that they might ... *aid and assist each other, create a mutual demand and supply, and extend themselves into the interior, or with capital to beat the enormous expenses of first improvement. Security against want, and extravagant prices of the necessities of life, would do much to attract the labourer, who is of paramount importance*" (35–36, italics original). This focus on growing the population of the town does not, surprisingly, come with the wholesale slaughter of the indigenous Australians, at least not at first. *That Deadman Dance* is in large part the story of Bobby Wabalanginy, a young Aboriginal man who befriends the white invaders and later tells the story of their arrival when he is an old man in Albany. Bobby, who is a talented dancer, typically begins his stories, Scott tells us, by "telling of when he was but a baby and the black man and the white man first lived together here in this very place and why he had remained unafraid and been so trusting" (74). Bobby's read on the cooperative nature of the early days of the settlement is backed up by that of Dr. Cross, who, with his superior, "agreed their colonial outpost needed to build strategic relationships. We are outnumbered, they said. It is their home. And we do not know what is planned for us or how long our colonial authorities require us to remain" (87).

These embryonic colonization efforts mimic the on-the-ground situation at the time. In the Australian news source the *Conversation*, Tony Hughes-D'Aeth writes of the novel that it "takes place through these years of informal colonisation, in which the fragility of those arriving was felt more acutely than it would be later in the colonial timeline." It was this point in history, Hughes-D'Aeth argues, that there "was a moment where the absolute guarantee of cultural supremacy was not fully assured for the coloniser, and in that shadow of a doubt something briefly flickered into existence. Just the tiniest of counter-historical possibilities comes to life, that things may have been otherwise." This is supported by the novel: characters or the narrator frequently say things like "We must work together, together is the only way we will survive" (231), or emphasize their communal links, or highlight the ways in which the communities depend on one another. Cross, especially, forms strong friendships with the local community, and he is even buried next to Wunyeran, a tribal elder. In its early years, King George's Town is like an integrated version of Botany Bay as portrayed in *The Secret River*; unlikely alliances, unheard-of at home, are formed to survive in a new world.

Quickly, however, fissures in the forced story of goodwill begin to form (unsurprisingly, as even cooperation is built on colonial exploitation) and the settlement takes on the features of the more typical Australian colonial criminal city. Wunyeran has died of a coughing sickness brought by the white men, and his name is not even put on the shared grave's cross; land begins to be parceled out according to capitalist logic; and ideas about policing begin to be imported from London, specifically the recommendations of Robert Peel, who founded the first modern police service in London. The local reliance on whaling begins to break down, as the omniscient narrator observes: "King George Town was a growing village, spreading upwards from the shore of the harbour. Might not need whales, the way its people were" (353). Gradually, King George Town begins to become a recognizably European city, with the attendant implementations of capitalism, colonial law, and social organization. The transition from the early days of mutual cooperation to the later era of more recognizable colonialism is marked by the destruction of Wunyeran and Cross's grave: "Floods would carry away the bones of Wunyeran and Cross," we are told. "All along this coast of ours, bones were plucked from riverbanks and tumbled together to the sea" (351). Without these grounding histories, marked through bones, the integrated community begins to fall apart. The advent of the (European) modern age, marked through colonialism and European invasion, runs corollary to the inscription of novelistic forms of representation; as Lukács writes, "The composition of the novel is the paradoxical fusion of heterogenous and discrete components into an organic whole which is then abolished over and over again" (84). The novel form, and the modern age, decimates the "organic whole" as a matter of course.

One of the first changes is linguistic, marking how the community begins to change its approach to race and how the white colonizers begin to implement the racial contract. Enlightenment approaches to racial categorization creep in: "The difference in their skin colour had seemed just one among so many other things—but maybe it was the most important, after all. No one said Noongar any more: it was all *blackfellas* and *whitefellas*" (353). In opposition to Bobby's outlook on life—that he "was raised to be proud and be friendly . . . My family thought we could be friends and share what we had" (159)—the Europeans start to weaponize ideas of private property as their criminal city continues to grow in terms of population and prosperity, developments that cause resources to become stretched thinner and thinner. Carol Birch notes, "As the sea is over-fished and the land over-hunted, the Noongars find out the hard way that the colonists do not share their views on the communal nature of supplies. Helping themselves to their share, they come up against the alien concept of 'private property,' and the response is brutal." A newer arrival, Chaine, begins to implement the stress on individual rights: "When I first arrived at this place, said Chaine, we were on friendly terms with the natives, although they were largely disrespectful of our habits and considered their right to enter our huts to be the equal of our own. And they were very numerous. I was the first settler to make a stand against them in this regard" (359). As the town continues to shed its early convict past, categories become more and more regimented and European modernity becomes more and more entrenched, until, as Bobby notes, "Chaine and them, they seemed to divide the world up into black and white people, and despite what they said, they put all black people together, and set to work making sure they put themselves in control, and put their own people over the top of all of us who've always been here" (362). The racial contract has been fully implemented in that the white community of Albany has begun to coalesce around shared ideals of white supremacy and colonial domination.

The very form of the novel reflects the dialectic between the European and Aboriginal modes of being in the world. It's true that, as Carol Birch points out, "the non-linear structure emphasises the numinous quality of Noongar perspective. We go back and forth in time freely." Yet it's also true, as Colin Johnson [Mudrooroo] notes, that the novel form "presents a problem [for Aboriginal writers], not only as to length, but also as to content. In a sense, novelists are people isolated from their community" (27). Though *That Deadman Dance* does try to tell the story of a community, it remains largely the story of Bobby, and it is through him that the effects of crime in the narrative are realized and made explicit.

As noted above, in its early years, King George's Town runs into a "problem of labour, especially acute now the prisoners were gone" (39). A town founded on the work of transported convicts needs some mechanism, some social organization, to keep it running on the principles on which it was founded. Because the Europeans continue to pursue a penal-oriented form of urban planning and social organization, the community begins to break down; one of the biggest breaking points in the criminal city comes with the forced imposition of European customs, specifically laws, that categorize Bobby Wabalanginy as a criminal.

Late in the narrative, Bobby attacks a constable who had tried to arrest a tribal elder, and is himself arrested for what he views as an act of self-defense and of tribal honor. He does not fully understand the implication of his arrest or his criminal status: when he is released from jail and asked to sign a statement admitting to his complicity in what the Europeans have declared a crime, he thinks of himself, "Hadn't he escaped the lock-up just from a few words on paper? Child's play. What was that against dance and song?" (390). Failing to comprehend that the words on paper have tangible effects, and that those effects will follow him in the form of a criminal record for the rest of his life, he comes up with an idea to choreograph and perform a dance that will show the Europeans "how people must live here, together" (390). After he is done, he thinks, "He'd sign their paper. We will sign a paper with them about how we might live. There will be no more gaol" (390). Bobby thinks that the rights available to Europeans are also available to him; he believes himself to be able to dictate what goes into rights and treaties, and his highest priority is to ensure the abolition of the jail. He also thinks he can win the Europeans over by dancing for them, a sacred and important rite for the Noongar.

Bobby performs the dance and loses himself in the movement, loses his sense of individuality to a bigger ideal of community. When he has finished, he is elated. "Yes," Scott writes, "Bobby Wabalangingy believed he'd won them over with his dance, his speech, and of course his usual tricks of performance-and-costume stuff. He was particularly pleased with the red underpants, worn as a concession to his audience's sensibility" (394–95). All of a sudden, however, "he felt not fear, but a terrible anxiety. Faces—other than those of Jack Tar and Binyan—had turned away from him. Bobby felt as if he had surfaced in some other world. Chairs creaked as people stirred, coughing. Chaine led them to their feet. Figures at the periphery of Bobby's vision fell away. And another sound: a little dog yelping" (395). In short, the Europeans failed to understand Bobby's dance, and all contemporary readers know the implications of that failure.

Hughes-D'Aeth declares *That Deadman Dance* "a great book because it makes from an impossible situation a possible way forward. This is a moral achievement as much as it is an aesthetic or literary one.... He doesn't give us hope based on platitude, but a mechanism through which to build a better world, a world in which things can survive together." This hopeful cast on the novel unfortunately fails to take into account the fact that the world depicted in *That Deadman Dance* has been shattered with the arrival of European capitalism, colonialism, and modernity. It has been broken through the crime of colonialism, and the crimes colonialism insisted on codifying into law. *That Deadman Dance* doesn't provide the reader with a sense of hope so much as a window into a past world when cooperation may have been possible, but likely was not, given the Europeans' reasons for establishing the criminal city of King George's Town in the first place. Any imperial project that involves claiming land for your own cannot be inherently just, and especially an imperial project that relies on the labor of forcibly transported convicts, accused of crimes and sentenced under codes mandated by an imperial, capitalist court. This is not a straightforward story of hope or a narrative that gives us tools to build a just society in the neocolonial twenty-first century; to say otherwise is naïve.

In an interview with Anne Brewster, Scott offers a slightly more tempered vision of what he believes his own book can accomplish. "The literary stuff," he says, "is about provoking and trying to open doors to a much wider audience, arousing interest in this other stuff" (Brewster 229). This "other stuff," he believes, are community-oriented actions that have tangible influence on the physical world: "community work, the regeneration and consolidating of culture in its own community, and empowering people through the sharing of that in a controlled way" (229). This is better aligned with what this novel about this criminal city might be able to accomplish. *That Deadman Dance* can spur people and groups into structural action; it is not itself a roadmap to building a better world. Besides the fact that it ends on a note of disconsolate almost-hopelessness, readers who become interested in this chapter of Australia's past might have their interest "in this other stuff" aroused, which in turn can perhaps spark interest in more communal solutions and changes. It might point the way to "an ethic of incommensurability, which guides moves that unsettle innocence" (Tuck and Yang 35), which could in turn move self-professed decolonial projects past the stage of metaphor.

This is in contradistinction to *The Secret River*, which wallows in a kind of narcissistic self-indulgence. When asked about white Australian historical fiction, Scott answers:

> I think part of the impulse is to find heroes for oneself, to go back and to re-work the most readily available historical narrative that you're given. . . . That's what Kate Grenville was doing, I think, with *The Secret River*: trying to find a place for herself that she's comfortable within this pretty harsh history. There's a difference though for the colonized people, carrying the legacy of oppression; the imperatives are I think greater. The impulse is to re-work, to find a story you can tell yourself and your people. And, I guess, the more shook up the current times are, the more dispute there is about the question: what is that historical narrative? (Brewster 237)

The Secret River remains too mired in individual self-absorption to be able to achieve the kind of communal emotional outpouring that is necessary for catharsis. On the other hand, *That Deadman Dance*, told from the point of view of "the colonised people, carrying the legacy of oppression," is able to plumb the depths of historical injustice in a deeper way. Sue Kossew writes, "Scott's return to this period of history is an assertion of the power, adaptability, and transformative survival of local Indigenous culture in the fact of the colonizing process rather than only a mourning of its passing. It is, of course, both memory and mourning" ("Recovering the Past," 176). It is through processing layers of historical crimes, as well as coming to terms with how crime has been wielded as a weapon against Aboriginal Australians, often by those victimized in the same way back in England, that catharsis really becomes possible.

Why is this important? Because, in many ways, we are still living in the society empire created. Ghassan Hage writes of twenty-first-century Australia, "As the state retreats from its commitment to the general welfare of the marginal and the poor, these people are increasingly—at best—left to their own devices. At worst, they are actively portrayed as outside society. The criminalisation and labelling of ethnic cultures, where politicians and sections of the media encourage the general public to make a causal link between criminality, poverty and racial or ethnic identity, is one of the more unethical forms of such processes of exclusion" (20). We often conceive of these kinds of injustices happening in the past; in fact, both Kate Grenville and Kim Scott set their depictions of criminalization, capitalism, and race in the past, and they are far from alone in doing so. But as anyone with even a passing understanding of white settler colonial societies is aware, the past is never over; it isn't even past. Colonialism is a structure, not an event. The current Aboriginal population of Australia is just under 3 percent of the total population (a sign of the violence of colonialism by itself), but vast disparities in health, education, treatment by police, and other categories are widespread. Even fifty years after the end of the "Stolen Generations" period, when indigenous children were forcibly taken from their parents as part of a larger assimilation project, Aboriginal people in many places lack the basic nutrition, education, and housing that many white Australians take for granted, not to mention the often-brutal treatment of Aboriginal people by the police and the much higher incarceration rates. Given the shocking inequalities that persist after the initial era of settler colonialism, it seems a reckoning with the violent past is far past necessary. Whitewashing the past, or a "longing for the dissonance to be resolved, affirmed and absorbed into the work [that] may be so great that it will lead to a premature closing of the circle of the novel's world" (Lukács 72), is not an effective strategy, but reinscribing the importance of communitarian and public catharsis might work. One way to accomplish this reckoning is through cathartic texts about criminal cities that challenge the readers into tangible, communal, structural action: texts that take into account positionality, orientation, responsibility, and privilege, ideas that are further elaborated on in a study of the literature of Bombay.

FOUR

"SHOT THROUGH WITH CRIME"

—

Bombay after Mumbai

Gregory David Roberts's 2003 novel *Shantaram* tracks the experiences of Lin, an Australian man (later rechristened "Shantaram" by villagers in rural India) who has escaped from prison in his home country and fled to Bombay to avoid detection and capture. Lin's initial impressions of his new city are striking in their lack of self-awareness: seeing an urban slum on the way from the airport into the city center, Lin thinks, "*What kind of a government . . . what kind of a system allows suffering like this?*" (7, italics original), seemingly oblivious to the homelessness and despair that persists in Australia's own lack of social supports. Just a few minutes later, Lin has changed his tune, musing instead, "To my eyes, the city was beautiful. It was wild and exciting. Buildings that were British Raj-romantic stood side to side with modern, mirrored business towers. . . . Even the flare of shame I'd felt when I first saw the slums and the street beggars dissolved in the understanding that *they were free*, those men and women" (21, italics mine).

About a quarter of a century before *Shantaram* was published, Edward Said defined Orientalism as "a way of coming to terms with the Orient that is based on the Orient's special place in European Western experience" (1). Lin's characterization of Bombay as being "romantic" as it relates to imperialism, and "wild and exciting" due to his own reasons for being there, and, most alarmingly, his patronizing depiction of inhabitants of slums and people who may be unsheltered or precariously sheltered as "free" are his way of situating his experience of Bombay within his own experiences as a Westerner, a way of dissolving his own shame. Lin's refusal to feel any sense of complicity in his or the West's own making of this city in which he now resides as a way to escape his own crimes in his own land is a consistent theme throughout *Shantaram*, although a theme that neither the narrator nor the author directly acknowledges.

Later in the novel, Lin is arrested and taken to jail, where he is singled out for special punishment due to his position of privilege. In one scene, he is beaten by a warden for some small infraction:

> "British built this jail, in the time of Raj," he hissed at me, showing teeth. "They did chain Indian men here, whip them here, hang them here, until dead. Now we run the jail, and you are a British prisoner."
>
> "Excuse me, sir," I said with the most formal politeness that the Marathi language offers, "but I am not British. I am from New Zealand."[1]
>
> "You are *British!*" he screamed, spraying my face with saliva.
>
> "I'm afraid not."
>
> "Yes! You are British! All *British!*" he replied, the snarl moving outward to a malignant smile once more. "You are *British*, and *we* run the jail. You go through *that* way!" (413–14, italics original)

This scene's linkage of the Australian and British experiences are not how these two countries would be understood in Australia, as we have seen in the previous chapter. But *Shantaram* provides a useful way of conceptualizing how crime in literature is understood in a postcolonial age, as we make a leap from the settler colonies of Ireland and Australia to what is often thought of as Britain's most representative colony, India. Western eyes frequently perceive Bombay in a romantic, condescending way, much as Lin has done, when colonial legacies they may be unaware of snake barely below the surface, requiring very little to bring them back up.[2] As we transition from Australia to India, it is helpful to keep in mind the words of Stephen Knight, who writes, "What we see in Australian crime fiction is evident elsewhere. Crime fiction is an early, often the first, voice to respond to new social and cultural encounters generated by the colonial situation. The crimes that were realised as personal and domestic were also projected directly or indirectly as social and political" ("Crimes," 25). Though I am not writing about crime fiction as the genre specifically, the connection between Australia and Knight's "elsewhere" (for these purposes, India) is instructive: crime functions as a way of telling the reader something about a particular place's "social and political" situation.

Westerners often frame the social and political experiences of Bombay in their own experiences of time or politics. Lin articulates a vision of the rise of Shiv Sena, a right-wing Hindu nationalist political party, in a way common among those used to Westernized teleologies: he writes of his years in the city that "those years, as Indian pride was rising like new green, white, and orange vines from the scorched post-colonial earth, were the last years when being foreign, being British, or looking and sounding British was enough to win hearts and intrigue minds" (874). Lin is referring to the idea that Shiv Sena's ascent to power, which was closely followed by sectarian riots and bomb explosions in the early 1990s, which in turn led party leadership to officially rename "Bombay" "Mumbai," "left many wondering if Bombay's cosmopolitanism had been just a façade, now as charred as the buildings damaged by explosions" (Prakash 10). To many Western or Westernized audiences, the transition of the city from "Bombay" to "Mumbai" signals many things: the end of a kind of supposed carefree cosmopolitanism, the official end of the colonial era, and the beginning of a new and dangerous right-wing movement to claim Hindus as the only legitimate citizens of the city. Thomas Blom Hansen writes in *The Saffron Wave: Democracy and Hindu Nationalism in Modern India*, that Shiv Sena's Hindu-centric narrative, what he calls "the real fiction at work here," has been imposed by Orientalism, the idea that there exists "the notion of a single Hindu culture, incommensurable with Islamic or western epistemes and forms of organization" (12). The Shiv Sena–endorsed logic that led to the name change, and the Westernized *understanding* of that name change, rely on Enlightenment notions of teleology and progress and are Orientalized versions of history.

This narrative of events is often told and seems like a commonsense understanding of how the city has changed in the past fifty years. It is neat, tidy, and easily digestible. It is cathartic in the sense that it views the name change as a release valve for the buildup of tension within the city. This narrative also lines up easily with a Western teleology in that it follows a simple chain of events—this happened, which led to this, which led to this, which led to this—as well as with common understandings of how crime works in literature, which is that crime literature as a genre "affirms values of scientific reason, logic, and teleology, and the Enlightenment idea that society is progressing towards a perfectible point" (Chambers 31). However, the story of the name change is more complicated than this gloss, and is reflected in recent literature of the city that does not afford the kind of cathartic properties of the popular narrative and refuses to portray this story in a straightforward linear manner. David Scott writes in *Omens of Adversity*, "There is, I think, a profound sense in which the once enduring temporalities of past-present-future that animated (indeed, that constructed, even *authorized*) our Marxist historical reason, and therefore organized and underwrote our ideas about historical change, no longer line up quite so neatly, so efficiently, so seamlessly, so instrumentally, so—in a word—*teleologically* as they once seemed to do. That old consoling sense of temporal *concordance* is gone" (6, original italics). Much as Lukács writes that "the circle within which the Greeks led their metaphysical life was smaller than ours" (33), necessitating the need for the novel to take over from the epic, the sense of cause-and-effect-driven telos or narrative has broken for the postcolonial criminal city and novel. In the criminal city of Bombay/Mumbai, Thrity Umrigar's *The World We Found* (2012) and Vikram Chandra's *Sacred Games* (2006) map this broken sense of "temporal *concordance*," to again quote David Scott, and simultaneously wrestle with the question of the name change from "Bombay" to "Mumbai" and what this means for notions of "progress" and forward movement. I argue we can read these novels most effectively through the lens of crime and how crime combines with transportation to foreclose opportunities for catharsis in a city bereft of "that old consoling sense of temporal *concordance*." Umrigar and Chandra's treatment of teleology, time, and crime complicates the story of Bombay[3] as it has been envisioned, told, and retold through Orientalized Western frameworks.

"THE GREATEST CRIME IN ALL HISTORY": BOMBAY, THE BRITISH, CRIME, AND NEOLIBERALISM

Put simply, Bombay would not exist without imperialism. In the precolonial era, Bombay consisted of seven islands, which operated as independent fishing colonies controlled by various empires over hundreds of years. In the seventeenth century, the Portuguese briefly took control of the islands that would become Bombay, only to cede them relatively promptly to the British East India Company.[4] The British are the European imperial power most typically associated with the history of Bombay and with India in general, and it is with them that the modern history of Bombay begins.

In the late eighteenth century, the British governor William Hornby undertook an immense civil engineering project to unite the seven islands into one single landmass. The project was successful, creating the urban agglomeration we recognize today. Prakash notes that Bombay is thus doubly colonized: the "seizure of lands from the sea for the urban settlement went hand in hand with the conquest of the territory and the people by European colonialism" (27). This makes Bombay an especially rich territory from which to explore the city that empire made, as the colonial powers continued to remake the city according to their own preferences. Mariam Dossal points out that "by 1875, Bombay had been significantly restructured [by the British]" (3). Writing of the nineteenth century, Tristram Hunt notes, "If a visiting European tourist avoided the insanitary rookeries, he might not even think his steamship had landed him east of Suez" (263). The very construction of Bombay, as well as the similarities between it and English cities, might account partly for what Alex Tickell points out, that the city holds a vexed place within "Indian nationalist discourses" (198). The existence of the city (when many nationalists, like Mahatma Gandhi, held up the village as the apogee of Indian life), combined with how Bombay specifically came to be, marks Bombay as particularly imperially inflected.[5]

The heavy hand of the British in Bombay can be understood through less tangible infrastructures as well: Shashi Tharoor has pointed out that "the sight of Hindu and Muslim soldiers rebelling together in 1857 and fighting side by side, willing to rally under the command of each other and pledge joint allegiance to the enfeebled Mughal monarch, had alarmed the British, who did not take long to conclude that dividing the two groups and pitting them against one another was the most effective way to ensure the unchallenged continuance of Empire. . . . The British had a particular talent for creating and exaggerating particularist identities and drawing ethnically-based administrative lines in all their colonies" (121).[6] The British legacy in Bombay, then, is marked not only by physical infrastructure but also by the forced creation of arbitrary divisions among the populace. These divisions were reified by informational technologies, such as the census, that deliberately directed attention away from the hybridity many see as integral to the city. Shiv Sena, in this reading, is a continuation of imperial logics, translated into twenty-first-century hard-right ideologies.[7]

Though Bombay was never the official capital of British India (that role fell to Calcutta and later, Delhi), its status as the primary western harbor gave the city an extremely important role within the colony: Urbs Prima in Indis, one of the British tags for the city. Bombay retained its status as necessary to the smooth functioning of the British Empire, primarily for its role in globalized capital and the exporting and importing of products. The British capitalist enterprise had so wracked India and Bombay by 1930 that a young American historian and philosopher, Will Durant, upon disembarking in India, wrote that Britain's "conscious and deliberate bleeding of India" amounted to the "greatest crime in all history" (quoted in Tharoor 2). This crime would continue to simmer for years, and the literary examples of cathartic crime studied in this chapter are, in many ways, an attempt to process or deal with the harms done by the original crime of imperialism.

When the British left India after World War II, Bombay ran no risk of being lumped into the new state of Pakistan, but Partition still deeply affected the city: millions of refugees from Kashmir, Gujarat, and other border regions poured into Bombay, and the violence and instability that resulted from the hastily drawn-up, poorly imagined, and sloppily executed plan that was Partition roiled the city in the 1940s and 1950s. This is reflected in the literature; as Priyamvada Gopal writes of "the Bombay novel," "In its polarities and contradictions, this vibrant city embodies the promise and the betrayals of Independence, a theme that would emerge repeatedly in the spate of anglophone fiction inspired by [*Midnight's*] *Children* [by Salman Rushdie, 1981]." (116). One of the most lasting effects of the post-Independence Partition was the public emergence of imperially engendered crises and hardenings of identity, primarily into a Hindu/Muslim binary framework but with other identity considerations as well.

Shiv Sena, a Hindu nationalist political party, was founded in 1966 by a former cartoonist named Bal Thackeray. The party was ostensibly founded out of a fury over the presence of non-Marathi-speaking "foreigners" in the city of Bombay and the state of Maharashta, its formation providing a convenient locus for the rage of the part of the city that was in the grips of general populist nativist sentiment. Shiv Sena, like many right-wing, nationalist, and fascist movements throughout history, is often associated with violence, stereotypically masculine values, and a gut appeal to the "common man."[8] The xenophobia and attraction to violence the organization helped inculcate in certain sectors of Bombay society propagated a mentality of hypermasculinity, violence, purity, and "us vs. them." Violence, in the form of riots, became normalized throughout the 1970s and 1980s, leading to what many regard as the quintessential "turn" in the history of Bombay, the 1992–93 Hindu/Muslim riots.

These riots came about due to the demolition of a mosque in Ayodhya, which Muslims interpreted as an escalation of tensions against their community. Muslims were overwhelmingly the victims in the riots; many were targeted for their identity, and many scholars have suggested reframing the "riots" as instead an attempt at ethnic cleansing or genocide. The initial riots were followed by retaliation bombings orchestrated by a Muslim leader of an organized crime syndicate. Thomas Blom Hansen writes in *Wages of Violence: Naming and Identity in Postcolonial Bombay*, "If we are to understand the transformation of Bombay into Mumbai, and the nature of the Mumbai dreams growing out of a violent movement like Shiv Sena, we need to see the importance of social imaginaries, of desires of recognition, and the attraction of the public spectacles of violence and assertion that Shiv Sena has employed so successfully over the years" (7). We do, indeed, need to understand social imaginaries, and I hold that analyzing the representation of crime in literature is one way to do that, and one way to "understand the transformation of Bombay into Mumbai," as well as what comes after.

These riots and subsequent retaliation bombings, for many people, signaled the "official" embrace of violent, fundamentalist, parochial identity politics by a substantial portion of Bombay's population. Only a few years after the 1992–93 riots, Shiv Sena felt empowered enough to push through the name change to Mumbai, which was inspired by the name of a Hindu goddess, Mumbadevi, further solidifying, in many people's opinions, Shiv Sena's push to "Hindu-ize" the city. Yet the story is more complicated than that: the name change did signal a shift away from the nomenclature of the British Empire, an empire that many who mourned the loss of an ostensibly formerly liberal and cosmopolitan Bombay disproportionately benefited from. Thomas Blom Hansen explains in *Wages of Violence*, "At a first glance, the change of the name was a rather straightforward assertion of the nativist agenda of claiming Bombay and all its symbols of modernity and power to be the natural property of local Marathi speakers.... However, the renaming also resonated with broader and nationalist concerns with decolonization of the mind" (3), a concern shared more with anticolonial leftists than right-wing fascists. Those who mourn the loss of a liberal and free Bombay tend to fall somewhere between these two poles, most likely affluent liberals who occupied the position of the middle class or "native elites" who had the least to gain by disruption to the status quo.

The name change, complexities and all, came only a few years after the Indian national government liberalized the economy in 1991, which opened India and Bombay up to international currents of capital and globalization processes to an extent not seen before. This liberalization represented the final nail in the coffin of the Bandung movement, of which India had been a key instigator and which had sought to maintain non-alliance with either First World capitalism or Second World socialism. Naomi Klein has written of neoliberalism[9] that "this fundamentalist form of capitalism has always needed disasters to advance" (9). After the twin disasters of the riots/pogrom and the bombings, it was easy to ramp up existing and nascent neoliberal economic policies in the city, policies that widened the income gap, snaked the logic of capitalism more deeply throughout the city, and encouraged individualist, rather than communitarian, approaches to life. These market reforms have also had a great deal to do with how crime is portrayed in the literature of Bombay.

Crime is often represented in Bombay novels as being inextricably tied to larger movements, such as the gangs or "underworld"; it is also often written about in terms of "official" political or governmental elites. Both of these frameworks are integral to Bombay; as Arjun Appadurai says, this is a city "where crime is an integral part of municipal order" (628). Though important parts of the local scene, these large criminal and political organizations also typically have international ties and are linked to global circulations of capital, while also being reliant on imperial structures and identities. As Rashmi Varma phrases it, "Underneath these new projects of accumulation [in the postcolonial city] lie older logics of colonial rule even as the postcolonial state and social movements seek to foreground the postcoloniality of these cities—colonial buildings, spaces, trade networks, social rules, and street names constitute the postcolonial city as a palimpsest of a messy colonial history and a postcolonial present in crisis" ("Gleam and Darkness,"

200). The palimpsest of the city of Bombay necessitates that "older logics of colonial rule," fashioned as neoliberal economics/market fundamentalism, continue to crop up in the city, though these structuring elements are splashed over by the louder, seemingly more urgent actions of identitarian religious groups. What may look like an atavistic return to identity tribalism is in fact deliberately fostered by the neoliberal regime's simultaneously modern and neocolonial character. Bombay in the twenty-first century is both a place where colonialism "remains a relevant factor in understanding the problems and the dangers of the world in which we live" (Tharoor 277) and a place that has successfully constructed a uniquely damaging neoliberal society. As we will see from the readings of *The World We Found* and *Sacred Games*, catharsis is often unavailable due to the knotted histories of imperialism and economic liberalization, which fold in on each other and do not allow for straightforward teleologies or that (Westernized) familiar, "consoling" sense of forward progression and straightforward movement.

Gyan Prakash addresses the intersections among Shiv Sena, the renaming of the city, and the continual return of the colonial era by writing, "Bombay is now Mumbai. The colonial era is abolished, dismissed as history.... A striking statue of the warrior [seventeenth-century Shivaji], mounted on his horse, sword in hand, stands near the Gateway of India. The Maratha chieftain could never have imagined that his seventeenth-century wars with the Mughal Empire would one day earn him a place in the gateways to a modern city. But there he is, miraculously installed as the city's icon, greeting visitors, commuters, and passersby today with the memory of centuries ago" (25–26). Prakash goes on to note that Shivaji's original placement in the city's geography was in Kala Ghoda, where a large statue of King Edward VII once stood. Though Shivaji now stands at the Gateway of India, Kala Ghoda was paved over to make a parking lot, and the statue of King Edward was placed in a museum, "legends abound that the vanquished king lives on" (26). In these legends, Shivaji and King Edward engage in duels all over the city, duels that never establish a clear winner. In the morning, Prakash writes, "Shivaji returns to his triumphant Gateway home and King Edward to the museum, both vowing to resume their duel" (26). There is no cleansing of the past, no catharsis to shed the weight of imperial history—the two opposing forces just repeat their actions, over and over and over again.

The position of the precolonial Shivaji is in line with one theory behind the renaming of Bombay to Mumbai: to signify, as Prakash writes, that "the colonial era is abolished, dismissed as history" (25). Yet, as the legends that would have King Edward and Shivaji fight to a stalemate demonstrate, that belief is not entirely true. Ghosts of the imperial past haunt Bombay: King Edward, thought to be consigned to a museum, instead roams the city freely, engaging in a fight against his precolonial counterpart. There is no linear story here; because imperialism has never been fully dealt with or reparated, injustice still lingers, but never in a clear or tangible way that could lead to a kind of catharsis. These imperial legacies intermingle with contemporary concerns like right-wing Hinduism and economic liberalization to create a particularly Bombay image of crime, colonialism, capitalism, and the city; as Caroline Herbert says, both Chandra and Umrigar's work engage thoroughly with how the city has reacted to "the rise of communal conflict" while "[demanding] that we embed our critiques within the materiality of everyday urban living" (945). In the readings that follow, I consider what that means for literature: why contemporary Bombay literature is so focused on crime, and what Thrity Umrigar's *The World We Found* and Vikram Chandra's *Sacred Games* have to say about lingering imperial crimes and contemporary local ones.

Yumna Siddiqi writes of colonial "fictions of intrigue" that "an impetus to maintain or reestablish order drives the stories at a thematic or textual level," noting a common "impulse toward narrative closure with the establishment of order and intelligibility" that is combated by "the persistence of residual, returning problematic elements that require that problems be 'solved' and anxieties allayed again and again" (10). This happens frequently in these Bombay fictions: Umrigar and Chandra present stories of crime in the contemporary city that are not easily resolved in terms of answers, time, or teleology; they grapple with recurrent problems born of unsolved imperial legacies, much like the ghostly King Edward. In many ways, these novels are wrestling with the problem David Scott has articulated in *Conscripts of Modernity*, when he wrote that, in a post-Bandung world, "the collapse of the social and political hopes that went into the anticolonial imagining and postcolonial making of national sovereignties" has created a tension between a "dead-end present" and "an imagined idiom of future futures that might reanimate this present and even engender in it new and unexpected horizons of transformative possibility" (1). Is it possible, these novels ask through their depictions of crime and mobility, to move out of the "dead-end present" of retrodden imperial legacies and into a brighter vision of the future?

"LIKE BLEDDY COLONIALISTS OR SOMETHING": THRITY UMRIGAR'S *THE WORLD WE FOUND*

The World We Found (2012) tells the story of four friends—Armaiti, Laleh, Kavita, and Nishta—who went to college together in Bombay in the 1970s. The four women, who were very active in socialist and left-wing circles during their undergraduate days, have gradually fallen out of touch throughout the years: Armaiti has moved to the United States, Nishta's husband has gradually secluded her from the world due to his fundamentalist interpretation of Islam, Kavita has thrown herself into her work as an architect and her relationship with a German woman, and Laleh has moved firmly into the upper classes with her marriage to Adish, an engineer who works on many construction and real estate projects and who is another former member of the circle. The women are thrown together again with Armaiti's news that she has been diagnosed with terminal cancer and wishes her friends to come visit her in the States one last time. Laleh and Kavita are free to leave immediately, but they must engage in subterfuge to get Nishta (renamed Zoha) out of her husband's home, as he will not allow her to travel or even leave the house without him.

The narration of the novel rotates among the four women, and trades between contemporary travel machinations and memories of their college days. Those days were difficult, as Kavita reminisces: "It was India. It was the late 1970s. The West, with its women's movement and gay liberation movement and its permissiveness and promiscuity, was at least a planet away. It was India in the late 1970s, and the country was still coming to grips with the nightmare of the Emergency years, and corruption was endemic and food prices and college tuition were rising, and public services were breaking down" (31). Amid all the turmoil, the four women have discovered leftist politics—"the only boys we talked about were named Lenin, Marx, and Mao," Kavita recalls (32)—and view it as the solution to their city's issues, frequently participating in large-scale protests in their city. The friends are operating within a post–Bandung Conference world, where India helped to pilot the non-alliance movement but where, simultaneously, much of its populace was being drawn closer to the ideals of socialism and communism.

One night, the four of them, along with Adish, and Iqbal (who will later marry Nishta) take part in a protest, the aftermath of which still haunts them forty years later. "Over the years," Kavita thinks, "she had worked hard to suppress the memories of that horrific night. But now she remembered the suffocating, claustrophobic feeling" (67) of being trapped in a jail cell after their arrest. Kavita and Nishta were arrested on some trumped-up charge (the others were not arrested for various reasons), and no one ever specifically names what happened to them in the police precinct, but it is very clear that a key inflection point in their lives came with being charged with some ostensible, unnamed crime, being thrown into jail, and trying to go back to normal life a few days later. It was a day that Adish believed "they had tucked away, like an old letter in a shoe box, until Laleh had dug it out again" (77), with the news about Armaiti's diagnosis and all the memories that surface alongside this news. Armaiti's illness brings up memories of this day and the accusations of crime that have come along with it. But there is another event that has lain buried in everyone's mind, one more recent and closer to the surface: that of the 1992–93 riots in their city and what they have meant for what the group of friends, and their city, have become.

The riots, coming as they do on the heels of the liberalization of the economy in the early 1990s and just before the official name change of the city from Bombay to Mumbai, are often lumped in with neoliberal economic policy and the name change as one large, undifferentiated event. Indeed, Rashmi Varma notes, "what we see in the transmutation of Bombay into Mumbai is an example of such a contradictory articulation in which the globalization of capital confronts the provincialization of citizens within the postcolonial state" ("Provincializing," 83). In *The World We Found*, this correlation between neoliberal economic policy—"the globalization of capital"—and the rightward swing of a city's culture—"the provincialization of citizens"—is best examined through the character of Iqbal, Nishta's husband, and another former leftist from the university days.

Laleh and Kavita have fallen out of touch with Nishta, though she remains living in Bombay as they do. Armaiti's news means they feel compelled to track Nishta down and ask her if she would like to travel to America with them for one last visit with Armaiti. They discover that Iqbal has forced her to convert to Islam (she was born Hindu) and has changed her name to Zoha. She wears a burqa, lives in purdah, and generally must live her life according to Iqbal's extremely strict understanding of Islam. While the women are trying to reach Nishta and convince her to talk to Iqbal so she can make the trip, Adish takes Iqbal to lunch to try to do his own autopsy on what has happened to his former friend. Speaking of the riots, Adish offers, "The secular, easygoing city that I had known changed forever during that time" (89). It soon occurs to him, however, that the riots have affected Iqbal far more deeply: it hits Adish that "he was gazing upon a broken, tormented man, whom secular society had failed completely" (92).

For Adish, a Parsi, the riots were a shock to the system, indicating that his city was more xenophobic and more racist than he had previously believed. It was not easy for him to come to terms with the realization that darker currents than he realized ran under the streets of Bombay. For a Muslim like Iqbal, however, the riots were something far more earth-shattering: the riots, which targeted Muslims above all other populations, were much more like an anti-Muslim pogrom or an ethnic cleansing attempt[10] than they were a two-sided act of violence. Indeed, they were sufficient catalyst for Iqbal to totally change his worldview. He muses to himself, "How wrong their analysis in college had been. Back then they had seen the fight as between rich and poor, a global class struggle. Maybe the world had changed since then, or maybe Allah had seen fit to drop the scales from his eyes, but everywhere he looked these days, someone was out for Muslim blood. Iraq. Afghanistan. Chechnya. Kashmir. Sudan. Gujarat. Even on the streets of this cursed city. Hadn't he seen it firsthand?" (147).

In addition to having his sense of community shattered by the riots, Iqbal has also had his material well-being ripped out from under him: the riots have impoverished his community, he resigned his well-paying job due to increasing prejudice, and he and Nishta have had to move flats and neighborhoods so that they now live in an overcrowded, impoverished, majority-Muslim area. This is despite the fact that the economy has supposedly been "opened up" in the intervening decades, a liberalization brought in by the dissolution of the Soviet Union. Adish, clinging to this belief that liberalization was a net good, reminisces with Laleh:

> Do you remember the day the Soviets invaded Afghanistan[?] . . . And do you remember what we all said? That the days of the American Empire were over, that the Soviet Union was the new imperial power. . . . Do you realize how wrong we all were? A few years later, the Soviet Union breaks into a thousand pieces, disappears like a child's dream. Just like that . . . we also thought that liberalizing the economy would destroy India. Instead, look at what happened. The economy is booming. Shit, there's so much construction going on in Bombay itself, my firm can't keep up with it. (40–41)

In return, Laleh snaps back, "And in the meantime, farmers are killing themselves in record numbers . . . there are food riots breaking out in the countryside" (41). Economic liberalization may have helped people in positions like those held by Adish and Laleh; the effects are far different on those less privileged, such as their former friends Iqbal and Nishta.

Naomi Klein has termed the forced imposition of neoliberal economic policies "the shock doctrine." By this, she means that the implementation of neoliberalism's "policy trinity"—"the elimination of the public sphere, total liberation for corporations, and skeletal social spending" (15)—"shocks" the community into submission. This "policy trinity" was achieved in Bombay after the early 1990s economic reforms, though the reforms predate the riots; as such, the way economics and the riots work here do not line up neatly with Klein's shock doctrine theory, which holds that "for economic shock therapy to be applied without restraint . . . some sort of additional major collective trauma has always been required, one that either temporarily suspended democratic practices or blocked them entirely" (11). Still, economic reforms were able to pick up the pace after the shock of the racist nightmare that was the riots, resulting in Rupal Oza's argument that "in the context of India's intensified encounter with global capital, the concomitant loss of sovereignty has resulted in the displacement of control onto national culture and identity" (2). In other words, neoliberal economic reforms have combined with a rise in Hindu nationalism to create a newer version of Bombay, an iteration later concretized by the name change from Bombay to Mumbai. The city of the friends' youths, one where a socialist, egalitarian future seemed possible, has been replaced by a city of deeply unequal living standards and opportunities: the type of city that "[embodies] the most extreme instances of economic injustice, ecological unsustainability, and spatial apartheid ever confronted by humanity" (Dawson and Hayes Edwards 6). In *The World We Found*, these changes have played out against the backdrop of the collapse of the communist movement. Thomas Blom Hansen argues in *The Saffron Wave: Democracy and Hindu Nationalism in Modern India* that anti-communism and Islamophobia are linked, that economic liberalization and the riots were made possible by Hindu nationalist elites convincing people that communism and Islam were "foreign ideologies" that "had prevented their societies from finding their true and essential cultural identity" (174), thus opening the door for acts of violence committed against either or both of these populations.

This is why *The World We Found* swirls around these two inflection points—the "crime" that lands the friends in jail as part of an anticommunist action back in the 1970s, and the criminal, violent riots that have, combined with economic policy, created the city in which most of them live today. These ideas are all dialectically linked: Shiv Sena, Arjun Appadurai writes, "succeeded in identifying with the interests of Mumbai's growing Marathi-speaking lumpen proletariat while also actively destroying its left (communist) union culture" (646). This loss of a socialist future and the bleak forecast of a xenophobic outlook are expressed in Umrigar's novel through the lens of crime: both that of the 1970s and the 1990s, and finally one that takes place in the present day as an expression of these, and some even older, troubling legacies.

As part of a flashback to a dinner party Adish and Laleh hosted shortly after the riots and before Iqbal and Nishta disappeared from their friend group, Iqbal hisses to Nishta upon leaving, "Did you see how they live? . . . The people who called themselves Socialists just a few years ago? Like bleddy colonialists or something" (167). Imperial divides have reconstituted themselves in contemporary Bombay, and not just by the instantiation of a "native elite" that mimics the wealth and power of the British of times past. Legacies of the British Empire also crop up in contemporary expressions of racism caught within the framework of crime, most publicly in the riots/pogrom, but also in smaller, one-on-one interactions, like one between Adish and Iqbal at the end of the novel.

Laleh and Kavita have managed to construct an elaborate plan to smuggle Nishta out of India; she plans to stay in the United States and begin a new life, away from Iqbal, after their time with Armaiti. The three women make it to the airport, but a flaw in their plan means that Iqbal is alerted to Nishta's attempt to leave, and he follows them to the airport to try to prevent her from boarding the plane. Adish, who has given the women a lift to the airport, sees Iqbal and attempts to detain him, but Iqbal is undeterred. Adish's instinctual move is to point at Iqbal, who with his beard and dress, codes as stereotypically Muslim, and shout, "Help. Terrorist. This man has a weapon. Help" (285).

Of course, it has the desired effect: airport security rushes over immediately, and though Adish demurs instantly, saying he must have been mistaken (the security guard scolds him, "False accusation is a criminal offense" [285]), the women have managed to make it through security and are no longer in danger of being tracked down by Iqbal. Ruminating on his choice to throw his former friend under the bus, Adish thinks, "How easily he had exploited the reflexive dislike and fear that many Indians had for Islam" (290), a "dislike and fear" created initially by the British and sustained by their years of colonial divide-and-conquer tactics. He builds on this by thinking of himself as "the Parsi as middle-man, as trickster, as the cool, suave, immoral asshole who played one party against the other" (290), another stereotype created by the British and their preferential treatment of the Parsi community. A Hindu man even tells Adish later he'd seen what Adish had done and congratulates him on his "courage," noting, "A model community, the Parsis" (292). In this short scene, Adish has managed to reconstitute much of the racial logic created by empire. The neoliberal world after Bandung, "the horizon that made that erstwhile story [of anticolonial revolution] so compelling as a dynamo for intellectual and political work has collapsed. It is now a superseded future, one of our futures past" (David Scott, *Conscripts*, 210). The heady intellectual future the students had engaged in during the 1970s is gone; in many ways, the characters are now repeating the past.

Imperial racial logics, legacies of crime from the past (1970s and 1990s), accusations of crime from the present, and transportation all come together in this scene, with transportation being stymied for one person (Iqbal) but made possible for three others (Laleh, Kavita, and Nishta). As noted, transportation is closely linked with catharsis; both concepts rely heavily on the idea of moving productively through space, of going forward rather than staying still.[11] Who gets to move forward in this scene is a comment on the possibility for catharsis and closure in contemporary Bombay; you can get it or closely mimic it if you have the money or access to money, but lack of resources keeps you trapped in the liminal space of the airport, in a historically dense matrix of interweaving political, cultural, religious, and economic logics.

Catharsis is not possible in this scenario for Iqbal, because none of these crimes and imperial legacies have ever been fully reckoned with. An independent India did not solve "reflexive dislike and fear" of the Muslim community; none of the women arrested in the 1970s have fully reconciled themselves to what they experienced, to the extent they can't fully speak or even think about what transpired; the riots have caused lasting damage; and all of this has congealed together to create a scene where Adish accuses his former friend of being a terrorist, a criminal. The failure of this friend group, of the city as a whole, to reckon with what has happened speaks back to what *The World We Found* presents as the original postcolonial failure, the failure of socialism to deliver what it promised in Bombay. As David Scott says in *Omens of Adversity*, "The once enduring temporalities of past-present-future that animated (indeed, that constructed, even *authorized*) our Marxist historical reason . . . no longer line up quite so neatly, so efficiently, so seamlessly, so instrumentally—in a word, so *teleologically*—as they once seemed to do" (6). Western Marxism, and its attendant reliance on logical progression of history and teleology, is no longer possible in the criminal city of Bombay. The socialist dream dangles as an unfinished project, one that was a promise of hope for so many but was ultimately abandoned, leaving the characters without a satisfying sense of finality, of conclusion. After all, what's more satisfying than the socialist premise of a dialectic that reaches its desired conclusion? Very little, but that desired outcome hasn't happened for any of these individuals, or for the city as a whole. In Umrigar's novel, the failure or desertion of socialism means that neither the readers nor the characters have the opportunity for cathartic crime.

Shortly after the women are arrested in their college days, Armaiti receives a trip to Prague as part of an essay prize. The trip thoroughly disillusions her of her political ideals. "Upon her return," Umrigar writes, "she had described to them in hushed tones how dark and drab Prague was, the soldiers with machine guns on the streets, the old ladies in black coats standing in food lines, the ever-present surveillance cameras in the hotel elevators" (150). The Soviet Union, the beacon of socialist hope for many Third World students at the time (Adish's "a child's dream"), was, to put it mildly, a huge disappointment; the collapse of that empire led to a growth in neoliberalism and a swelling of the ranks of the economic liberalizers (Klein 18). Those economic reforms in India, combined with right-wing Hindu nationalism, have created the contemporary criminal city of Bombay, where all action swirls around talk and memory of crime but no satisfying conclusion is ever completely reached.

Jan Morris writes that "the most potent legacies of empires are immaterial things" (1), something remarkably true even of Bombay, a city marked with plenty of material legacies of empire (trains, names of buildings, the Gateway of India). In contemporary Bombay, a friend's simple request to see her oldest friends before she dies must be navigated by asking questions about "Who has the power? Who has the money?" (Itani). The answers to these questions are alarmingly similar to how they would have been answered in the colonial era, with existing privilege and power structures compounded by the lack of a more idealistic or equitable future; as we see in the airport scene, progress or a move away from these entrenched logics is possible for those who have access to money and power, not to those who don't. Those who don't stay in stasis in the city, locked in interminably by the power and weight of past and present crimes.

This story is more complicated than the one that says "Bombay used to be cosmopolitan; then Shiv Sena came in, and now it is hard-right, identitarian, and racist." That narrative actually has cathartic properties of its own, in that it allows the (usually Western) tellers to soothe themselves with the story of those *other* people who do those bad things over *there*; it's an easily digestible morality tale. Accounting for the full scale of things turns up a more knotted story, a truth further realized in Vikram Chandra's *Sacred Games*.

"ROTTED BY IT": VIKRAM CHANDRA'S *SACRED GAMES*

Vikram Chandra's hard-boiled detective novel *Sacred Games* is a nearly thousand-page epic dealing with the city of Bombay in all its frenzied, convoluted, palimpsestic glory. At the center of the action is Sartaj Singh, a Sikh police inspector who is called to negotiate with the notorious Hindu gangster Ganesh Gaitonde through the door of Gaitonde's underground nuclear bomb shelter. As Gaitonde variously threatens to kill himself, turns melancholic, and threatens Sartaj, the two men open up about each of their personal histories, recount how they got to where they are now, and discuss the current state of politics, crime, and culture (especially Bollywood movies) in contemporary Bombay. After Ganesh eventually dies by suicide, also murdering his friend Jojo in the same bunker, Sartaj learns of Ganesh's entanglement with a mysterious guru (Guru-ji), and it is by following this thread that the police inspector is introduced to an entire species of widespread, historically rooted crime that he previously had no idea existed. The characters in the novel are implicated in corruption, riots, bombings, and terrorist plots, many on international scales; the criminal underworld is allowed to flourish in the way it does because of historical conditions that have undergirded its establishment and continued existence, and Sartaj's investigation of these crimes turns up the knotty interweavings of imperial legacies, postcolonial Indian history, and recent political restructurings in the city of Bombay.

As Sartaj is investigating Jojo's murder and Ganesh's suicide, he comes into contact with a woman named Anjali Mathur, who works for Research and Analysis Wing (RAW), India's foreign intelligence agency. Sartaj learns that RAW is involved in this investigation because the agency has come across an impending threat from "an underground Hindu organization called Kalki Sena" who, according to Anjali, plans to "set up a Hindu rashtra. . . . After the war, which will be the frightful end of Kaliyug [in Hindu theology, the final of the world's four stages], there will be a perfect nation, run according to ancient Hindu principles" (509). When Sartaj asks whom this war will be against, Anjali replies, "Muslims, communists, Christians, Sikhs. Anyone else who doesn't like this perfect nation" (509). Essentially, Kalki Sena plans to set up the perfect cathartic crime and cleanse the city of what it perceives to be un-Indian and foreign (colonial) elements.

The Kalki Sena's aims and ideologies seem closely linked to that of the real-world Shiv Sena, who envisions Bombay and the state of Maharashtra as being for Hindus only. This is compounded by the fact that the Kalki Sena organization has been presenting itself as an Islamic terrorist organization, based out of Pakistan, playing on stereotypes created by the British and cemented by Partition; "if there's a bomb in the city," Sartaj's partner, Kamble, says, "it's got to be the Muslims who brought it in" (520).[12] Mathur, speaking of the false front Kalki Sena has set up, notes that they utilize quotes from the Qur'an like "Closer and closer to mankind comes their Reckoning: yet they heed not and they turn away" and formulate threats like "A great fire will take the unbelievers, and it will begin in Mumbai" (556). Even as the right-wing Hindu movement plans to destroy the city and begin entirely anew, they still marshal imperial and postcolonial stereotypes to deflect attention from their plans, knowing that this will be an effective move.[13] Mukund Belliappa writes that the novel wants to prove to its readers that gang warfare in the city can be telescoped out to be understood as "a proxy war for control of the subcontinent, a proxy war in the expansion of fundamentalist and aggressive Islam, a proxy for the global war being fought by stable, law-abiding societies against terrorism" (350). The novel insists on a conflation between the local and the global, though I am not sold on Belliappa's point that any one nation is positioned as a "stable, law-abiding society"; rather, *Sacred Games* wrestles with the crimes that imperialism has created, and considers what happens when we are forced to live with them instead of eviscerating them.

The international dimensions of the planned bombing are illustrated well by a scene in which Anjali approaches her mentor, K. D. Yadav, as he is on his deathbed, for help with the case. Yadav tries to help her as best he can, and after she leaves, lost in his memories of past crimes and criminals, he muses to himself, "The world is shot through with crime, riddled with it, rotted by it" (326). He goes on to contemplate the kinds of crimes he has encountered in his long career: "The Pakistanis and the Afghans run a twenty-billion-dollar trade in heroin, which is partly routed through India, through Delhi and Bombay, to Turkey and Europe and the United States. The ISI [Inter-Services Intelligence, in Pakistan] and the generals fatten on the trade and buy weapons and mujahideen warriors. The criminals provide logistical support, moving men and money and weapons across the borders. The politicians provide protection to the criminals, the criminals provide muscle and money to the politicians. That's how it goes" (326). Given his life's work, Yadav is of course very interested in the international dimensions of crime, and, though he does not articulate it specifically, it's clear that the contours of the crimes he is thinking about are treading similar patterns to those established by the British Empire. The heroin trade he thinks about was fostered by the British, and relies on ancient trading routes the British fought hard for control over; the very creation of the state of Pakistan is a British invention; and the kinds of corruption he thinks about in terms of cozy relationships between politicians and criminals are the result of a weak postcolonial state and the poorly organized British withdrawal from the subcontinent. The criminal city of Bombay did not spring out of nowhere with the rise of Shiv Sena and the Bombay-Mumbai name change; it's been part of the story from the very beginning of the empire.

Caroline Herbert writes that *Sacred Games* reflects "on canonical reference points in narratives of the city: the legacies of colonialism and Partition; the limits of Nehruvian socialist secularism; the rise of a regional strain of militant, masculinist, Hindu nationalism; the uneven impacts of economic liberalisation; the emergence of a criminal underworld" (948). Through four insets, Chandra tells the story of a young Sikh woman driven out of Pakistan by Partition (who we later realize is Sartaj's mother); of K. D. Yadav's career in the days immediately following India's independence; of poverty in rural India compounded by economic liberalization, poverty that forces migration to the city; and of the disappearance of the young Sikh woman's sister (Sartaj's aunt), who was separated from her family at the time of Partition and has been living in the United States, pretending to be a Pakistani Muslim her entire life. These insets underline the criminal city Chandra creates, as history hidden just below the surface but that goes ignored as just one story among the millions of people who call Bombay home. A sense of frustration that these problems and difficult legacies are unfixable permeates the book, a sense that Bombay is too broken to be fixed. "You want to save *this*?" Sartaj thinks. "For what? Why?" (877).

It is this kind of frustration, born of the problems created and sustained by empire, that Guru-ji draws on when planning his bombing of the city. When asked why he wishes to destroy the city, Guru-ji responds,

> All these United Nations, these dreamy-eyed do-gooders who rush to stop conflicts, they don't understand that some wars must be fought, that killing must happen. They think they have stopped war, but all they ensure is a state of constant, smouldering war. Look at India and Pakistan, bleeding each other for more than fifty years. Instead of a final, glorious battle, we have a long, filthy mess. These well-meaning idiots always chatter on about the progress of the human race, but they don't understand that progress cannot occur without destruction. Every golden age must be preceded by an apocalypse. (838)

Guru-ji believes that the only way to stop the "long, filthy mess" of postcolonial violence is to cause an apocalypse so that the world may begin anew, free of what he views as the original sins of imperialism and pluralism, and he plans to cause just such an apocalypse by setting off bombs, a plan implemented by his close personal friend Ganesh Gaitonde. "You told me every story needed a climax," he says to Ganesh. "Read the signs in this world, the signs from all over this life we lead, and see what it needs. It wants an ending, Ganesh. It needs a close, so we can start over again" (838). Guru-ji's crime story is geared toward an imagined future resolution: an almost Leninesque dialectic of hastening the revolution, the ending, by bringing all these strands of crime and imperialism to their logical, cathartic ends of total and immediate destruction.

Rupal Oza points to the Indian government's development of nuclear weapons as a key stage in India's neoliberal evolution. She further articulates that the "demonstration of masculine pride and of restored virility following the tests to the nation's colonial history of emasculation and the manner in which the Hindu Right was able to harness and deploy this sense of impotence in contemporary India" (115) is tied to "the colonial and postcolonial construction of masculinity" (121) and "middle class aspirations" (121). The Hindu Right, aggressive displays of masculinity from both the male-dominated police force and the heavily masculine criminal underworld, colonial history, and neoliberal economics all swirl around the issues of bombing, violence, crime, and the underworld in *The World We Found* and *Sacred Games*. It is not possible to understand the dimensions of crime in Bombay without taking all these issues into account; Guru-ji's crime of bombing the city has multiple imperial legacies, heavy overtones of toxic masculinity, and a clear link to the global circulation of capital, itself a process instigated by past imperialisms.

The planned bombing also plays into another part of contemporary Bombay life, the Bollywood film industry. The plot of the novel is what Belliappa calls "Bollywood's holy grail" (346), in that Ganesh Gaitonde is a living embodiment of the "country to the city" narrative (he grew up in a very rural village); this "holy grail" narrative keeps gender roles and "traditional values in place" (346); and it allows the country to "[forget] its wretchedness in burlesque simplicities" (346), with the bombing failing, the police triumphing, and the city being saved once again. Well-worn narratives are trod again, with the idea being the presentation of a final resolution everyone has been expecting.

Ganesh himself gets involved in the film business, financing what he envisions will be an international smash hit but is ultimately a gigantic flop. In the process of this project, he hires a communist film director named Manu, who both argues with him about politics and teaches him about filmmaking. "The art-film types keeping saying they're doing new-new things," Manu says, "but they also have to obey the rules. It's just a different set of rules, and a different audience. You can't get away from the rules" (676). Ganesh understands, and thinks to himself, "This is why the screenplay had to move in its cycles of sequences, but inevitably towards a climax, after which there would be nothing. Or, as Guru-ji was implying, maybe something, but only after the world of the screenplay had vanished" (680). The narrative structure of *Sacred Games*, the plotline (and lack of success) of the fictional movie, and the (eventual) failure of the bomb all mimic the same big idea: grand scenes built on centuries of history that build toward a climax but that ultimately fizz out and fade away, denying the satisfying closure that the Western narrative of Bombay demands.[14]

Guru-ji's grand vision of the bomb, one that relies on imperial histories and legacies, is that the city of Bombay will be completely leveled. "We are approaching a time of great change," he tells Ganesh. "It is inevitable, it is necessary, it will happen and has to happen. And the signs of change are all around us. Time and history are like a wave, like a building storm. We are approaching the crest, the outburst. You can feel it, I know you can, it is a build-up of emotion in your own body as well. The events are mounting in their intensity, they come one after another. But in this maelstrom is the promise of peace. Only after the explosion, we will find silence and a new world. This is sure" (730).[15] But what happens when the police are called in for a controlled demolition of the bomb, which they have managed to track down due to Sartaj's police work? After a warning from Kamble that "the climax is about to happen" (730), very little actually does. "Nothing changed in the room," Chandra writes, "but then, from far away, came a series of pops, and then another, phap-phap-phap, phap-phap-phap-phap. A moment passed, and then from the front of the room, a cheer grew and spread. Anjali Mathur came running through the clapping crowd. 'We're safe,' she said. 'We're safe'" (876).

An anti-cathartic conclusion to the crime, to be sure. Why didn't anything happen? Why didn't we get something more spectacular? If this were a Bollywood film and the audience were denied the special effects of a bomb, no one would be pleased. Theodore Martin writes that this crime, along with a comparable crime in a Michael Chabon novel, "[leaves] things, quite literally, open-ended: by preventing apocalypse, each detective transforms the end of his narrative into a nonevent, the perfect absence of any climax. . . . Forestalling the apocalypse, Landsman [of the Chabon novel] and Sartaj realize, does nothing to resolve the political and religious tensions that give rise to the threat in the first place" (169). Indeed, even when it's all over, Sartaj is left with a vague sense of unease. He "didn't feel any safer," Chandra writes. "Inside, him, even now, there was that burning fuse, that ticking fear. He leant against a post in a wire fence and tried to feel satisfaction" (877). The growing sense of unease, the sense he is still not safe, is due to the fact that none of the problems that led to this bomb have been solved; the bomb may not have gone off this time, but we know this isn't a straightforward, teleological story. From a formal, Aristotelian point of view, without any kind of violent rupture, there could be no catharsis. In terms of this novel specifically and the themes it develops, there's nothing to stop history from coiling back in on itself and repeating once again.

Writing about, in part, *Sacred Games*, Megha Anwer makes the argument that this novel "[challenges] the mania for an epiphanic, all-revealing, transformational key episode as the structural basis of a fiction's textual logic. The way is then cleared for a strategically loose, counter-discursive fictional structure" (9). This challenging of the key logic of catharsis and cathartic crime—that something will *happen* to clear out all the gunk that has blocked up the works for so much of history—opens the door for a novel that resists Orientalist logics that read Bombay after Mumbai as provincial, right-wing, fascist, a departure from the carefree days of yore. The crime forces a spotlight on buried histories that challenge this reading, and that open the door for a kind of failed catharsis, an anti-Western progressive or teleological understanding of history. Even the title of the novel, as Pankaj Mishra points out, speaks to this kind of recursive logic: "Chandra's genial mood of acceptance," Mishra writes, "seems part of a Hindu vision of human affairs as *leela*, or sacred game, which transcends easy distinctions between good and evil—a world view that both major and minor characters in the novel, spies and cops as well as criminals, magnify." If there's no overwhelming, single force of evil over which to triumph, and instead we must wrestle with the results of multiple causes of crime, it is not possible to present a single cathartic moment.[16]

There's no great moment that will "fix" Bombay, the novel says; there's too much to sort out, too much gummed up in there, for one big moment that will act as a collective catharsis for both readers and characters. We don't get the "old consoling sense of temporal *concordance*" (David Scott, *Omens*, 6) that we want and that a crime novel typically provides, nor is that even desirable. And again, this lack of temporal satisfaction is mapped through understandings of travel and of space. At the very end of the novel, Sartaj is caught in a traffic jam, "hemmed in by a BEST bus and two autos, and there was nowhere for anyone to go, so they all waited companionably" (946). Chandra describes the scene, taking note of the office commuters, the students, the beggars, the street kids, the construction workers, painting it all in a chaotic but convivial light: "Sartaj drank it all in, incredulous that he had missed all this while he had been away, and that he was glad to be back. Even this particular stench of exhaust and burning and heated tar, even this was delectable. I must be mad, he thought. And then he remembered Katekar, who had been crazy in the same way, who had complained endlessly but had confessed to yearning for the city when he went to his in-laws' village. 'Once the air of this place touches you,' Katekar had said, 'you are useless for anywhere else'" (946). Besides being a touching portrait of contemporary urban life, this scene underlines the fact that a single cathartic event does not make sense for Bombay. There's no big moment after an irrepressible progressive thrust forward, no one solution that will clear the way for everything and make it all better. The traffic jam, like the bomb, doesn't go anywhere, but not because of one singular cause. Instead, there are a series of smaller events that build on history, that repeat again and again in what Gyan Prakash describes as "a tapestry of different, overlapping, and contradictory experiences, imaginations, and desires" (348). The city refuses to centralize itself, or any one part of itself, which means crime will happen and repeat discursively but without any one clear catharsis. The novel ends with Sartaj entering the police station, with the final lines, "He was ready. He went in and began another day" (947).

Fredric Jameson writes of the concept of closure in narrative that it represents "the sign that somehow all the bases have been touched, and that the galactic dimensions and co-ordinates of the now global social totality have at least been sketched in" (31). This certainly does not happen in the Bombay of *Sacred Games*. This city offers no closure, no sense that we have sketched out a full understanding of the international and historical elements that continue to structure this city. We don't get that pleasing narrative of "Mumbai used to be the freer, more lovely and cosmopolitan Bombay," nor the fascistic ethnocentric narrative of "Mumbai is now ethnically cleansed" that offers closure in a different and obviously horrifying way. We aren't allowed that satisfaction of the easily wrapped-up story from either the hard right or the cosmetically liberal.

So what does it mean to say, "Bombay after Mumbai"? A refusal to sway to right-wing, identitarian demands, certainly, but also a reminder that there is no easy answer: a reminder that history repeats, that colonialism and its legacies have not disappeared from the cityscape, that the Bombay/Mumbai name change was neither the cathartic event for Shiv Sena nor the traumatic occasion for liberals who tend to view it as the final nail in the coffin of the city's supposedly cosmopolitan and carefree past. It's a reminder that imperialism is still alive (it might even be a troublingly romanticized longing for the Raj), and it's a way to emphasize that time folds in on itself and repeats in this criminal city. It's a way to think of the city in terms of opportunities as well as losses. These novels signal to the reader that if the past isn't closed off completely, there is still a chance to go back and revise it to be something better. There are, to take the words from David Scott, "new and unexpected horizons of transformative possibility" (*Conscripts*, 1). This place may follow the narrative beats of other places (like Bollywood films or the novel's own narrative structure), but it refuses to be fully forced into this mold. Indeed, as Herbert writes, "Sartaj's success is not framed as the triumph of knowledge and rationality, or as a reassertion of social order, departing from the narrative drive of much detective fiction" (965). Bombay may, on the surface, seem as though it follows the rules, but at the end, its citizens inscribe their own logic and mapping, similarly to the tactics seen in the criminal city of Johannesburg. This type of postcolonial urban novel makes sense for a city where "the once enduring temporalities of past-present-future" (David Scott, *Omens*, 6) have been undercut by economics, history, and urban development.

FIVE

NEOLIBERAL CRIMINALITY

Post-Apartheid Johannesburg

Ivan Vladislavić's 2001 novel *The Restless Supermarket* is set in the Johannesburg neighborhood of Hillbrow in 1993, right on the brink of the end of the apartheid era (which formally ended just a year later, in 1994). The novel's main character and narrator, Aubrey Tearle, is a cantankerous and rigid retired proofreader, who is extremely upset that the version of the city he understands, with its orderly apartheid rules and categories, is changing as he watches helplessly. Standards, he holds, are slipping, leading to societal downfall. He muses, "Standards of proofreading have been declining steadily since the nineteen-sixties, when the permissive attitude to life first gained ground, and so have standards of morality, conduct in public life, personal hygiene and medical care, the standard of living, and so on. All these are symptoms of a more general malaise. Decline with a capital D" (84). Tearle goes on to explain that, because he believes "the solution to the problem of declining standards lay with the individual" (84), he has begun to visit various establishments in his neighborhood to offer his unsolicited advice on their signage's grammar. He sees this behavior as a public service, for it is his firm belief that upholding his personally determined standards of correctness is of the utmost importance for the well-being of his city. Tearle makes a connection between what he deems to be "correct" grammar and the general orderliness of the world around him, exclaiming to one acquaintance at the end of the novel, "Once you're free to spell a word any way you like, chaos comes marching in. . . . The decline in the standard of proofreading is linked directly to the decline in standards everywhere else" (284–85).

For Tearle, a significant effect of this "decline in standards,"[1] being linked to words on the page, means that the relaxation and eventual abandonment of legal (written) apartheid rules and codes will spell doom for his neighborhood of Hillbrow and Johannesburg as a whole, though he personally is "either oblivious to or disingenuous about the ways in which his systems of imposing order on chaos very much resemble the methods that the apartheid state used to impose social control on the black population" (Shane Graham 81). He is deeply anxious over the loss of a strictly ordered society and how this loss might introduce chaos and what he deems criminality into his circumscribed little world. He thinks, "I felt—I had to stop myself from quaking—that we were *in mortal danger*. We were on the verge of extinction, I realized, and the fact seemed chillingly explicit. But what did I really mean? Who were 'we'? The human race? People of good sense and common decency? The ragtag remnants of the Café Europa? Was it a royal 'we'?" (155). Tearle's uncertainty about who gets to be included in the "we" (ranging from the entire "human race" to the fellow patrons of the appropriately named café where he spends his time to just himself) is, given his time period, primarily a reference to the racial codes and structures of apartheid, but we can see in this quotation a projection into the future, where the criteria for inclusion in the "we" no longer are based solely on race, but have moved on to the more slippery and ostensibly colorblind category of criminality. Tearle's choice of the phrase "people of good sense and common decency" points not necessarily to skin color, but to acceptable standards of behavior, which presumably those accused and convicted of crimes would not exhibit. A byproduct of this seemingly colorblind language, of course, is that those of "good sense and common decency" are often understood to be white Europeans, and anyone outside this supposedly behavioral norm becomes cast as suspiciously other and potentially criminal.

In an excerpt from a short story Tearle writes about a proofreader, Fluxman, who can change the layout and demographic makeup of his city simply by "correcting" or revising texts written about it or maps drawn of it, Fluxman (who is modeled on Tearle) is confronted with the question about what to do about what he deems the disorderly elements of his city, Alibia:

"And then it was the human detritus he found in the margins of the city, the erroneous ones, the slips of the hand, the tramps, the fools, the congenitally stupid, the insufferably ugly. They were incorrigible, he reasoned, and doing away with them, at one painless stroke, was more humane than trying to improve them" (224). Tearle sympathizes with Fluxman and similarly wishes to rewrite Hillbrow to remove what he considers "human detritus"—again, not explicitly a racial category, but ostensibly a behavioral one—from the area. Vladislavić's studied refusal to have Tearle utilize racial language and categorization makes *The Restless Supermarket* an interesting jumping-off point for the study of how cathartic crime works in Johannesburg. Though set during the final days of the apartheid era, the text's colorblindness establishes a framework wherein it can be argued that Tearle, though a man with a strong impulse to exclude, does not necessarily or explicitly view the rubric for inclusion or exclusion into the "we" as being based on race, as the apartheid system would; rather, Tearle's constant inveighing about standards of behavior and declines in propriety might easily be viewed as his desire to exclude those he, personally, deems messy, low-life, criminal, poor, in the post-apartheid, postcolonial world order.

This chapter will argue that, as apartheid began to be recognized as a crime by the international community and then South Africa itself, that system of clear-cut rules and structures was discarded in favor of the more fluid and neoliberal system of criminality. This looser system of criminality was utilized in order to help white South Africa "cope" with the end of apartheid by sliding in a new form of ostensibly colorblind exclusion and oppression on top of an older, more explicitly racist one, thus relying on a type of emotional processing or catharsis. By shedding light on the ways in which discourses and conversations on crime, race, and poverty map and undergird the contemporary South African city, Lauren Beukes and Phaswane Mpe use their novels to spur readers into thinking about the larger systems that structure the post-apartheid environment.

APARTHEID, NEOLIBERALISM, EMPIRE, CRIME

Christopher Heywood writes of contemporary South African literature, "The twenty-first century may view the wars of the colonial past and the struggles of the later twentieth century as incomprehensible, yet modern nightmares such as disease, privatised crime, and unemployment, are rooted in the past" (20). Tracing how these "modern nightmares," especially "privatised crime," connect back to their historical roots will shed light on the ways crime is weaponized and used as a form of catharsis in the present, and must be understood in light of the crimes of empire and its racial system of apartheid.

Johannesburg is the largest city in a country that has seen Portuguese, Dutch, and British imperial influence and, until the late twentieth century, operated under a system of strict racial segregation known as apartheid. Though not formally instituted until 1948, apartheid built upon systems of racial segregation initially put into place by both British and Dutch imperial rule. Apartheid's intensities and formal codifications into strict law were a post-imperial innovation, but apartheid can be seen as an imperial legacy in that its general purpose was to solidify the hold white Europeans enjoyed over indigenous Black Africans and the mixed Coloured population once the formal protections of European imperial rule had left the country. Moreover, because "land had been a critical factor in the colonial encounter" (Welsh 30) and apartheid focused heavily on controlling access to land and space, "apartheid can surely be grasped," argues Rita Barnard, "as a deliberated and anachronistic perpetuation or reinvention of the spatial and epistemological distortions of imperialism within one country's borders" (47). Apartheid, simultaneously a system of domestic imperialism and a hangover from imperial rule, was also tied up with discourses of criminality from early on, both in the sense that the system was a crime, a violation against any basic understanding of human rights, and in that it instituted a wide and far-ranging set of crimes in the sense of "legal concept[s] [and] what is or is not against the law" (Roth 8). Because of apartheid's many rules and regulations regarding what people could or could not do based on skin color, it was virtually impossible to keep abreast of the many ways one could violate apartheid law and thus be classified as a criminal. As Loren Kruger writes, "The apartheid order . . . created instead a determinedly *provincial* [italics original] *criminal city* [italics mine], not merely in the broad anti-apartheid sense of a regime that violated international human rights, but also in the classification of most inhabitants as actual or potential offenders against a host of laws defining Group Areas, Separate Amenities, and Urban Areas and thus, as foreigners deserving expulsion" (146). Perhaps the starkest rendering of this institution of criminality may be found in the title of the South African comedian Trevor

Noah's autobiography, *Born a Crime: Stories from a South African Childhood* (2016). The first page consists of a reprinting of the 1927 Immorality Act, which was intended to "prohibit carnal intercourse between Europeans and natives and other acts in relation thereto." Noah, as the child of an African woman and a European man, was thus "born a crime," and is only one of several examples of how crime could be and was defined in apartheid South Africa. The criminal city of Johannesburg relies, then, on a historically dense matrix of legal codes and apartheid-era definitions of crimes, updated for the twenty-first century to function as a space deeply concerned with narratives of "crime," one that is ostensibly colorblind but just as racially coded as the "official" apartheid era.

The operation of apartheid both as a system of domestic imperialism and as a crime was particularly sharply felt in South African (criminal) cities, including and perhaps especially Johannesburg. David Welsh writes that "one of apartheid's principal aims—if not *the* principal one—was to abort the urbanisation revolution among Africans by deeming urban Africans to be 'temporary sojourners'" (212). Classifying Africans as such meant that they had no right to the city and could not live within its limits; further legal technologies, such as pass and identification laws, meant that Africans could only be inside the Johannesburg city limits during certain times of day (usually business hours) before they had to return to the townships, located on the urban fringes. It is at least partially for this reason that Irikidzayi Manase asserts that the South African city, Johannesburg included, "evolved and assumed its characteristics due to the impact of European colonialism, white social, political and economic domination, and, currently, the policies of the ruling majority and nationalist governments as well as the impact of changes in the world economies" (101). Though it is true that "in spite of its appearance of fixity, Johannesburg was never a totally foreclosed city even at the height of apartheid" (Mbembe, *Aesthetics of Superfluity*, 48), the contemporary city of Johannesburg remains shaped by the legacies of the systems of imperialism and apartheid, leading to contemporary examples of cathartic crime.

Because the outright, explicitly racist attitudes that were acceptable in the apartheid era are now discouraged, the divisions and exclusions of contemporary South African cities are based less on racial categorizations than on crime. The economics of neoliberalism, by which I mean the expansion of supposedly colorblind market logic, insidiously works to replace apartheid by presenting itself as more open to racial difference, the idea being that neoliberal regimes reward hard work, no matter the racial or ethnic background of the individual. This system, which took root in South Africa after the dismantling of apartheid, also leads to unequal societies, which in turn lead to crime, especially property crime; on a more theoretical level, fretting about crime helps to sustain the spatial logic of apartheid in contemporary Johannesburg. The city today functions much as it did under the official rule of apartheid: Edward W. Soja argues that "the lasting effects of the apartheid system are vividly expressed in contemporary urban landscapes of the independent and African-led Republic of South Africa" (*Seeking Spatial Justice*, 39). In the contemporary city of Johannesburg, he notes, white neighborhoods now house a smattering of "black elite" but are "still fortressed with high walls and guarded entranceways running continuously block after block, street after street, like a massive agglomeration of residential citadels signaling obsessive protection against a perceived threat of invasion" (39). This atomized vision of society, in which the wealthy must always be on guard against the racialized criminal "Other," works as a cushion and a cathartic salve to protect those who feel threatened by the end of the security of apartheid and who need a new way to process and articulate their preferred vision of society.

Due to the massive demographic changes that took place in Johannesburg in the 1990s—from white flight into the suburbs to the increase in migrants from other parts of Africa—crime and security and the languages surrounding these concepts became a socially acceptable way to process the end of apartheid and the rise of the "new South Africa." Because, moreover, "South Africa's democratic breakthrough coincided with the highpoint of neo-liberal triumphalism" in the 1990s (Green 326), and crime is often committed due to the economic disparities and shredding of social services that are the goals of neoliberalism, fear of crime is often expressed in language closely linked to some of the main tenets of neoliberal philosophies: individualism, personal responsibility, defense of property, competition and market logic, and so on.

One way, I argue, that writers have tried to map Johannesburg is by understanding the urban space through first the crimes of apartheid and, later, the ostensibly colorblind codes of criminality. Its turbulent history, from apartheid to crime, means that Johannesburg as a city is often seen as incomprehensible, its social problems contributing to its inability to be properly understood by "rational" observers. Loren Kruger writes, "From its early years to the present, Johannesburg has escaped the strictures of literary as well as civil decorum. The city has appeared to planners and artists alike to be *unimaginable* as well as unmanageable" (141, italics original). Unpacking an allegedly colorblind neoliberalism turns the city from unmanageable and unimaginable by tracing discourses of crime to excavate imperial and apartheid legacies that help resituate us in the city.

The literary texts analyzed in this chapter—Ivan Vladislavić's *The Restless Supermarket*, Lauren Beukes's *Zoo City*, and Phaswane Mpe's *Welcome to Our Hillbrow*—are all set in the Johannesburg neighborhood of Hillbrow. Together, the texts comprise a constellation of literary Hillbrow narrated and presented by vastly different subject positions. The neighborhood of Hillbrow holds a vexed place within the larger city. Hillbrow is a high-density area, unusual for Johannesburg, which is generally a sprawling, low-density city, notable for its lack of infill. In the apartheid era, Hillbrow moved from being a "whites-only" area to being designated a "gray area," where people of different ethnicities lived side by side. During this "gray area" phase, Hillbrow was known for its cosmopolitan, intellectual, progressive atmosphere, as well as its (unusual for the time) LGBT scene. However, with the white flight that was common to many inner-city areas of Johannesburg in the 1970s and 1980s, Hillbrow became marked by the same problems that plagued many cities, both in South Africa and around the world, in this time period: poverty, unemployment, and crime. Today, Hillbrow is generally known as an area for people in transit, hosting migrants from rural South Africa as well as the rest of the continent of Africa. It has been compared to London's East End: hosting newcomers to the city until those newcomers are able to get on their feet, so to speak, and move elsewhere in the city. The contemporary neighborhood, due to its immediate post-apartheid image and its current home as a landing space for immigrants, is stereotyped as being dirty, dangerous, and full of the Other. For reasons based in these historical and contemporary stereotypes, Hillbrow is also frequently pointed to as the epicenter of Johannesburg and South Africa's problems with crime.

Lindsay Bremner notes that Johannesburg in the post-apartheid era "has become a field of violent contestation between extreme wealth and extreme poverty, between luxury and subsistence, idyll and inferno, excess and need" (51) and that "into this [neoliberal] situation, a new discourse and set of practices have emerged—those of crime" (53). Crime and the moral panics that surround the subject can be considered a subset of neoliberalism in many ways: sometimes actual crime is committed due to material inequality under neoliberalism, or the panic over property crime is linked to neoliberalism's insistence on the value of personal, private property. But, especially in South Africa and places like it, discourses surrounding crime allow people to express themselves in coded racist ways; Jean and John L. Comaroff note that, in a post-apartheid South Africa, "crime becomes racialized and race criminalized" ("Criminal Obsessions," 804). In the post-apartheid era, it is considered inappropriate (in many settings) to articulate the explicit racism that was a key part of the apartheid order. For this reason, not-so-subtle concerns about security and crime have edged into the public discourse and can similarly be seen in contemporary Johannesburg literature in order to continue to prop up the racialized order Aubrey Tearle and so many others hold dear. Yet in *Zoo City* and *Welcome to Our Hillbrow*, Lauren Beukes and Phaswane Mpe offer subtle rejoinders to the moral panics surrounding crime and security in contemporary Johannesburg and suggest ways forward for Johannesburg to reimagine itself. In the sections that follow, I consider these two novels—both set in the inner-city suburb of Hillbrow, though during different time periods—to think about the ways these novels can excavate imperial legacies and neo-apartheid structures in order to dissect how they are related to contemporary discourses of crime and its cathartic properties.

"NO OFFENSE TO THE ANIMALLED": LAUREN BEUKES'S *ZOO CITY*

Lauren Beukes's 2010 novel *Zoo City* is a futuristic, science fiction text set in a dystopic Johannesburg. Elements of the real history of Johannesburg have been carried through into the speculative city of Beukes's novel—for instance, apartheid seems to have happened in the history of *Zoo City*, and the titular "Zoo City" is the real-life Johannesburg neighborhood of Hillbrow. But, given the genre, many elements of the world of *Zoo City* are fantastic; some residents of the city, known as "zoos" or, more derogatorily, "apos," the novel's narrator Zinzi December included, are constantly accompanied by animal familiars (Zinzi's familiar, for example, is a sloth). Though various theories abound as to why these "zoos" (who exist all over the world, not just in Johannesburg) have come to be, the one variable common to all zoos is that they are all formerly incarcerated persons, or as Zinzi wryly puts it, "Criminals. Murderers, rapists, junkies. Scum of the earth" (15). Because of her criminal history, Zinzi is forced to make her living on the black market, by finding lost things for clients and by taking part in the ultimate neoliberal venture, internet scams. But besides the commonality of a criminal history, neither the scientific community nor the world at large has managed to figure out how or why the zoos have these familiars, and zoos face significant social, economic, and political discrimination in their day-to-day lives.[2] This fantastic projection of a hyperbolic Johannesburg operates as a hyper-real parallel to the contemporary criminal city's preoccupations with security, crime, and neoliberal capitalism, offering an amplification of the cathartic properties of the post-apartheid crime narrative.

Residents of Johannesburg use "Zoo City" to refer to the part of the city where the zoos are effectively forced to live. Zoo City is what was previously (in its Former Life, or FL, before the zoos arrived) referred to as Hillbrow, an inner-city suburb that, in both our history and the history of the novel, was viewed as glamorous and cosmopolitan in the apartheid area, and that fell into hard times with the end of apartheid and subsequent white flight to the suburbs. By designating Hillbrow as the area where the zoos, people with criminal histories, must live, Beukes draws a connection between apartheid and criminality; in the "real" history of Johannesburg, post-apartheid Hillbrow is often stereotyped as being dirty, dangerous, and full of Others, due to its post-apartheid demographic makeup; the same is true of the speculative Zoo City and its criminal zoos. Neville Hoad writes of the neighborhood that while it "continues to enjoy a lively street life," this is "coupled with a high crime rate, and [the neighborhood] is considered a no-go zone for respectable white people and tourists" (113) (note the deliberate pairing of the ostensibly colorblind, behaviorally influenced language of "respectable" with the color-conscious use of "white people"). In both our Hillbrow and in the world of *Zoo City*, the neighborhood is a site of post-apartheid segregation, with the new postcolonial divisions based on a neoliberal language of crime; Lisa Propst writes, "Unable to escape the visible stigma of criminality, this animalled become the new underclass" ("Information Glut," 4).

For an example of the continuities between the eras of apartheid and post-apartheid in the novel, consider how much of the language in post-apartheid *Zoo City* remains the same as in the apartheid era. For instance, when Zinzi is meeting with one client, the old woman snaps, "'If you would be so kind as to let me finish? . . . I hid in the bathroom and took all my jewellery off because I know how *you people*—criminals that is,' she added hurriedly, 'No offense to the animalled'" (8). We see a slippage here between the racist, apartheid-era language of *"you people"* to the quick clarification that she means "criminals," and of course, not the animalled, and *certainly* not Black Africans. Though the deep structures have not changed, in a post-apartheid and neoliberal era, Zinzi's client must clarify that she is not racist in the sense of judging the physical characteristics of the animalled, but that she is simply prejudiced against "criminals." By presenting this lightly masked corresponding city to actual twenty-first-century Johannesburg, Beukes removes the reader to a still-proximate distance that allows us to understand how the city has processed crime as a kind of catharsis for the end of apartheid and the associated changes in the urban landscape.

The fictional Zoo City's past matches that of the real Hillbrow: for instance, Zinzi talks about "back when this part of town was cosmopolitan central, with its glitzy hotels and restaurants and outdoor cafes and malls packed to the skylights with premium luxury goods" (51), an image that would reflect the real history of apartheid-era Hillbrow. In the time of the novel, however, Zinzi informs us, "Gunfire has always been part of the nocturnal soundscape of Zoo City, like cicadas in the countryside. But it's only recently that it's become part of the daytime routine" (59). The danger associated with the neighborhood, Beukes suggests, has come about in the immediate post-apartheid era, much like in "actual" Hillbrow. The colonial system of apartheid has given way in both the speculative future of *Zoo City* and its close parallel, our contemporary Johannesburg, to a less strict, more neoliberal system of segregation and control. Neoliberalism's looser rules and privileging of economic, rather than strictly racial, segregation creates a Hillbrow/Zoo City that is the de facto, rather than de jure, home to those left behind by years of the apartheid order.

When we first meet Zinzi December, she is waking up next to her Congolese migrant boyfriend, Benoît, and his animal familiar, a mongoose, in her bed in Zoo City, in a building that was "condemned years ago" (8). One of the first things readers learn about her is, "I'm precious about my work. Let's just say it's not entirely legal" (7). Zinzi, as previously mentioned, contracts herself out on the black market, receiving payment under the table, to find lost things. In this way, she fashions herself as a kind of detective: she notes that "everybody's lost *something*" and that the key to success in her field is "all about figuring out which string to tug on" (13). Zinzi gives her readers a kind of framework for untangling the mystery of why her city is structured the way that it is—we know, because she tells us that, "some lost things can't be found . . . like . . . property values once the slums start encroaching" (13), but what we don't immediately know is *why* the "slums" are "encroaching," or why Zoo City—both the neighborhood and the novel—are organized and structured in the way that they are.

As the colonial legacy of structured apartheid gave way to the more fluid rules of the post-apartheid era, neoliberalism took over as the defining organizational structure of the city, in both our Johannesburg and the criminal city of *Zoo City*. Critics have noted the failures of neoliberalism that are apparent in *Zoo City* and its coincident depictions of crime and danger in Johannesburg. Matthew Eatough observes that the novel engages with the African National Congress's post-apartheid decision to "move to a market-driven logic in state planning" (696) and that it portrays "an eerily familiar South Africa in which money, resources, and respectability have been apportioned into a two-class system" (703), composed of ordinary humans and zoos. In this neoliberal framework, Eatough contends, "the category of criminal has subsumed that of race in discussions of inequality" (708) in a move "eerily reminiscent of apartheid's race-based system" (709). Jayna Brown similarly notes that *Zoo City* "revels in the underside of capitalist hyperconsumption" to create "a new aesthetic . . . marked by a focus on class" (7). As such, the race-based system of apartheid that targeted the non-white has partially given way to market-driven, capitalized logic in both our own world and in that of *Zoo City*, though the logic of segregation promulgated by apartheid retains its hold; in Zinzi's words, "that's the thing about ghosts from Former Lives—they come back to claim you" (68). In the world of the novel, this variant of neoliberalism, like a ghost from imperialism and apartheid, has specifically targeted those with criminal histories, opening the door for the discourse of crime—a key anxiety in the real world of twenty-first-century Johannesburg—to create space for new postcolonial possibilities.

For imperialism and apartheid have structured a society that, on first glance, seems very grim. Zinzi recounts the chain of events that led her to living in Zoo City, after she has been arrested for drug offenses:

> They call prisoners clients these days. It's all in the semantics. "Clients" still get served slop and *pap*, still have to sleep fifty-seven to a room

designed for twenty, still have to exercise in a grim concrete yard with the outside world taunting, only a mesh fence and a gun turret away. Clients still get kicked out onto the street when their compulsory state-funded vacation is up. With zero support except for an overloaded parole system that can't keep track of who you are, let alone what you're supposed to be doing....

It was inevitable that I'd end up in Zoo City. Although I didn't realise that until after the fifth rental agency had sneered over their clipboards at Sloth [Zinzi's animal familiar] and told me they didn't have anything available in the suburbs—had I tried Hillbrow? (60-61)

Surface-level jargon aside—clients instead of prisoners, etc.—the deeper effects of neoliberalism are evident from this passage. For instance, Zinzi's incarceration and subsequent labeling as a criminal once she is released reminds the reader strongly of Michelle Alexander's argument in *The New Jim Crow*: that individuals belonging to discriminated-against classes of people (Zinzi is Black) are branded as criminals in a neoliberal age to keep the prison-industrial complex humming. Once released, without state supports (Zinzi, like many others formerly incarcerated, is estranged from her family and cannot rely on them), people with criminal histories have nowhere to go, no one to rely on. Without laws or safety nets in place to mandate some sort of reintegration into society, or robust housing assistance, all the people with criminal histories, the "zoos" are forced together into Hillbrow. This may no longer be due to the official policies of the apartheid regime—actual laws mandating who may live where have been repealed—but the logic of the market, combined with individual and structural prejudice and bigotry, mandates that there's nothing available in desirable areas and that the zoos must live in Hillbrow/Zoo City, the place of last resort.

Because of this neoliberal segregation, Zinzi is effectively barred from legal, non-black-market work, which is why she must become a neoliberal entrepreneur and begin her finding business, planting herself into the 419 internet scamming trade. Rather than being a drag on her productivity, her sloth familiar actively assists her in finding lost things and in navigating the 419 world, by acting as a sort of conduit through which discoveries may pass to Zinzi. Matthew Eatough contends, "As the novel progresses, the zoos and their *mashavi* [familiars] quickly crystallize into a metaphor for the privatization of infrastructure under neoliberal economic policy" (704) because the zoos rely on their familiars, rather than the state, for services ranging from "household security . . . to medical care . . . to freelance employment" (704–5).

This neoliberal, segregated, "criminal," and individualistic environment Zinzi and her sloth are effectively forced to navigate provides the motor for the novel's main action. Her skill at finding things is established very early as she manages to find an old woman's (Mrs. Luditsky) ring. She is on her way to return the ring when she gets word that Mrs. Luditsky has been murdered. The two individuals who give her this information outside Mrs. Luditsky's apartment, a man with a Maltese poodle familiar (whom Zinzi refers to as "Maltese") and a woman with a marabou stork ("Marabou"), seemingly innocently engage Zinzi in conversation and, hearing what she does for a living, tell her that they run a "procurement" business and hire her to find a missing person, the pop star Songweza, who is managed by a reclusive music producer named Odi Huron. Though Zinzi despises finding lost persons, the death of the old woman and her subsequent loss of that paycheck, combined with her segregation from legal markets, means that she is left with no other choice than to accept the job.

Zinzi's Johannesburg is founded on crime and the lasting effects of empire: colonial legacies have made it so that the economic and social structure and functioning of the city is built upon a continuation of apartheidesque codes of segregation and urban organization, with the criminal now occupying the space formerly designated for Africans in Zoo City's "inegalitarian division of basic services eerily reminiscent of apartheid's race-based system" (Eatough 709). But Beukes positions Zinzi so that she at first assists in propping the system up, but then navigates the system in such a way as to bring to light subsumed ideologies. This places the reader in the position of detective to figure out the base, underlying structure of a society where the bones of colonial legacies are still visible for those who know where to look.

Zinzi begins looking into Songweza's case by pretending she is an investigative journalist for a popular music magazine in order to gain access to those in the upper echelons of the entertainment and music industries. This positioning allows her to delve into areas where a criminal zoo would typically not be allowed, and as she falls deeper and deeper into her investigation, Zinzi begins to realize that the disappearance of Songweza closely mirrors the cases of other missing people in recent years; when she discovers all those people (except for Songweza) were animalled, she begins to become convinced that the prior murders in the pattern were committed to kill the familiars, not the human zoos they were attached to. She realizes that the familiars have been killed to make *muti,* or a potent kind of medicine believed to treat diseases like HIV/AIDS that are thought to be uncurable. The familiar *muti* murders in *Zoo City* have a real-life parallel in contemporary South Africa, in that a moral panic not unlike the one kicked up around the prevalence of crime has sprung up around supposed *muti* murders of humans. Zinzi notes that "someone's always buying in this city. Sex. Drugs. Magic" (301). By tying the fictional *muti* murders of familiars to the extremely-rare-but-it-does-happen phenomenon of *muti* murders of real-life humans, Beukes further solidifies the link between the speculative future of *Zoo City* and real Johannesburg. Neoliberalism and its accompanying hyperbolic rhetorics of crime have taken over where apartheid left off to continue the categories and structures set in place by apartheid's racial codes.

Though she doesn't articulate it in quite these terms, Zinzi works out the connections between apartheid, imperialism, and crime when she arrives at Odi's mansion to accuse Marabou and Maltese of keeping Songweza and her twin, S'bu, hostage for a purpose that remains murky, but that Zinzi knows has something to do with the *muti* murders. Maltese tells her frankly that he and Marabou have killed two "unlucky street kids who match the general physical description" (322) of Songweza and S'bu and framed Zinzi for their murders. He explains, over her protestation of "No one's going to believe this," "Won't they? A psychotic junkie zoo bitch who killed her brother? Who was so celebrity-obsessed she pretended to be from a bigshot music magazine so she could get closer to the twins? Whose fingerprints were all over poor Mrs Luditsky's apartment, who took her little china cat home with her as some kind of trophy? Are you kidding me?" (322). Songweza's disappearance was planned by the Maltese and the Marabou; they framed Zinzi from the beginning, killing Mrs. Luditsky to snare Zinzi into the criminal structure. Though Songweza and S'bu are not zoos, the murders of the "street kids who match the general physical description" have been plotted to make the pop stars' impending murders look as though they fit the pattern of *muti* murders. The purpose of murdering the twins at all is revealed when we learn that Odi Huron is a zoo and is hiding this from the public; he is "sick to death" of his familiar, a crocodile, and believes that murdering zoos for their familiars, followed by killing one of the twins, will allow him to transfer his familiar to the remaining twin and rid himself of the stigma of being a zoo. Then, by murdering the twin who he has forced to take his crocodile, Maltese and Marabou will kill the crocodile and "chop you up for *muti*" because, as Zinzi explains to the animal, "Monster like you? You're probably worth a fortune" (340).

This complicated plotline would make sense nowhere except in the context of a Johannesburg shaped by neoliberalism, imperialism, crime, and apartheid. The discrimination against zoos that would make Zinzi a believable suspect for a series of murders and that forced her to work in illegal activities to begin with is one element of the narrative, but so is the neoliberal criminal city that pushed her out of jail onto the streets with nothing resembling state supports, nudging her into a life of constant evasion of the law. Large patterns shape the world Zinzi is operating within: the undying quest for profit above all else that would make these serial murders possible, the segregation brought about first by apartheid and then by the unequal distribution of wealth and privilege encouraged by neoliberalism that drives crimes like these murders forward by providing convenient cover stories. Beukes uses a speculative future with many parallels to our own world to demonstrate that fears and anxieties over crime have taken over contemporary Johannesburg in the eroding of the formal codes of apartheid. *Zoo City* allows the attentive reader to see how the city is processing the seismic shift of the end of apartheid: by essentially swapping out one racist discourse for another.

Though Odi may seem like a monster, it's made clear that he was being used by the true criminals, the agents of the neoliberal, neo-apartheid, neo-imperial state: the Marabou and the Maltese. When Odi is killed by his own crocodile, the Marabou says, "A pity to lose the Crocodile, but what can you do?" to which the Maltese says, "Oh, sweetie, there'll be other procurements" (343). They make no mention of Odi; it is clear he was merely a tool for them to use the crocodile, which they planned to sell for *muti*. Operating entirely outside law and morality, at the end, they are not punished—they "simply" vanish into thin air (343), never to face the consequences of their actions. "Zinzi," writes Lisa Propst, "may be able to solve the murders, but her discovery does not alleviate the suffering of the victims" ("Information Glut," 8); nothing structural changes as a result of Zinzi's detective work. The Maltese and Marabou escape all consequences.

In the world of *Zoo City*, people like Odi or other low-level agents of the world order, from those who harbor individual prejudice against the zoos to those who cordon off their homes with the help of gates and security wire to others who are simply cogs in the neoliberal machine, are not the ones who ultimately prop up the structure of the criminal city (though their presence and actions certainly don't hurt). Rather, those like the Maltese and Marabou—who do not seem terribly threatening through most of the novel—are the true players in the criminal city, along with the neoliberal order itself. The Maltese and the Marabou remind us that systemic injustices and crimes in both our Johannesburg and *Zoo City* can often be so subtle as to go undetected except by those, like Zinzi in her investigative work and the reader of *Zoo City*, with an eye toward discovering it (and yet, those who prop up the criminal city order often escape all consequences). Beukes, in her imaginative future of *Zoo City*, encourages us to become detectives in our own cities and open up opportunities for uncovering and combating these realities, even if her main character does not fully follow through on that opportunity for herself or her city, and if no cathartic crime is reached in Zinzi's particular narrative.

Zoo City ends with Zinzi escaping the dangerous hellscape city for a drive across Africa. She maps out a journey for herself in eight days, from Johannesburg to Harare to Lusaka to Mbeye to Dar es Salaam to Nairobi to Jinja to southern Uganda to Kigali (348).[3] Once in Kigali, she plans to assist Benoît's family, who are stuck in a refugee camp there. As for her plans for what to do after she helps them, she muses, "Maybe I'll get lost for awhile" (349), giving no indication to the reader she intends to return to the city that she has left behind her. Beukes, and by extension Zinzi, Andrew Pepper notes, "demonstrate[s] no faith in the idea that capitalism can be directly confronted and overturned" (229). Rather, the opposition to capitalism and neoliberalism comes via "narratives that hyperbolically show the worst excesses and depravities of capitalism" (229) without providing the reader with any cathartic or wholesale solutions. Zinzi's rejection of the city and gesture of pan-African solidarity is one way to escape the crime that has so damaged the city, but, as we shall see, *Welcome to Our Hillbrow* represents another response.

"WORLD OF OUR CONTINUING EXISTENCE": PHASWANE MPE'S *WELCOME TO OUR HILLBROW*

First published in 2001, seven years after the formal dismantling of the apartheid system, Phaswane Mpe's novel *Welcome to Our Hillbrow: A Novel of Postapartheid South Africa* paints a rich portrait of Hillbrow as it existed in the years immediately following apartheid. The novel "has become one of the formative textual markers of the post-apartheid period" (Frenkel 31) by giving readers a post-apartheid map of one of the central neighborhoods of the city. Though the novel switches between the points of view of two characters, Refentše and Refilwe, it is continuously narrated in the second person, which has the effect of drawing the reader in and interpellating him or her in the day-to-day functioning of Hillbrow; in Ronit Frenkel's words, "The reader becomes *a part* of the story and is inextricably implicated as a member of the ever-expanding community the novel maps out" (32, italics original). Frenkel continues, "Mpe anticipates and utilizes the fear that the inner-city neighborhood of Hillbrow summons as an icon of criminality" (32). Going into the novel, readers expect a degree of criminality and danger from the neighborhood; Mpe knows this, and, as the novel progresses, writes accordingly to resist our preconceived notions of Hillbrow as a bastion of lawlessness and immorality to allow for a different kind of catharsis than readers attempted to negotiate in *Zoo City*.

Though set in the late 1990s (Mpe's present), the Hillbrow portrayed in *Welcome to Our Hillbrow* initially comes across as dangerous as the dystopic future Hillbrow of *Zoo City*. One of the first impressions readers receive of the neighborhood is filtered through a radio report "broadcasting snippets of car hijackings and robbers' shoot-outs with the Johannesburg Murder and Robbery Squad every news hour" (5). The text goes on to list further crimes broadcast on the radio, including but not limited to (ellipses original):

> Five men were found with their ribs ripped off by what appeared to have been a butcher's knife . . . Two women were raped and then killed in Quartz Street . . . Three Nigerians who evaded arrest at Jan Smuts Airport were finally arrested in Pretoria Street for drug dealing . . . Street kids, drunk with glue, brandy and wild visions of themselves as speeding Hollywood movie directors, were racing their wire-made cars through red robots, thus increasingly becoming a menace to motorists driving through Hillbrow,

especially in the vicinity of Banket and Claim Streets ... At least eight people died and thirteen were seriously injured when the New Year's Eve celebrations took the form of torrents of bottles gushing out of the brooding clouds that were flat balconies ... (5)

The list of crime and violence goes on, but the unnamed narrator caps it off with a dryly ironic "Welcome to Our Hillbrow..."

As seen in the excerpt above, *Welcome to Our Hillbrow* does not shy away from tackling crime and other contemporary topics; indeed, Mpe has stated he wanted the novel to address what he called "taboos" or "sensitive issues," and he refers to Hillbrow as a "monster" on page 3, noting "the lure of the monster was ... hard to resist." However, by taking those issues on and demonstrating that Hillbrow certainly has problems but also inherent value, Mpe is able to construct a very real, relatable space that works to unearth and address some of the discourses and preconceptions inherent in that space. As Shane Graham points out, literature can reimagine "the postmodern, post-apartheid city"; *Welcome to Our Hillbrow* does just that though the mechanism of cathartic crime.

When reimagining the city through literature, a great boon to Mpe's readers is that we feel part of and invested in the literary map of Hillbrow he creates for us. The second-person narrative voice has the effect of interpellating the reader into Mpe's imaginative city; we as readers are not afforded the distance from the text usually granted to us. Take one of the earliest scenes of mapping the neighborhood. The unnamed narrator seems to be talking to Refentše, giving him directions to Refentše's cousin's place. Refentše is newly arrived from the countryside, from a town called Tiragalong, and the narrator's directions seem to have the pride of knowledge of the recent transplant to the city as well:

> If you are coming from the city centre, the best way to get to Cousin's place is by driving or walking through Twist Street, a one-way street that takes you to the north of the city. You cross Wolmarans and three rather obscure streets, Kapteijn, Ockerse and Pieterse, before you drive or walk past Esselen, Kotze, and Pretoria Streets. You will then cross Van der Merwe and Goldreich Streets. Your next port of call is Caroline Street. On your left-hand side is Christ Church, the Bible Centred Church of Christ, as the big red letters announce to you. On your right-hand side is a block of flats called Vickers Place. You turn to your right, because the entrance to Vickers is in

Caroline Street, directly opposite another block, Da Gama Court. If you are not too lazy, you will ignore the lift and walk up the stairs to the fifth floor, where Cousin stays. (6)

I highlight this quote for a number of reasons. First, note the effect of the "you"—though we know it is technically Refentše walking to his cousin's house, the narrative puts you, the reader, in the position of imaginatively charting that same path to Cousin's house (with a big C, indicating that character's knowability to you). This very detailed map grounds the reader in the physical space of Hillbrow, while also pointing out some of the more obvious imperial legacies present in Johannesburg—the street names.[4] Note the Kapteijn, Ockerse, and Pieterse Streets to reflect the Dutch/Afrikaaners/ Boers, as well as the Caroline Street and Vickers Place for the British. The neighborhood even reaches far back to the days of Portuguese contact in South Africa with Da Gama Court. Though imperialism, of the Portuguese, Dutch, or British variety, has not been a reality in Johannesburg for quite some time, the city retains its legacies, as Refentše's walk shows us.

Similarly, apartheid is not a physical, contemporary presence in the novel, but its legacies are certainly felt. Sarah Nuttall writes, "Hillbrow, for Mpe, is figured as a partial and now patchy inventory of the old apartheid city and as a revised inventory of a largely black, highly tensile, intra-African multiculture" (206). Though the characters are able to walk or drive anywhere in the city they please without being stopped at checkpoints or being forced to carry papers, it is clear the racial segregation system still deeply haunts the city. The full title of the novel is *Welcome to Our Hillbrow: A Novel of Postapartheid South Africa*, but that "post" should not be read as a strictly temporal marker, saying apartheid is done, dusted, and dealt with. Rather, the "post" in "postapartheid" can be read similarly to how *Criminal Cities* reads the "post" in "postcolonial," in that it urges readers to be attentive to the legacies of the system being described.[5]

The legacies of imperialism and apartheid retain a potent hold on late twentieth-century Hillbrow and Johannesburg, and they are excavated by the novel's use of cathartic crime. Though, as Ghirmai Negash says in the introduction to the novel, Mpe does not "dwell on apartheid's material exploitation and violence" (xvi), the years of apartheid have clearly marked the city in which *Welcome to Our Hillbrow*'s characters dwell. Structures of apartheid have carried over into post-apartheid Johannesburg. As previously mentioned, Hillbrow is typically thought of as being a neighborhood for migrants from the South African countryside or other countries in Africa. Non-native South Africans are pejoratively referred to as the *Makwerekwere* and often discriminated against, in similar ways as the zoos are in *Zoo City*. Neoliberal lack of attention to urban planning has much the same effect on city geography as apartheid did; with no state supports to assist recent migrants to the city, they are forced to coalesce in specific areas, where they will be stereotyped and discriminated against, much as the native Africans were during the years of apartheid. This repeat of apartheid-era structures and organizational patterns often serves as a launching pad for characters in the novel to expostulate on other subjects, notably their own perceptions of crime and how crime helps them process their surroundings.

For instance, when Cousin and Refentše are having a discussion on soccer ("Like most Hillbrowans," the narrator tells us, "Cousin took his soccer seriously" [17]), we learn that Refentše and Cousin disagree strongly on the subject of supporting "foreign teams—especially those from elsewhere in Africa" (17). During these arguments, "Cousin would always take the opportunity... to complain about the crime and grime in Hillbrow, for which he held foreigners responsible: not just for the physical decay of the place, but the moral decay" (17). Refentše, on the other hand, believes that "the moral decay of Hillbrow, so often talked about, was in fact no worse than that of Tiragalong" (17). Cousin refuses to agree with him, insisting instead "that people should remain in their own countries and try to sort out of the problems of these respective countries, rather than fleeing them; South Africa had too many problems of its own" (20).[6] By positioning this issue as an argument between Refentše and Cousin, Mpe is able to point out to the reader the untenability of Cousin's position and the ways in which he is (either knowingly or unknowingly) drawing on the legacies of apartheid and imperialism to replicate their structures in the present against a similar, but different, population. In this way, Cousin acts as a sort of unwitting accomplice to prevailing racialized ideas about crime, in that he is one of the "useful idiots," to borrow the Cold War term, who assist in shoring up the contemporary order by buying into and spreading propaganda and moral panics.

Refentše's rebuttals to Cousin, though unheeded, reflect the ways in which the novel positions the *Makwerekwere* as having been slotted into positions similar to that of the Africans under the apartheid state, and the ways in which neoliberalism perpetuates this new/old societal order. Refentše points out to Cousin that "there are very few Hillbrowans, if you think about it, who were not originally wanderers from Tiragalong and other rural villages, who have come here, as we have, in search of education and work" (18). This, of course, would not have been possible during the apartheid era, when access to the city was strictly limited and Africans were relegated to townships on the outskirts of the city, but now, under the neoliberal regime, it is not only accepted to leave home villages for the city to compete against others for education and work, but encouraged. Moreover, though, the narrator, again seemingly addressing Refentše and the reader simultaneously, thinks, "You would want to add that some *Makwerekwere* were fleeing their war-torn countries to seek sanctuary here in our country, in the same way that many South Africans were forced into exile in Zambia, Zaire, Nigeria, and other African and non-African countries during the Apartheid era. You would be reminded of the many writers, politicians, social workers and lecturers, and the endless string of South Africans hanging and jumping from their ninth floor prison cells because the agents of the Apartheid government wanted them to" (19). The narrator's and, by extension, Refentše's explicit comparison of the *Makwerekwere* with the treatment of South Africans during the apartheid regime, as well as the apartheid-era suicides that mimic Refentše's own future suicide when he jumps out of his apartment window, mark Hillbrow and Johannesburg as clearly still influenced by the not-so-long-ago apartheid era. As Emily S. Davis writes, "Subject to constant police harassment and reliant upon illicit trades such as prostitution and drug dealing for their income, the *Makwerekwere* occupy a position uncomfortably similar to that of black South Africans under the apartheid regime" (104). Manase agrees, saying, "The South African city is therefore fictionally mapped as fragmented socially: it pits the community as segmented between the perceived diseased and dislikeable foreign migrants and the suspicious and contempt-filled local migrant characters" (96). The conjunctures between assumed (and actual) lawlessness, apartheid logics, and criminal classifications are too glaring to ignore; much like in *Zoo City*, when the postcolony could not explicitly rely on the Africans to subjugate, as was possible in the apartheid era, it had to reach for some other population, and as such tags crime into contemporary conversations in order to process the end of apartheid. In *Zoo City*, the target was the zoos, and in *Welcome to Our Hillbrow*, the *Makwerekwere*; both are marked as Other, alien, criminal.

In short, the two Hillbrow texts of *Zoo City* and *Welcome to Our Hillbrow* both utilize crime and those who get classified as criminals as a way to explore how crime is weaponized to create Others and process seismic shifts in the postcolonial world order: in this case, a postcolonial, post-apartheid city space. Though, obviously, the specifics of the two novels are quite different, both think through ways in which apartheid and imperial legacies still linger, and offer differing ideas of how its logics have been carried through to either our very recent times or a hypothetical future dystopia. However, while *Zoo City* does not offer a rooted, Hillbrow-specific vision for the future, *Welcome to Our Hillbrow* uses its vision of the neighborhood, as well as its incorporation of a Heaven where deceased residents of the neighborhood may go while remaining invested in Hillbrow, to articulate a space of a local solution for resisting these discourses of crime.

Zoo City, as discussed above, ends with a rejection of the specific city of Johannesburg and an embrace of the larger African continent and its urban spaces. Given what we have seen of Hillbrow's deaths and prejudices, the reader could be forgiven for assuming the characters in *Welcome to Our Hillbrow* might plot similar escapes: it seems at first glance as though Mpe's Hillbrow is hardly a place one would wish to be welcomed to, even less want to stay in, much like Beukes's initial portrayals of Zoo City. It would even seem as though characters are actively looking for a way out. For instance, the first main character we encounter, Refentše, commits suicide after discovering his lover in bed with his best friend. He jumps off the roof of his building, a move that, as noted, will be eerily echoed in the text during discussions of crimes committed by police and other agents of the state in apartheid South Africa. After his death, the book turns to the experiences of his former lover, Refilwe, without any explicit explanation, change in style, or break in stride. Refilwe, in turn, leaves Hillbrow to go and study in Oxford, seemingly signaling an exit from the criminal city. However, both Refentše and Refilwe return through Hillbrow—one spiritually and one physically—as the novel continues, presenting Hillbrow as a textured, welcoming, and *real* place, one worth living in and coming back to.

Welcome to Our Hillbrow constructs a literary, physical Hillbrow that is premised on human dignity and the politics of belonging and locality, incorporating migrants from the countryside, Hillbrow natives, and *Makwerekwere* alike. Indeed, shortly after we are presented with the earlier-cited radio report on the horrific crimes being committed in Hillbrow, Mpe writes (the "you" is again Refentše, shortly after he has arrived in Hillbrow),

> So far, you have not seen any car chases or witnessed a shoot-out. You did meet some semi-naked souls whom your guide, from the same village of Tiragalong, called prostitutes. Otherwise, the thing that stands out in your

memory is the extremely busy movement of people going in all directions of Hillbrow, seeming to enjoy the neon lights of the suburb, while others appeared to be in a hurry to get to work—or yes, to *work*. Now, you were not in a position to say what *the work* was. You knew, though, that a student's guide to careers in South Africa would probably not have listed it as an entry. It amazed you that there should be so many people jostling one another in the streets at nine in the evening. When did they prepare their meals and go to sleep? (7)

By creating this vision of Hillbrow for his readers and refusing to let Refentše give into the hysteria surrounding crime and violence to which so many of his co-citizens have succumbed, Mpe constructs a Hillbrow full of people, life, and enterprise to rebut Kruger's claim that Johannesburg presents as unmanageable; rather, Mpe's novel makes the neighborhood legible and manageable. By mapping the neighborhood and populating Hillbrow with "so many people jostling one another in the streets," Mpe is signifying that Hillbrow is a real place, one with life, one with a story to tell, not the scary hellhole riddled with gunfire and violence that is too often imagined and portrayed. The *Makwerekwere* are not identified as being separate from the "real" Hillbrowans; they are simply part of the city, there just like everybody else. No one in this excerpt is causing crime, no one is perceived as dangerous, and, however briefly, the logics of apartheid and imperialism are overcome via this streetscape. Mpe's Hillbrow is not a place from which to flee; rather, it is a place where it is possible to set down roots and live companionably with one's neighbors, a place where even readers are interpellated into the community. In this way, *Welcome to Our Hillbrow* is able to imagine an earthly, localized alternative to the postcolonial city that is too often thought of as corrupt, violent, dangerous, and criminal by demonstrating that, even in this criminal city, there remains room for resistance and recovery.

Yet *Welcome to Our Hillbrow*, even in the excerpt above, is still captive to the logics of neoliberalism—note the implication that one must "hustle" to survive, which thinkers such as Lester K. Spence and others have noted is neoliberal in nature, and the subsequent acknowledgment that the residents of Hillbrow are completely dependent on individual work and striving and the amassment of capital. This feeling is magnified when, for instance, we learn that "the concrete pavements here, like those of inner Hillbrow, teemed with informal business, in the form of bananas, apples, cabbages, spinach, and other fruits and vegetables" (8). The need to rely on "informal" (and likely illegal/illicit, like Zinzi's shady finding-lost-things setup) business ventures may be viewed by some as a testament to the Hillbrowans' ability to survive and prosper; while it may be that, it also points to the ways in which the former apartheid city currently utilizes neoliberal logics to continue to classify some people and some neighborhoods as less-than or "criminal."

But Mpe's novel offers solutions for this as well. Neoliberalism relies strongly on the notion of the individual's will and work ethic determining success (or lack thereof); as is evident even from the title of the book, however, the Hillbrow of *Welcome to Our Hillbrow* is far more interested in the communitarian possibilities that lie in contemporary urban life. Ronit Frenkel notes that the novel "[asserts] a sense of communal ownership for Hillbrow and its attendant vices" (32), while Neville Hoad asks, "Who is the 'our' of our Hillbrow? Both the potential expansiveness of the 'our' and the geographic place to which we are being welcomed (Hillbrow) work against the elite overtones of the cosmopolitan to invoke the lineaments of an insurgent and rooted, yet open, cosmopolitanism" (113). Though some people, like Cousin, view the *Makwerekwere* with suspicion and code them as potential or actual criminals, the novel as a whole offers a vision of the neighborhood that points to the possibilities of what could happen if urban residents viewed themselves as part of a community, rather than as a collection of individuals.

The second chapter, titled "Notes from Heaven," develops this theme explicitly, by utilizing the space of Heaven as a metaphysical parallel to Hillbrow. In the earthly neighborhood of Hillbrow, Refentše had had a relationship with a woman named Lerato, who was both from Hillbrow originally and thought to be a *Makwerekwere*, marking her as doubly disadvantaged in the eyes of many from Refentše's home village of Tiragalong. Though on earth, Refentše's mother "hated the Hillbrow women with unmatchable venom" (39) and was none too pleased about Lerato's supposed foreigner status, once in Heaven, his mother accepts Lerato warmly. Mpe writes, "You [Refentše] watched your mother's eyes contracting. They scrutinised Lerato from the feet, slowly moving up until they reached the level of her eyes. Your mother fixed a long stare there. And a gentle smile announced itself" (70). Though on earth, Refentše's mother despised even the idea of Lerato, in the Heaven that lies above Hillbrow, the two are friendly and warm with each other. The earthly, individualist prejudices do not exist; Heaven functions as the community that Mpe's literary Hillbrow on earth aspires to be. Because Heaven is a reflection or extension of Hillbrow, Mpe uses this trope to develop a vision of a city where divisions born out of apartheid, imperialism, neoliberalism, and crime discourses can be transcended and overcome. Refentše, as well as other characters who have died throughout the novel, moves to his new residence of Heaven, but he and the other characters are able to look down on the goings-on in earthly Hillbrow much as if watching a television. Though they cannot intervene in the events on earth, they seem very interested in observing what is happening in Hillbrow, and Mpe paints their reactions and emotions for us in great detail. As noted earlier, we as readers feel preternaturally connected to Hillbrow via the narrative voice and mapping of the city; we feel similarly interpellated into and invested in Heaven via those same narrative tools.

Note how different this vision of Heaven is from the "rhetoric of sameness" (Mahon) flattenings of imperial constructions of power.[7] Though it is true, as David Scott writes in *Omens of Adversity*, that after colonialism, "victims and their persecutors are urged to adopt an attitude of *reconciliation* toward each other" (14), that's not what is happening here. Black South Africans aren't being forced to "conjure a reasonable, shareable *modus vivendi*" or to "[accommodate] the past" (14). That method of reconciliation can stagnate a city, ensure that it remains "stranded in the present" (14); Mpe's vision of Heaven does something different, in that it appears the former persecutors are basically left out of the equation entirely and the victims of the apartheid regime allowed to seek reconciliation, reparation, and succor on their own.

By virtue of this tool of Heaven, as well as Mpe's portrayals of life on the ground in Hillbrow, Refentše and other deceased characters, unlike Zinzi, stay in the neighborhood, "crime and grime[,] . . . physical . . . and moral decay" (17) and all. Though *Welcome to Our Hillbrow* functions in a similar post-apartheid, neoliberal city as *Zoo City*, Mpe's novel offers a radical vision of a space without the need for the kind of cathartic crime that is used to negotiate the end of apartheid. Both the vision on the ground in Hillbrow and the vision in the space of Heaven combat the harmful effects of imperial legacies and neoliberal economics that structure the current city of Johannesburg.

However, for a complication of this position, consider Refilwe, Refentše's old girlfriend. When she is diagnosed with AIDS,[8] she moves from Oxford, where she was doing postgraduate work,[9] back to Hillbrow. Upon arrival back home, "she remembered Refentše telling her how the superintendent of his building hated *Makwerekwere*: It used to be fine in Hillbrow, until the Nigerians came. Now she herself was, by association, one of the hated *Makwerekwere*. Convenient scapegoat for everything that goes wrong in people's lives" (118). Her last days on earth, in the space where she moved home for comfort and healing, are thus marked by apartheidesque divisions put in place by the neoliberal world order. The novel ends with Refilwe's welcoming into Heaven, which the narrator tells us is

> the world of our continuing existence, located in the memory and consciousness of those who live with us and after us. It is the archive that those we left behind keep visiting and revisiting; digging this out, suppressing or burying that. Continually reconfiguring the stories of our lives, as if they alone hold the real and true version. Just as you, Refilwe, tried to reconfigure the story of Refentše; just as Tiragalong now is going to do the same with you. Heaven can also be Hell, depending on the nature of our continuing existence in the memories and consciousness of the living. (124)

Refilwe's arrival back in Hillbrow is announced by her new status as an outsider and perhaps a coding as a criminal; with her medical diagnosis, she becomes a type of *Makwerekwere*, a scapegoat, someone outside the law and moral code of her society. Any hoped-for peace in Heaven may not be delivered, as Refilwe is told "Heaven can also be Hell": the Miltonesque line indicates that the space of Heaven is dependent on how it is cast in the minds and imagination of those left on earth. Refentše and Lerato were welcomed into a Heaven that straightened out and smoothed over the postcolonial, neoliberal world order, but it does not look like the same option is on the table for Refilwe. Mpe's casting Heaven as an "archive" means that Heaven is necessarily edited: materials that go into archives are carefully chosen, smoothed around the edges, made to fit a particular narrative. That narrative closely mimics the one in existence on earthly Hillbrow: Refilwe is bad, damaged, a criminal, her story to be "reconfigured" by those left on earth. Heaven, it turns out, is subject to the imaginations, the "memories and consciousness," of those left on earth; it is not the space of perfection we as readers were at first led to believe.

And because we, as readers, have become interpellated into Heaven and Hillbrow, we are to some extent responsible for this perpetuation of the criminal city, and we have to go through our own process of catharsis as a way to reparate. We are participants in the archive; we continue to shape what is considered to be "the real and true version." To return to the text that opened this chapter, *The Restless Supermarket*, and its protagonist, Aubrey Tearle, we as participants in this literary text, like Tearle in his obsession with printed words and proofreading, have become complicit in the perpetuation of colonial crimes. In an interview with Mike Marais and Carita Backström, Vladislavić says that what fascinates him about Tearle is

> the places where Tearle and I are similar. . . . A sense of ordering is certainly something that comes out of my own personality. And the impulse to exclude, which I think is very powerful here. . . . What I try to do with Tearle, perhaps, is to take to extremes positions that I, and people I know, might hold in a milder way. A concrete instance of this is how people who experienced the orderliness and tidiness of formerly white Johannesburg overreact, now that the city has become more relaxed, when they encounter a bit of "chaos," a little bit of "dirt," a little bit of "disorder." People react in a very extreme way. (120)

By interpellating us into Hillbrow, Mpe points out to us the ways in which we reconfigure stories, suppress certain parts of the archive, highlight certain narratives and bury others. We are thrown into Hillbrow, welcomed, but then asked at the end to consider the ways in which our presence perpetuates "the world of our continuing existence" where "Heaven can be a Hell." How do we react to such a realization that we are complicit in these systems?

We have a number of options for a kind of catharsis. Vladislavić notes that there is a bit of Tearle in all of us, that people can "overreact totally" when confronted with the seeming chaos of the postcolonial reordering of the world. On the other hand, we can create new worlds, patching up narratives in the archive, as was done for Refentše and Lerato, or reinforce harmful suppositions, as was done for Refilwe. By using discourses of crime, neoliberalism, urban spaces, and imperialism to provoke us into these realizations, Vladislavić, Beukes, and Mpe open up various postcolonial possibilities for their readers to consider—ways to live in the African postcolonial criminal city, with Nairobi offering a related but different perspective.

SIX

"THIS LINE CREATED A COUNTRY"

Nairobi, Father and Son

In 1903, and perhaps apocryphally, the British colonial administrator Sir Charles Norton Edgecumbe Eliot proclaimed of the imperial British railway project in Kenya, "It is not uncommon for a country to create a railway, but this line actually created a country." Eliot was referring to what became popularly known as the "Lunatic Express," or a series of railway lines that linked the Ugandan and Kenyan interiors to the Indian Ocean port city of Mombasa. Though his quotation contains staggering colonial arrogance, the railway actually did help to create modern Kenya, and, by extension, modern Nairobi. In terms of a European-style nation-state, Kenya did not exist prior to the twentieth century; nor did its capital and most populous city, Nairobi. Both of these entities, as we understand them today, were created by British colonial infrastructure projects, such as the railroad. Later in the twentieth century, after independence, the Kenyan government began to prioritize the building of roads over the construction and maintenance of railways. The transition away from rail travel and toward highway and personal automobile travel marks a break with the formal colonial era. Even later in the twentieth century and into the twenty-first, a shift toward the importance of international travel began to take place. These changes in travel occurred alongside changes in how crime is portrayed in literature, from the crimes of empire to those of neocolonial, nominally independent governments, to transnational formations in the twenty-first century.

In his 2017 novel *Dance of the Jakaranda*, Peter Kimani writes of the arrival of the first train in the Kenyan countryside: "It was a monstrous, snakelike creature whose black head, erect like a cobra's, pulled rusty brown boxes and slithered down the savanna, coughing spasmodically as it emitted blue-black smoke" (7). The ominous language present in the description of the train is echoed by the narrator noting later in the text, "The elders saw the construction of the railway as a continuation of the slave trade" (156). The slave trade, of course one of the most destructive components of European colonialism in Africa, is integrally linked to imperial infrastructural and travel projects, with the potential for future and continual damage on the continent. Locals "foresaw the train as a beast whose belly would require communal feeding for an eternity, accurately presaging the years of colonialism that lay ahead" (233). They were certainly right; transportation infrastructure was a colonial priority precisely because it eased extraction and exploitation. As well as the link between railways and colonialism has been documented—in fields ranging from literature to history to political science to history—what is missing is the parallel attention to imperial constructions of crime that were developed alongside imperial travel infrastructures such as railways. Social and colonial understandings of crime have contributed to the criminal city of Nairobi, which is "criminal" in that it has been thoroughly marked by structures of colonialism and neocolonialism. The city has grown up alongside the railway and has acted as a harbinger for how crime is understood in Kenya as travel infrastructures have shifted and adapted in the postcolonial era.

In the world of *Dance of the Jakaranda*, the colonial administrator Ian Edward McDonald oversees the construction of a jail in colonial Kenya. The highly stratified building is described in the following passage:

> There were three levels to the building. The top floor was well lit and ventilated and had a beautiful view of the endless sea. In his notes, McDonald had labeled the top floor *White*. The lower floors were labeled *Others*. Even his jail was designed according to racial hierarchy. Whites took the best available space; other races would take what was left. The middle floor was poorly lit although some light from the *White* area filtered through, and one could see the outline of the sea where crevices had not been filled in with

weeds. The bottom level was cloaked in virtual darkness—echoes reverberated when the workmen spoke as bats flitted about soundlessly. When one got accustomed to the dark, one noticed the stone walls were perspiring from the intense heat and poor air circulation. (112)

Colonial Kenya's racial hierarchy is mapped into this jail, this infrastructure for the containment of imperial constructions of crime. McDonald has a plan in mind for the floors labeled "Others," what he calls in his mind a "divide-and-rule policy" (128): "A new compartment was created in the dungeons. Now there were three dungeons, with *White* at the top, *Brown* in the middle, and *Black* at the bottom. He decided to wait and gauge the Arabs' attitudes. If they were hostile to the British presence, he would lump them together with the Africans in the *Black* section. But if they behaved properly, they would be categorized as *Brown* and grouped with the Indians" (128–29). This jail, and the corollary explanations of Kenya's racial caste system, were being developed right alongside Kenya's railway system. They are twin travelers, bound together through parallel colonial logics. By understanding how crime and travel are mapped in Nairobi literature from the era of independence to the twenty-first century, we can get a handle on how imperial structures still persist, opening up opportunities for catharsis where previously those chances had been foreclosed.

The parallel tropes of crime and travel infrastructure track how Nairobi has developed in the literary imagination. The father-and-son pairing of Ngũgĩ wa Thiong'o and Mukoma Wa Ngugi[1] have written works in which crime acts as an animating focus to mark transition points in a city and a literature's history. Both father and son are interested in charting the material exploitation of colonialism and its legacies; the foundations and outcomes may change, but both look to history for thorough groundings for their claims. Attention to travel infrastructure, depictions of Nairobi, and crime in the novels of these two authors demonstrates how a city and a nation have been denied a necessary postcolonial catharsis in the past and explores what possibilities for the future might exist.

Ngũgĩ wa Thiong'o is practically synonymous with postcolonial Kenyan literature: his oeuvre as both a creative writer and an academic spans fiction, drama, critical theory, essays, and nonfiction. Much of his work is concerned with language, and primarily the use of Gikuyu as a tool for decolonization: however, this chapter will consider the English-language *Petals of Blood*, a novel centered around the crime of murder, to argue that Ngũgĩ's focus on crime says as much about the postcolonial city of Nairobi as it does about issues typically associated with his work, like language and village life.² His son, Mukoma Wa Ngugi, is an academic and creative writer as well, who counts among his works the detective novel series consisting of (so far) *Nairobi Heat* (2009) and *Black Star Nairobi* (2013). These works by two different generations of Kenyan authors circle around the nexus of ideas around transportation and crime that is so necessary for a full and layered understanding of the criminal city of Nairobi.

In his conclusion to *Aesthetics and Politics*, Fredric Jameson writes that treating an artistic endeavor such as literature as a "change-oriented activity" (204) has been a centerpiece of Marxist aesthetics at least since the days of Bertolt Brecht. Both Ngũgĩ wa Thiong'o and Mukoma Wa Ngugi are Marxists in this sense, as both of their literary outputs envision a changed world. By mapping how crime, travel, and imperial legacies all work together, both father and son help us to understand Nairobi's predicament more concretely, specifically where catharsis has failed and how it might succeed in the future. In the criminal city of Nairobi, catharsis can be slippery when oppressive neocolonial structures are adaptable and resilient, from the post-independence days of Ngũgĩ wa Thiong'o to the more transnational and postmodern city of his son, Mukoma Wa Ngugi.

"A PROCESS OF BRUTALIZATION": NAIROBI, RAILWAYS, AND THE BRITISH

Nairobi and Kenya's history with the British must be understood through a matrix of several complementary and overlapping factors: the crimes of imperialism, the creation of urban centers, racism, capitalism, and the construction of transportation systems such as railways. The British formalized their rule in Kenya fairly late in terms of their empire, establishing the East Africa Protectorate in 1895. The colony never experienced the levels of white settlement that, say, South Africa did, but throughout Kenya's colonial history, there was a substantial white minority presence in the country. After the Second World War, the Kenyan fight for independence ramped up considerably, most famously marked by the appearance and eventual success of the Mau Mau revolutionary fighters,[3] who waged a guerilla war for almost a decade. Kenya achieved independence in 1963, though several elements of the government remained unchanging, as Ngũgĩ wa Thiong'o and others have pointed out; in many ways, post-independence Kenya is a case study in neocolonialism.

British imperialism in Kenya was marked by particular brutality. Caroline Elkins has documented the extremely harsh methods by which the empire attempted to put down the Mau Mau rebellion, writing, "with the onset of Mau Mau settler conservatism and overt racism would harden, and local European opinion would collectively move farther and farther to the right" (28). Nairobi was a particular focal point for British ethnic cleansing. Elkins tells of the events of April 24, 1954, when "Britain's military forces, under the command of General Sir George Erskine[,] ... launched an ambitious operation to reclaim full colonial control over Nairobi by purging the city of nearly all Kikuyu living within its limits" (121). The violence Britain deployed to maintain its grip on Kenya lines up with the history Achille Mbembe outlines in *On the Postcolony*, when he explains, "It was through the slave trade and colonialism that Africans came face to face with the *opaque and murky domain of power*, a domain inhabited by obscure drives and that everywhere and always makes animality and bestiality its essential components, plunging human beings into a never-ending *process of brutalization*" (14, italics original).

This "process of brutalization" reached its apex during the Mau Mau rebellion with its internment camps, summary executions, and British crackdowns on movement and liberties, but for decades, the British had been imposing their will on Kenya in ways that did violence to the people, the landscape, and the ways of life of the indigenous peoples who inhabited the colony. One of the most tangible legacies of British imperialism in Kenya is the railway. Vladimir Lenin thought "railways are a summation of the basic capitalist industries[,] ... a summation and the most striking indices of the development of world trade and bourgeois-democratic civilization" (5), an observation that lines up neatly with British colonialism and railway building. In Kenya, the insistence on railway building, in particular the Lunatic Express, "sparked a series of developments which transformed Kenya into an important British colony and center for European settlement" (Soja, *Geography*, 16). Even more directly for our purposes, "the railways established the general urban pattern of Kenya, fostering the growth of important centers at key points along their route" (Soja, *Geography*, 29). Without the railways, there would be no criminal city of Nairobi.

Nairobi originated as a stop on the railway line between the Indian Ocean port city of Mombasa and the British interior colony of Uganda (Varma, *Postcolonial City*, 76). Nairobi, established in the late 1890s, was quite literally a colonial creation, and it became evocative of both the crimes of the British and the neocolonial tendencies of the independent Kenyan government over the next half-century. Nairobi occupies a place somewhat similar to many postcolonial cities: it is often seen as an alien imposition on the landscape, a European invention not in keeping with local histories and priorities. After independence, Nairobi became a kind of "model" postcolonial city, a place where colonial legacies would be overlaid with African stylings and where people from many different tribes and ethnicities could theoretically be subsumed into one national identity (Varma, *Postcolonial City*, 84). Nairobi was held to be an urban center where the "divide and rule" tactics of the British would be forgotten, and where a new national identity could be forged.

The novel, like the city of Nairobi, is a European import to Kenya. J. Roger Kurtz writes that these two structures, the city and the novel, act as "wrestling ground[s], in which expectations rooted in indigenous tradition and expectations raised by 'modern' importations struggle with each other" (155–56). Due to the city and the novel's connections in the Kenyan context (Kurtz 155), the contemporary Kenyan novel typically contains a "pronounced emphasis on the city" (Kurtz 3). If the novel is a bourgeois European product, it makes sense that this is the form used to represent a city created by Europeans via a transportation system used to shore up their hold on their colony. As Kurtz has pointed out, the novel came to East Africa as part of a larger European colonial apparatus (13); tying the novel in with railways, criminal infrastructures, and urban form provides readers with a firm matrix to understand the criminal city of Nairobi. The corollary European influences here are thrown into even higher relief when considering both Ngũgĩ wa Thiong'o and Mukoma Wa Ngugi novels, which either feature detectives or can outright be considered crime fiction; as Stephen Knight notes, "Crime fiction as a narrative form, especially in its detective-focused mode, has had quasi-imperial power in the publishing market and also possessed originary links to colonialism" ("Postcolonial Crime Novel," 166). Crime fiction, even more so than the typical European novel, carries strong connections to imperialism and its aftermath. All of these elements—the city, crime, the novel, transportation—are part of a larger bundle of British colonial legacies on the soil of Kenya.

But even after the British left, power structures and imbalances left in place by the empire have remained. Ngũgĩ in particular has been vocal about the injustices of the postcolonial Kenyan state, dividing the thirty years after World War II into three ages, "the age of the anticolonial struggle; the age of independence; and the age of neocolonialism" (*Writing against Neocolonialism*, 1), insisting that Kenya has been a particularly resonant case study of the dangers of neocolonialism. According to Kwame Nkrumah, who wrote of the phenomenon in 1965,

> The neo-colonialism of today represents imperialism in its final and perhaps its most dangerous stage. In the past it was possible to convert a country upon which a neo-colonial regime had been imposed—Egypt in the nineteenth century is an example—into a colonial territory. Today this process is no longer feasible. Old-fashioned colonialism is by no means entirely abolished. It still constitutes an African problem, but it is everywhere on the retreat. Once a territory has become nominally independent it is no longer possible, as it was in the last century, to reverse the process. Existing colonies may linger on, but no new colonies will be created. In place of colonialism as the main instrument of imperialism we have today neo-colonialism. (ix)

Neocolonialism presents in contemporary Kenya as the continued interference of the West in internal Kenyan affairs; as the propagation of Western-approved leaders of the country; and as the suppressing of dissent, as when Ngũgĩ was imprisoned in the late 1970s under the orders of the Western-aligned then vice president Daniel arap Moi.[4] It is tempting to believe that there is another stage of revolution against neocolonialism in the offing, as in a Marxist understanding of history. David Scott has written in *Conscripts of Modernity*, "Anticolonialism has been a classic instance of the modern longing for total revolution. . . . Colonialism [in defining texts of anticolonialism] was principally described as a negative structure of limiting and stultifying power to which the anticolonialists were obliged to respond with a positive and regenerative counter-power" (6). In other words, anticolonial thought, like that of Ngũgĩ's time, often presented as binary in that it sought to meet colonialism with an equal and opposite force, a type of equilibrium through catharsis.

However, as the critical theorist Achille Mbembe points out, "African social formations are not necessarily converging toward a single point, trend, or cycle. They harbor the possibility of a variety of trajectories neither convergent nor divergent but interlocked, paradoxical" (*On the Postcolony*, 16). In other words, there is no forthright anticolonial catharsis that is necessarily going to happen to break Nairobi out of its criminal city formation. Instead, we have a number of different, perhaps "paradoxical" routes that Kenya might use to resist its current neocolonial framework. Ngũgĩ wa Thiong'o's work on crime and the city in an immediate decolonization context points to these types of paradoxes, specifically in his 1977 novel *Petals of Blood*.

"A LAW OF CRIME": NGŨGĨ WA THIONG'O'S *PETALS OF BLOOD*

Ngũgĩ wa Thiong'o's *Petals of Blood* is a novel that grapples with the legacies of the British Empire in Kenya, as well as the failings of the new "independent" Kenyan government. It is set in Ilmorog, a small town that grows into a substantial city, as well as in Nairobi, and charts the relationships inhabitants have to their various urban spaces. The narrative centers around a crime—the murder of three Kenyan businessmen, all of whom act as the African directors of a foreign-owned brewery. When the *Daily Mouthpiece* breaks the news about the triple murder, the story declares, "The three will be an irreplaceable loss to Ilmorog. They built Ilmorog from a tiny nineteenth-century village reminiscent of the days of Krapf and Rebman into a modern industrial town that even generations born after Gagarin and Armstrong will be proud to visit" (6). Their murders, early in the text, set the stage for the story of Ilmorog, Nairobi, travel between those two places, and the narratives of the schoolteacher Munira, the shopkeeper Abdulla, the trade unionist Karega, and the sex worker Wanja, all of whom live in Ilmorog and live interrelated lives due to their past involvement with the Mau Mau rebellion, as well as their current connections to the three murdered businessmen. The novel flashes back to Ilmorog, in the days when it was a tiny village, and to an epic march many Ilmorogans undertake to Nairobi when their town is in the grip of a terrible drought. Through these flashback sequences, the reader learns more about what led up to the central crime, and how the murder is part and parcel of the travel infrastructure and urban growth that have shaped these particular Kenyan criminal cities.

Though Ngũgĩ had long been displeased with the shape of independent Kenya, and had been using his writing to document what Simon Gikandi calls "the rhetoric of failure" (139), *Petals of Blood* marks his turn away from merely registering this disappointment toward using his writing to actively push for change. The novel represents an opportunity for catharsis, a chance to move beyond documenting what is wrong with a situation and instead agitate for a dramatic release of tension to change it. It advances a new kind of political commitment for Ngũgĩ. A 1959 trip by train to Makerere University was the catalyst that changed Ngũgĩ's political philosophies, aesthetic sensibilities, and overall life direction (Isegawa xi). Traveling along the railway, a legacy of the British Empire, paradoxically had turned Ngũgĩ into a committed Marxist, a radical critic of the post-independence Kenyan government, and an activist for change in his home country. It was the train, the colonial infrastructure, that had made this possible; as he continued down this path, he eventually was imprisoned for his critiques of the government,[5] and when released, he eventually fled Kenya and began a life in exile.

His fourth novel written after the watershed moment on the train, *Petals of Blood* epitomizes the political direction in Ngũgĩ's oeuvre. It is a departure in form as much as intent, with its newfound focus on crime and political action. As Gikandi notes, *Petals of Blood* "seemed to exist both inside and outside the tradition of the European novel. For many of its early critics, the novel seemed to gesture toward familiar patterns of realism popularized by European novelists in the nineteenth century, but it also wanted to go beyond what Ngugi considered to be the limits of this kind of 'critical realism,' namely the inability of the bourgeois novel to transcend the social and cultural situation it represented and to function as an aesthetic agent of radical change" (128). This hope that the novel would "function as an aesthetic agent of radical change" is wrapped up in its portrayal of crime, travel, cities, and neocolonialism. Tracing these separate threads will help to untangle Ngũgĩ's wider political and aesthetic vision for a Nairobi that can break free of colonial structures. *Petals of Blood*, with its focus on how African elites continue structures of colonialism and its corollary animating concentration on crime, makes clear the paradoxes Kenya and Nairobi faced at the start of its independence: how to decolonize under neocolonialism, especially when European influences continue to prop up unjust structures.

To start, multiple scholars have observed that *Petals of Blood*, on its face, seems to be a kind of detective novel. J. Roger Kurtz notes that the novel "was clearly influenced by the new fad for detective stories; it opens as a murder mystery, and while it quickly becomes much more than that, it is clear that Ngugi was responding to the newly popular mystery genre" (103). This "newly popular" genre might help to answer Stephen R. Carter's questions, who in "Decolonization and Detective Fiction: Ngugi wa Thiong'o's *Petals of Blood*," writes, "Granting that there are at least some significant connections between capitalism, colonialism, and detective fiction, it becomes a question of considerable importance why Kenya's leading writer and radical, Ngugi wa Thiong'o, would choose to use the mystery form for a major attack on neocolonialism" (73). The question is fairly simply answered: if neocolonialism takes over from where colonialism left off, using a form influenced by capitalism and colonialism could be a subversive move. Ed Christian, however, is not impressed with Ngũgĩ's decision, arguing, "It seems to me that while *Petals of Blood* is an important novel, it is not a successful detective novel. Rather than pushing against the conventions and appropriating them, Ngugi simply uprooted them" (7). Christian's working definition of "successful" demands review. If the goal was merely to transplant the detective novel genre to Kenya, yes, probably Ngũgĩ did not succeed in this task. But if the goal was to push for a political and aesthetic catharsis, or a shift in moods and attitudes to lead toward a new kind of society, *Petals of Blood* begins to look more successful. It does not fully achieve its vision, as I shall lay out, but there is more going on here than just a simple "appropriation" of the conventions of the detective novel.

The detective in question is Inspector Godfrey, sent from Nairobi to Ilmorog to investigate the murders of the three businessmen. Godfrey, we learn, "had served in various capacities under various heads from the colonial times to the present. Crime for him was a kind of jigsaw puzzle, and he believed that there was a law to it—a law of crime—a law of criminal behavior—and he believed that if you looked hard enough you could see this law operating in even the smallest gestures" (52). The inspector is quite clearly a creation of the British Empire; he literally worked for the colonial authorities before they left Kenya, and his insistence on a sort of prescribed and orderly thinking belies his colonial education and job training. Because

Godfrey is unwilling to consider anything that goes outside the bounds of this predetermined "law," he misses a great deal of what goes on around him in Ilmorog, ultimately setting him up for failure in his investigation as he cannot comprehend a way of life or a way of thinking outside of his prearranged assumptions about what crime is and how it works.

Godfrey is, of course, a big-city man come to the small town in the country, and those classic tensions seem ready to be unpicked as well. However, by the time the inspector arrives in Ilmorog, it has transformed itself from a sleepy rural village to a modern, industrial town that almost rivals Nairobi. In large part, this is due to the Trans-Africa highway that is constructed to connect Ilmorog primarily to Nairobi, but also to other regions of Kenya and eastern Africa. What the railways were to the British, the highway is to neocolonial Kenya, and it builds Ilmorog in the same way the railway did Nairobi a century ago. Where once Ilmorog "started its decline and depopulation" (*Petals of Blood* 148), causing all its young people to flee to Nairobi, by the time of the murders, the highway had facilitated scores of growth and several reverse migrations back to Ilmorog.

The unnamed narrator declares, "How Ilmorog rose from a deserted village into a sprawling town of stone, iron, concrete and glass and one or two neon-lights is already a legend in our time" (313). That legend was made possible by the Trans-Africa road, which the narrator says "is justly one of the most famous highways in all the African lands, past and present" (311). The road is what Jaecheol Kim claims is a "spatial contrivance" that is "used to map the process of primitive accumulation on a metropolitan or multinational scale" (198). It is this road, along with the epic journey many of the characters take from Ilmorog to Nairobi to see their Member of Parliament and ask for assistance while the community is undergoing the repercussions from a terrible drought, that outlines how urban growth and travel infrastructure create the conditions that lead to the triple murder.

This journey is the novel's most direct engagement with Nairobi, and the trip there plus time spent in Nairobi is equivalent to about one-fourth of the novel. This setting, tripling together Ilmorog, Nairobi, and the highway, "delineates the theme of proletarianization which is part of the leitmotif of the novel" (Kamenju 133). The mobility between what was once a sleepy village to the big city and back again, seeing the sleepy village transform to a city in its own right, not only dramatizes Ngũgĩ's Marxist commitments, but also pulls Ilmorog into closer relationship with the city center; by the end of the novel, Ilmorog might be what we would today call an exurb of Nairobi, as the once-unimaginable distance between the two spaces has become much more easily traversed, thanks to the highway. The Ilmorog characters begin the novel by thinking of Nairobi as ludicrously far away, full of ludicrous people performing ludicrous customs; by the end of the novel, not only have most of them traveled there, but the currents of capital and neocolonialism have pulled Ilmorog further within the bigger city's orbit, and many Ilmorogans use this engagement with Nairobi to deepen their own political beliefs and actions.

In the old days, before the highway, Munira muses to himself, "the only thing that pained them was this youth running away from the land. The movement away had started after the second big war ... No ... before that ... No it was worse after the Mau Mau War ... No, it was the railway ... all right, all right ... even this had always been so since European colonists came into their midst, these ghosts from another world" (23). Ngũgĩ places the blame squarely on the British here, identifying World War II, the Mau Mau rebellion, the construction of the railway, and the appearance of the colonizers themselves as being at fault for pulling people away from Ilmorog and toward Nairobi. It gets to the point, during the drought, where "it seemed that authority, power, everything, was outside Ilmorog ... out there ... in the big city" (139). Nairobi occupies an almost imperial space as compared to Ilmorog, the place that takes in all of Ilmorog's labor and produce and gives them nothing in return. The characters decide to march to Nairobi to "confront that which had been the cause of their empty granaries, that which had sapped their energies, and caused their weakness" (139). Wanja puts the lure of Nairobi even more simply: "So why not become rich? How? And the answer came. Nairobi. Europeans" (157).

And thus begins a type of colonial conquest in reverse, the people from the hinterland marching to make a move on the metropole. This journey shifts some of their perceptions of Nairobi. Where a woman named Nyakinyua had previously "talked of how she had earlier imagined the city as containing only wealth," upon reaching Nairobi, she "found poverty; she found crippled beggars; she saw men, many men, sons of women, vomited out of a smoking tunnel—a big, big house—and she was afraid. Who had swallowed all the wealth of the land? Who?" (250). This realization, along with the realization many of the Ilmorogans have that their Member of Parliament is not interested in helping them, leads to a transformed political consciousness among the masses. As Rashmi Varma says in *The Postcolonial City and*

Its Subjects, "It is in the journey *between* the city and the country that the space for a renewed cultural and political struggle of the people is produced" (98). The journey makes the villagers aware of how capitalism and neo-colonialism are affecting their home, and marks the "acquisition of historical consciousness" that "proves to be solid and ever-lasting" (Masilela 21), even up to and including the time of the triple murder.

In the time between the journey and the murders, however, Ilmorog transforms greatly. What had been perceived as evils unique to Nairobi—capital accumulation, greed, individualism, selfishness—move into and pervade Ilmorog, largely due to the neocolonial decisions the three murder victims, among others, make. This is where Ngũgĩ could have stood the greatest chance of offering his reader a kind of cathartic crime; for example, the troublesome neocolonial businessmen could have been killed off, the town could have been saved, and peace would once again descend upon the land (in the style of a Disney Channel or Hallmark original movie). Yet, somewhat obviously, Ngũgĩ does not choose to do this, instead opting for a more complicated move that denies the reader, or his characters, any kind of political or aesthetic catharsis linked to the crime; this is, however, the point.

James A. Ogude has been critical of the novel because "the peasants of Ilmorog are not at the centre of the story"—a slight that echoes the marginalization workers suffer in "the new Ilmorog" itself. Ogude even considers Ngũgĩ's first-person-plural narration a poor performance of solidarity: "It is nothing less than a ploy for authorial intrusion; a strategy for asserting the ideological authority of the writer in the narrative" (6). It is true, as Ogude says, that neither a *collective* of peasants nor one of workers is at the center of the narrative, but it is undeniable that the four main characters—Munira, Abdulla, Wanja, and Karega—are themselves workers and peasants. Wanja is a sex worker; Abdulla runs a small shop; Munira is a teacher; and Karega is literally a union organizer. Perhaps they are not directly working the land, but these four are part of the laboring classes (particularly Wanja, with the possible technical exception of Abdulla), and it is their experiences and their voices that form the center of the story. Not only that, there might be a reason Ngũgĩ utilizes this "strategy for asserting the ideological authority of the writer in the narrative"—if he knows that catharsis won't be possible, due to Kenya's neocolonial structure, he cannot have the fictional workers successfully execute a revolution; if the point of catharsis is to purge emotion, such a fictional representation would foreclose the need to carry out this type of action in real life.[6] The kind of socialist realism that Ngũgĩ develops in *Petals of Blood,* where he uses a narrative to transmit his ideology, works well for his ultimate goals without getting him all the way there. Inspector Godfrey does not solve the crime; Ilmorog does not magically become a more just place; the problems of postcolonial Kenya are not overcome. Ngũgĩ, by denying the reader a cathartic crime, uses the narrative to outline the kinds of problems people will face if they truly wish to enact a revolution.

Neil Lazarus writes of *Petals of Blood* that Ilmorog "mutates over its course from a peasant village . . . into the horror of 'New Ilmorog,'" an industrial wasteland of factories and slums, leaving the bulk of its inhabitants ruined: "dispossessed, impoverished, and demoralized" (38). The murders, as they are both carried out and perceived in the community are in part an expression of this demoralization; as the narrator explains, "This was the society they had been building since Independence, a society in which a black few, allied to other interests from Europe, would continue the colonial game of robbing others of their sweat, denying them the right to grow to full flowers in the air and sunlight" (348–49). *Petals of Blood* is taking a cue from Frantz Fanon in this sense, and specifically Fanon's insights about "native elites" in postcolonial spaces; as Fanon outlined in *The Wretched of the Earth,* many postcolonial revolutions simply end with local bourgeoisie instating themselves in positions of power in order to continue the work the European colonists began. Indeed, Ngũgĩ himself wrote in "Petals of Love," "That is what I was trying to show in *Petals of Blood*: that imperialism can never develop our country or develop us, Kenyans" (97). Neocolonialism was so pervasive in Ngũgĩ's both real and fictional Kenyas that an honest attempt at catharsis for the reader could not be achieved in one novel.

By stopping short of offering his audience catharsis, however, Ngũgĩ actually creates a way for the characters in his novel to achieve the same. What is denied the reader and Inspector Godfrey is allowed for some of the novel's characters. Though Godfrey only partially solves the crime, the full truth is revealed to the readers by the unnamed narrator.[7] Munira has become deeply enmeshed in right-wing Christian theologies (themselves colonial impositions!), and becomes convinced that he must save the world from Wanja by burning down her brothel. This fire, which was intended to kill Wanja, instead kills the three businessmen; two die by fire, and Wanja kills the third with a panga. Munira is (logically and rightly!) denied his feeling of catharsis that would come at the expense of the death of a sex worker, though Karega, Abdulla, and Wanja know the truth and either help with the deaths or see the neocolonial native elites perish, while Inspector Godfrey has to take a melancholy train ride back to Nairobi, one where he "should now have been experiencing that inner satisfaction he always had felt whenever he put a crime jigsaw puzzle together; but instead he felt an inner discomfort, a slight irritability" (396). Because neocolonialism is a perpetuation of colonial systems under a local guise, of course Godfrey does not feel any kind of relief, nor is he allowed the pleasure of solving the crime; anything that might complicate his European-style thinking is not allowed to make it into his brain. And because this crime does not neatly slide into an easily understood paradigm, knottily wrapped up as it is with urban growth, transportation, and neocolonialism, it is not allowed to proceed further in his mind. For Godfrey, a man for whom "the system of private ownership, of means of production, exchange and distribution, was for him synonymous with the natural order of things like the sun, the moon and the stars which seemed fixed and permanent in the firmament" (396), any amount of chaos or unpredictability makes no sense; evil men have to be evil, and good men have to be good, and no gray areas exist in between for what it means to, for example, kill the wrong men when you had been intending to kill a sex worker, or that three people deeply harmed by the victims' decisions and choices are not particularly upset when they have died.

Yet, though Abdulla, Wanja, and Karega are somewhat satisfied by the deaths of the businessmen, the underlying rot in Ilmorog is not fixed. As Stephen R. Carter observes, Godfrey's "discovery that Munira set the fire that killed Chui and Mzigo solves none of the underlying social problems, and he even fails to discover that Wanja killed Kimeria with a panga after observing that her wood mansion was on fire" (76). The crime plot is "solved" by the detective in only the shallowest of ways; it is the local people, a subset of the working class, who know the full truth. What is more important, however, is what is revealed along the way: "The mystery around the murder case resolves itself as the narrative progresses. Toward the end, we grasp a clear neocolonial social picture with an explicit cognitive map" (Kim 191). We as readers grasp the picture but are denied catharsis; the characters in the novel are allowed a limited amount, but not much. The point is that Kenya and its criminal cities are still too rotten by imperialism, even in a postcolonial age, to truly allow for a societal transformation within the limits of the bourgeois European novel.

Ngũgĩ succeeds in demonstrating where the rot is, and in communicating his Marxist ideologies to his audience, but the novel is limited in what it can accomplish. Like Nairobi and the trains, the novel is a legacy of European colonialism: like Ilmorog and the highway, it can take those imperial impositions and translate them to Kenyan dictates, but, as demonstrated throughout the first wave of decolonization, clean breaks with Europe aren't as possible or as clear-cut as we might theoretically imagine. Catharsis will have to come through more nuanced understandings of the postcolonial situation.

Of course, Ngũgĩ would eventually demonstrate the power of such a clean break; both his eventual, and very famous, insistence on the importance of African languages over English, and his name change (he was born "James") testify to this political commitment. But there are hints even in *Petals of Blood* that the struggle is ongoing; that though catharsis was denied this time, it doesn't have to be in the future. J. Roger Kurtz has pointed out that the novel's section titles ("Walking," "Toward Bethlehem," "To Be Born," and "Again . . . La Luta Continua") echo William Butler Yeats's understanding of cycles of history as expressed in the poem "The Second Coming," with its famous ending query "And what rough beast, its hour come round at last,/Slouches towards Bethlehem to be born?" As Kurtz points out, the "rough beast" is the neocolonial society in which Ngũgĩ and his contemporaries found themselves mired; however, there is the fact that "La Luta Continua" points to the future and the hoped-for promise of a new, more just society. Ngũgĩ's insistence on looking to the future, even in this neocolonial society his countrymen have built, holds out hope for a future kind of catharsis. *Petals of Blood* offers some catharsis, but the picture is incomplete; in the twenty-first century, his son's fiction picks up the detective theme, presenting readers with a cognitive map for the twenty-first century.

"AN INTERNATIONAL CRIMESCAPE": THE DETERRITORIALIZED NAIROBI OF MUKOMA WA NGUGI

Shifting away from the disillusionment of his father, Ngũgĩ, to something more postmodern and less tangible, Mukoma Wa Ngugi has published a pair of novels taking up the question of neocolonialism in Kenya. Two of his novels, *Nairobi Heat* (2009) and *Black Star Nairobi* (2013), feature Ishmael, an African American detective from Madison, Wisconsin,[8] who later moves to the titular capital city and sets up shop with a Kenyan detective, Odhiambo, known simply as O. Together, the two solve first the murder of a young white woman who was killed in Madison but who has links to Nairobi (*Nairobi Heat*) and then a bombing of a hotel in Nairobi (*Black Star Nairobi*).

Mukoma Wa Ngugi's writing picks up from his father's, though Kenya has changed rather drastically in the intervening almost half century. The presidency of Daniel arap Moi essentially turned Kenya into a one-party state, and interethnic violence and tribal tensions ratcheted up through the 1980s and 1990s. A clean, neat teleology of progress post-independence was not possible; David Scott's "old consoling sense of temporal *concordance*" (*Omens*, 6) was not within reach.

In *Conscripts of Modernity*, David Scott has also written of the difference between anticolonial (Ngũgĩ wa Thiong'o) and postcolonial (Mukoma Wa Ngugi) narratives, arguing,

> I am going to suggest that anticolonial stories about past, present, and future have typically been emplotted in a distinctive narrative form, one with a distinctive story-potential: that of *Romance*.... They have largely depended on a certain (utopian) horizon toward which the emancipationist history is imagined to be moving. I do not take this conceptual framework to be a mistake. However, in the wake of the global historico-political and cognitive shifts that have taken place in the past decade or two, I have a doubt about the continued critical salience of this narrative form and its underlying mythos. Indeed, my wager in this book is that the problem about postcolonial futures—how we go about reimagining what we might become of what we have so far made—cannot be recast without recasting the problem about colonial pasts. (7–8)

Ngũgĩ wa Thiong'o's *Petals of Blood* was already starting to move away from the "distinctive narrative form" identified by Scott as being "typically" anticolonial, and his son picks up his project by continuing to think through "reimagining what we might become of what we have so far made." Mukoma Wa Ngugi's twenty-first-century novels tackle cathartic crime by "recasting the problem about colonial pasts" in a way inspired by, but divergent from, his father.

Nairobi Heat begins with a young white woman found dead on the doorstep of the African peace activist and Rwandan refugee organization head Joseph Hakizimana, who has accepted a position on the faculty of the

University of Wisconsin. Hakizimana is famous for rescuing hundreds of people during the Rwandan genocide of 1994 by providing shelter for them in his schoolhouse (a kind of riff on the story of *Hotel Rwanda*). Ishmael is put on the case, and soon receives a mysterious call telling him, "If you want the truth, you must go to its source. The truth is in the past. Come to Nairobi" (27). Ishmael does as instructed, and upon arrival in Nairobi, he is paired up with O from the local police force.[9] Together, the two trace the mystery of the anonymous young woman, who she was, and what her links to Joseph were, eventually moving out of Nairobi proper to rural Kenya and eventually, to Rwanda itself in order to uncover the mystery of her murder. Through his travels in the criminal city and throughout East Africa, Mukoma expounds upon many of the threads his father explored in an earlier era, notably ideas surrounding crime, urban form, transportation, and neocolonialism/colonial legacies.

One of O's earliest ideas to track down who the woman is and to learn more about Joseph is to pay a visit to Lord Thompson, an old British settler who still lives on a plantation outside the city. As the two detectives wind farther and farther down country roads, Ishmael expresses his disbelief that anyone could possibly live so far away from the city. O replies, "After colonialism, they were supposed to remain invisible, and we were supposed to forget what they did. . . . So they hide out in places like this" (54). This early indication that British colonialism is hidden, tucked away, and needs to be sought out is an early indication by Mukoma that his Nairobi is not that of his father's: instead of the ravages of colonialism being near the surface, the two must actively seek out the remnants of empire.

The pair reach Lord Thompson's home and have a less-than-fruitful conversation with the old man; he does not give them much information, and they leave dissatisfied. However, upon arrival back in Nairobi, someone tries to kill the two in a bar, and he reveals he had done so on Lord Thompson's orders. This seals O and Ishmael's certainty that Lord Thompson holds the information that links the victim and Joseph; he's "the link we had been looking for" (65). They return to his estate and are let in by Thompson's older Kenyan servant, in a kind of updated Mau Mau attack. "Terror registered on the old man's face," Ishmael notes. "Betrayed by his black help, the nightmare that his whiteness had protected him from was standing before him" (69).[10] No longer does Lord Thompson live in a place where his white skin affords him the ability to dominate and rule over the African population—the echo of the Mau Mau "invasion" of white settler spaces is paired with twenty-first-century concerns surrounding vengeance and continued European interference in African affairs. Lord Thompson admits that he had been told to arrange for O and Ishmael's death by a man named Samuel Alexander, who works on the board of Joseph's Rwandan refugee organization. After this admission, O kills Thompson, in part as revenge for his own attempted murder, and in part revenge for the Africans Thompson has killed on his property throughout the years. The two leave the estate and return to the city.

There is certainly an element of Ngũgĩ's observations about neocolonialism present in this storyline: Ishmael thinks to himself, "Sure, the old white man was dead, but it wouldn't be long before some rich African bastard ended up with the farm, and then they would be right back where they started. It was the way of the world everywhere" (73). It's clear that Mukoma shares a lot of his father's (well-justified) cynicism in this regard. But the death of Lord Thompson marks the end of one of the last vestiges of Ngũgĩ and his compatriots' understanding of Nairobi. Lord Thompson does not have any sons, and there do not seem to be any young ex-British settlers about; it's the end of an era. His murder means we have moved from an anti- or postcolonial time that is marked by resistance to the British and their "native elite" legacies to something that requires a more global and sprawling form of resistance to formations a lot less tangible than the formal British Empire and its associated white settlers. Though David Scott has argued that postcolonial theorists are still too reliant on a "conception of colonialism . . . [that] has continued to bear the distinctive traces of anticolonialism's conceptual preoccupations" (*Conscripts*, 6), we see a move in Mukoma's work away from that type of binary thinking and toward a more diffuse and loose understanding of oppression and how to respond to it.

The kind of revolution that Ngũgĩ and his contemporaries envisioned is not possible now; we are not in the age of Mau Mau. The murder of the young white woman is not directly linked to the British Empire; it is instead linked to the Rwandan genocide, the roots of which can be laid at the feet of the French, who controlled that particular part of East Africa and who encouraged divisions between the Hutus and Tutsis that led to the eventual bloodshed, but also at the feet of the postcolonial Rwandan government and post-genocide NGOs and "humanitarian" organizations. In his first novel, Mukoma's identifying of a kind of transnational imperialism is a bit of a riff on Michael Hardt and Antonio Negri's concept of Empire: "Sovereignty has taken a new form, composed of a series of national and supranational organisms united under a single logic of rule" (xii). The legacies of the French and British empires, combined with the power of international humanitarian organizations that ostensibly claim to be working on behalf of Rwandan refugees, are a sort of proto-example of Empire. Because "Empire establishes no territorial center of power and does not rely on fixed boundaries or barriers" (Hardt and Negri xii), it is possible for this matrix of power to expand from Rwanda to rural Kenya to Nairobi to Madison. If the motor of Ngũgĩ's time was the highway, to take the Ilmorogans to Nairobi and to transform Ilmorog into a city in its own right, the travel in Mukoma's novels eschews this infrastructure in favor of international travel across oceans and continents.

There is no clear-cut anticolonial replacement theory as there was in *Petals of Blood*; this is not a story of "native elites" taking over for former colonials. It turns out that Joseph, though he did rescue some escaping refugees, used the pretext of his school to lure unsuspecting Tutsis into murder traps; he saved some of them in order to keep up the pretense, but his school instead functioned as a killing field.[11] The young white woman, Macy Jane, was the daughter of American missionaries whom Joseph's men murdered as well; she only lived because she was away at boarding school at the time. She had approached Joseph in Madison to confront him about his crimes, and he had killed her in response. This sets in motion a complex transnational cover-up, led by many people pretending to be humanitarians like Joseph and Samuel Alexander.

Though Ishmael and O finally get to the bottom of the mystery, they are dissatisfied with the conclusion. They realize they do not have enough evidence to convict Joseph of Macy Jane's murder, but also that there is nothing they can charge him with in regard to the genocide. Joseph's crimes do not fit neatly into established frameworks; they are not the crimes of the British Empire, nor of those depicted in *Petals of Blood*, even if there are transnational imperial roots. Ishmael takes matters into his own hands and arranges for the Madison chapter of the KKK to murder Joseph[12]; after that, there is nothing left to do but bury Macy Jane in Rwanda, after which, Ishmael thinks, "everything had come to an end. Everyone had some sense of closure" (185).

Of course, this isn't true; there's no closure, no catharsis, and the story of the criminal city of Nairobi picks back up again in *Black Star Nairobi*. Ishmael has moved to Nairobi and set up an independent detective agency with O.

They are called to investigate the murder of a man whose body has been left in the Ngong Forest, but they quickly realize this murder might be linked to the bombing of an American-owned hotel.[13] This novel is set in the lead-up to both the Kenyan and the American elections of 2007/8, elections that, in Kenya, led to violence between the Kikuyu and Luo against the backdrop of the American presidential campaign of Barack Obama, who is of course the son of a Kenyan father.

According to an interview with National Public Radio's *All Things Considered*'s Jacki Lyden, Ngũgĩ praised Mukoma for doing something Ngũgĩ was never able to do: namely, write a detective story. According to Mukoma, Ngũgĩ even mentioned *Petals of Blood*, saying *Black Star Nairobi* was a better example of the genre than his own novel. Mukoma goes on to say in the interview that the detective novel genre "allows you to look at very, very extreme situations, extreme violence, a society just about to explode in a way that I don't think you can do with realist fiction." This genre, then, is perhaps well suited for the Nairobi of the twenty-first century, a city that has expanded greatly since the time of Ngũgĩ's heyday to become a place even more marked by violence, traffic congestion, and international influences. Nairobi is still a place marked by colonialism, but Mukoma's writing looks beyond the British to map how international currents inflect crime in this city.

Ishmael and O figure out that there is a group of Western individuals at the heart of the bombing, though it takes them awhile to understand their motives for the violence. The leader of the pack, whom they call Sahara because he wears a tourist T-shirt emblazoned with an image of the Sahara Desert, has a map in his possession with a number of tourist landmarks circled: "The Jomo Kenyatta Conference Center, Nairobi National Museum, Fort Jesus in Mombasa, built by the Portuguese in the 1500s, Tree Tops Hotel, where in 1952 the then-Princess Elizabeth had learned that her father had died and she would be queen, and many others" (88). The emphasis on a mix of both colonial and postcolonial landmarks means that the key enemy in this text is not just the Europeans; we have, again, moved past the politics of disillusionment that were so key to Ngũgĩ's time, and even beyond identifying the enemy as the kind of Kenyan who takes the place of the colonizer. Mary, Ishmael's wife, suffers tragedy when her father is killed in election-related violence. He had fought for the British during the war of independence, yet, as Mary's mother explains, "that is not why they killed him. They killed him because his daughter married a Luo" (135). This shift from the colonial era is marked now, at least on its face, by intertribal violence, instead of violence against the British and their replacements, mystifying Ishmael and O as to Sahara's motivations even further.

Yet the roots of the violences and the crimes that pockmark Nairobi may be more genealogically linked to Ngũgĩ's era than they seem at first glance. As one of Sahara's colleagues explains, "The institution doesn't change with the leader" (230). The colonial deep state has not been fully abandoned, even in an era of Hardt and Negri's deterritorialized Empire. In *Black Star Nairobi*, Mukoma expands on the figuration he had initially established in *Nairobi Heat* to create "a 'crimescape' that spans Kenya, Mexico, and the United States" (Pahl 89), as Ishmael and O must sneak illegally into the U.S. through Mexico to continue to trace Sahara and his colleagues' misdeeds. The two continue their international escapades as they attempt to get to the bottom of the bombing, the murder, and the full story of Sahara and his crew.

As Mukoma creates this international crimescape, we must also pay attention, as Eleni Coundouriotis says, to "what he pushes aside: the logics of the long aftermath of colonialism, which haunt the causal explanations of the genocide, and the roots of the post-election violence in Kenya in 2007 that spurred the writing of *Black Star Nairobi*" (386). The lack of attention to the imperial causes of these violences, Coundouriotis explains, can be understood through the technique of "*unnaration*, or blotting out," the "historical dynamics" of empire that inform the making of the present-day city (386). Because his two Ishmael novels do not deal directly with the legacies of British colonialism in the way his father's do, Mukoma's writing works to "[orchestrate] a purge of colonial vestiges . . . that pushes his weighty literary inheritance into the background and along with it the shadow of his father's lived historical trauma of the war against British colonialism" (390). In David Scott's words, Mukoma has "[recast] the problem about colonial pasts" (*Conscripts*, 8).

Sure, this might read as all very *Anxiety of Influence*-y, but if we accept that both father and son are engaged in a Marxist, activist tradition of literature, it bears repeating that the targets of this kind of activism have necessarily changed in the thirty-plus years since Ngũgĩ published *Petals of Blood*. It isn't a straightforward colonialism that is the enemy, that is directly or indirectly responsible for many of the ills of the criminal city; now, it's a series of international cabals, a Hardt and Negri–esque empire, that latch onto humanitarian defenses and facades in order to continue to exert their will on a soil not their own. Both Ngũgĩ and Mukoma are interested in exploring the effects of colonialism by another name; but that "other name" changes and morphs to fit the particular contexts of each particular Nairobi.

In *Nairobi Heat*, this international organization is Joseph's Never Again Foundation. As his henchman, Abu Jamal, explains it to Ishmael and O, "All right, say you are a savvy businessman who realises that there is a lot of money to be made out of this guilt . . . a lot of money. Say you have a white face, but you find a black man, a hero who helps you tap into the community of refugees from this country that owns the guilt of the world, and you start a Refugee Centre. Say you then start a foundation called Never Again to tap into this guilt from all over the world" (108). A flimsy shell started by a war criminal, the Never Again Foundation is an attempt to offer a kind of catharsis to the world. And it works, for a time; people buy Joseph's story enough that he's offered a position on the faculty of a major American university. But the true motive for setting up this foundation, even more than sanitizing his image, is to make money. "How much can a guilty conscience be worth?" Ishmael asks himself as he pores over the foundation's records. "Millions, it would seem. . . . Anybody and everybody with money was in the game. This was the world trying to clear its conscience, and to do that it was prepared to pay close to seventy million dollars a year" (112). Again, the entity pulling the strings has changed since Ngũgĩ's Kenya, but a duplicitous colonial logic is still snaking through twenty-first-century Nairobi.

Black Star Nairobi also identifies an international cohort as creating the criminal city of Nairobi, but the details are more pronounced and specific. Ishmael and O finally realize Sahara and his colleagues are part of an association of middle managers to powerful individuals like Bill Clinton, Nelson Mandela, and Jimmy Carter. This association, known as International Democracy and Economic Security Council, or IDESC, wants to completely eviscerate places they have identified as "trouble spots" and rebuild them from the ground up in their own image. They all began as humanitarians and quickly became disillusioned with this kind of work. (Note, of course, Mukoma's focus on the duplicitous nature of the humanitarian industry or NGO-industrial complex in both of his novels.) As Ishmael understands it,

> Imagine all you want to do in this world is some good. You go from trouble spot to trouble spot and do your best to make a difference. You start in the Peace Corps in some village somewhere, drilling wells and building makeshift schools. When you leave, in spite of your efforts, the well dries up and the school decides to stop admitting girls because a local fat cat angling for

political office has decided it is against African culture. You get another job where you have more power and you continue up the do-gooder ladder until you land in some of the most powerful offices in the world—of former U.S. presidents, world monetary organizations, the United Nations—and still nothing is changing. (249–50)

In this vision, the Jimmy Carters of the world cannot take any dramatic action; they are constrained by their privileges, powers, and responsibilities. But Sahara and his men—nobodies who nevertheless are proximate to great power—can. Again putting himself in the position of IDESC members, Ishmael thinks, "You start dreaming of taking over one of these countries one day and showing the world how it can be done right. . . . If the cancer could be gutted out and replaced with Kenyans who really cared for their country, would that be so bad? It would be a revolution" (250). IDESC wanted to test out their ideas in Nairobi; it was to be their initial foray onto the world stage for this kind of work. They had identified Nairobi as the criminal city so corrupted it needed to be torn down completely and built again from scratch.

The sprawling, violent regime known as IDESC has some resonance in Ngũgĩ's disillusionment with the post-independence Kenyan elites—Ngũgĩ certainly would have liked to "gut out the cancer" of post-independence Kenya and replace the powerful with "Kenyans who really cared for their country"—but it has stronger links to old-style British imperialism. One is reminded of Marlow in Joseph Conrad's *Heart of Darkness*, musing that while colonialism is not a pretty business, "what redeems it is the idea only" (7). Sahara echoes this perverted idealism by pleading with O and Ishmael, "If you could open your eyes for a minute, if you could see what I see, you would be helping me create new men and new women, a new country, one that is not tied to the past. A society past the point of singularity, a people so far into a new and better future that there would be no going back" (256). This is the idea that Sahara has chosen to "set up, and bow down before, and offer a sacrifice to" (Conrad 7).

Ishmael and O foil IDESC's plans to level Nairobi; they realize that the organization was behind the murder and the bombing of the hotel, and that they have a plan to set off a bomb in the statute of Jomo Kenyatta[14] in Nairobi's largest convention center, where a great number of world leaders are gathering for a conference. But as Ishmael realizes, "IDESC was going to reconstitute itself. If Mpande [one of Sahara's men] was telling the truth, the organization existed in the memories of those involved. They would find another body, another organization. But for now, we had done our little bit" (259). There is no catharsis in this crime; the bomb never went off, but the story never ends, and colonial logics keep reinventing and twisting themselves to fit particular contexts, spaces, and times. We are given no closure.

Mukoma's Nairobi, therefore, expands its borders to an international scope. Whereas his father's treatment of cities was linked to colonial and early neocolonial technologies like railways and highways, enabling travel between Ilmorog and Nairobi and setting up highway-based development of the city's dusty outskirts, the twenty-first century breaks down city and national borders because criminal cities are now fully transnational. As previously noted, in *Writing against Neocolonialism*, Ngũgĩ breaks the years after World War II into three ages: "the age of the anticolonial struggle; the age of independence; and the age of neocolonialism" (1). If *Petals of Blood* documents "the age of neocolonialism," the last stage outlined, what age have we and Mukoma entered into in the long arc of colonialism and imperialism?

Mukoma wonders the same, writing for the *Los Angeles Review of Books*, "The legacy of colonialism's bifurcated world—on one side the European colonists, and on the other, the colonized Africans—its corrosive effects on both, and the ensuring culture clashes and alienation has given way to something harder to articulate than mere 'globalization': a metaphysical colonization in which language, and racial identity itself, gets scrambled." In this Hardt and Negri Empire-esque world, a Black Rwandan like Joseph can be part of a "metaphysical" and also physically violent colonialism; middle managers who were once in the Peace Corps can conceive of plans for unimaginable violence; technologies like air travel can enable colonialism and exploitation on levels never dreamed of by the British with their railways.[15] This has created conditions where criminal cities start to matter more than the nations they are housed in: Who cares for Kenya and India as abstract concepts when you can fly into Nairobi in the morning and on to Mumbai in the afternoon? The imperially defined nation-states of the world are, perhaps, beginning to break down in ways that would have been inconceivable to Ngũgĩ and his independence-era contemporaries; for his son in the twenty-first century, however, this transnational focus of the criminal city might open new doors for cathartic crime.

David Scott understands tragedy, the narrative form most closely linked to catharsis, as "[questioning] . . . the view of human history as moving teleologically and transparently toward a determinate end, or as governed by a sovereign and omnisciently rational agent" (*Conscripts*, 12). The world of both father and son, Ngũgĩ and Mukoma, similarly questions this emphasis on teleological and neat narrative catharsis. There is no "sovereign and omnisciently rational agent," but rather confusing networks, sprawling influences, multiple pathways, and forking histories. By studying the literary output of this father and son pairing, we can understand how Kenyan fiction focused on Nairobi has changed its understanding of the criminal city from the end of the anticolonial age to the twenty-first century.

One of the main characters in *Dance of the Jakaranda*, the novel that opened this chapter, is Rajan, the grandson of a man who moved from the Punjab to Kenya to work on the colonial-era railways. When India attains its independence, it becomes difficult for Rajan's grandfather to return to India, because Punjab, once an autonomous state, has been dissolved and split between the new nations of India and Pakistan. Rajan's father has no home country; he has nowhere to return to; he stays in Kenya, even though neither he nor his grandson attain Kenyan citizenship.

This makes it difficult for Rajan later in the novel, when he is to be deported from Kenya due to trumped-up criminal charges. Yet he, like his grandfather, has nowhere to go. He cannot go to India or Pakistan; Britain has ended its policy of allowing immigration from Commonwealth nations; and Kenya does not want him. In the words of an airport employee as Kenyan officials are trying to deport Rajan, "It is quite unusual for a man to lose three countries at once. If Britain is out of bounds, Punjab has been dissolved, and he failed to apply for Kenyan citizenship, the man is basically stateless" (334). He has nowhere to go, and no country to belong to—a case study of a colonial law, a "racist legal instrument" (340) being used to deprive people of spaces and contexts they are familiar with. Rajan's story of statelessness, and the layers of imperial history it exemplifies, is a vivid example of the burgeoning transnational nature of how imperial legacies continue to affect criminal cities all over the globe, from Africa to Palestine, and the paradoxes of breaking free from colonial history while remaining mired in neocolonial structures.

SEVEN

"HIS MEMORY RESISTS ORDERING"

—

The Difficulty of Catharsis in Palestine

Isabella Hammad's 2019 novel *The Parisian* follows the life of young Palestinian Midhat Kamal as he travels from Palestine to Paris and back again during World War I and its immediate aftermath. When Midhat leaves for Paris, his home city of Nablus is under Ottoman Turkish control; the war shifts the balance of power immensely, and he returns home to the British Mandate of Palestine. Hammad writes,

> At the Ottomans' overthrow, the streets of Jerusalem had flooded with revelers, and the citizens danced and whistled and cut down the telegraph wires to take home as trophies. But in Nablus the reaction was quite different. There the crowds gathered outside the municipal hospital, that symbol of Nablus's modernity, not to support but to protest the British capture of Jerusalem, and the Nabulsis had chanted their way to the temporary Turkish encampment to display their fervent displeasure. Although the city was a centre of Arab nationalism, her citizens still feared the defeat of the Empire. The known was better than the unknown, they said uneasily; the Ottomans had been bad, but who wasn't in a time of war? And besides, in those Turkish garrisons their sons were half the soldiers. And in addition Balfour had made his declaration: Nablus guessed what the British had planned for them, and they were afraid. (147)

This rendering of a historical moment speaks to the revolving door of empires Palestine has seen in its modern history, from the Ottomans until the early twentieth century to the British Mandate until 1948 to the contemporary Israeli occupation (assisted and sustained in large part by the United States). Nablus, in what we would now call the West Bank of the occupied Palestinian territories,[1] is an ancient Palestinian city, a home of Arab nationalism, and a space continually occupied by global empires that wish to use it for their own purposes. Palestine, and the cities of the West Bank in particular, is a place layered with years of imperial history, including, after World War I, the heavy hand of the British.

The British Mandate gave the British Empire rule over the areas we would now call Palestine and Israel (as well as some other areas of western Asia) for just under thirty years (1920–48). The Balfour Declaration, referenced above in the excerpt from *The Parisian*, combined with the Sykes-Picot Agreement that divided much of the Levant between British and French spheres of influence, are the two pieces of twentieth-century imperial legislation with the greatest effect on contemporary Palestine. The Balfour Declaration laid the foundations for the establishment of the state of Israel in 1948, while Sykes-Picot drew arbitrary lines to create nations that had no relationship to long-established communities and well-understood territorial markers. When speaking of Palestine today, it is common to hold Israel and the United States responsible for Palestinian suffering; while these two nations certainly deserve opprobrium, it is important to keep in mind British (and Ottoman) roots in the region, and how their policies continue to influence life today. Hammad's novel uses the past to demonstrate these post–World War I events to contemporary readers, which Hala Alyan's *Salt Houses* (2017) does as well, but for a post-1948 world.

The years since 1948 have been marked by bloodshed, oppression, and travel restrictions for the Palestinians who remain in the West Bank, not to mention widespread exile from Palestine to other countries in the Levant and beyond. Basma Ghalayini writes, "Israel's 70-year programme of systemic, ethnic cleansing is one long, ongoing extension of the event that took place in 1948, the origin of which lay in the liberties that Israel took that year when Zionist militias, supported by the British, took more than 78% of the Palestinian's land" (ix). This early support of "Zionist militias," combined with the British Empire's long-standing general ability to create and sustain ethnic and religious tension, has led to the contemporary occupation of Palestine by Israel, who is in turn supported by American foreign aid and military assistance. This means that Israel is an outpost of Western hegemony; it is a colonial power created by the British Empire and sustained by the American, and this in turn is represented in its urban organization. Today, Israel bears many resemblances to Western Europe and the United States (Cohen Lustig 25), particularly in its economic organization, and this economic organization leads to city planning that falls in line with "a global phenomenon of metropolitan sprawl and segregation into ethnically and religiously homogenous communities that [mirror] the American and South African gated communities" (Weizman 123). This method of city planning—these criminal cities born of imperialism, apartheid, and segregation—directly affects Palestinian livelihoods in that Israeli sprawl creates Palestinian exile, and these urban spaces feature prominently in many Palestinian postcolonial novels and narratives.

This chapter will argue that a long chain of imperial control over Palestine has resulted in an Anglophone literary and cultural understanding that relies heavily on the mechanisms and workings of crime to make sense of years of oppression, exile, and deprivation. Crime in the Palestinian context is typically defined from above (in other words, the Israeli occupying forces have the power and ability what constitutes a crime, and what does not). Palestinian writers are aware of this power imbalance, and play with it in order to disrupt the representational script, working to elucidate the elisions that exist between low-level Palestinian "crimes" such as marching and organizing, and the international silence around British and later Israeli war crimes such as ethnic cleansing, destruction of cultural sites, and the creation of displaced refugees. By articulating the immense gaps between perception and reality, Anglophone Palestinian literature, and specifically Hala Alyan's 2017 novel *Salt Houses*, works to reach a global audience to educate readers about how crime works in the occupied territories.

One of the clearest ways in which the crimes of Israel are most keenly felt is in mobility and movement (or the difficulty thereof). Raja Shehadeh's *Palestinian Walks* is an account of the author's travel through a Palestine that changes daily as Israeli settlements and sprawl encroach more and more on his birth city of Ramallah and its environs, and as more roads are constructed that are limited to Israeli usage. He writes of one particular walk, "It was no longer possible to get to the village using the short direct route, which would have taken twenty minutes. Instead I had to travel west then south then east again, in a big loop, through the villages of A'yn Arik, Deir Ibizi, Kafr Ni'ma,

Safa, Beit 'Ur El Tahta and finally after a ninety-minute tortuous trek over narrow winding roads through the hills and valleys to Beit 'Ur El Fauqa" (83). Due to the construction of Israeli-only roads and highways, Palestinian cities and villages have become ever-more cut off from other regions of Palestine, the rest of the Levant, and the world itself. Palestinians often must travel hours and miles out of their way in order to go even very short distances, meaning daily life is often incredibly difficult and arduous. This is not to mention the long-distance travel that many Palestinians have had to make since the Nakba of 1948, when many were driven from their homes and forced to become refugees in the West Bank, Jordan, Lebanon, Kuwait, and many other places. With this in mind, this chapter will also pay close attention to mobility and travel, and how these themes chime in with the ever-present reality of crime and how it is defined in Palestinian novels.

Oddly, even though there are many resonances between postcolonial studies and Palestine (and one of the most famous and original postcolonial scholars, Edward Said, was himself Palestinian), Palestine has been understudied and underrepresented in postcolonial discourses (Ball 4). Anna Bernard agrees, writing, "Israel/Palestine has played a minor role within the dominant formations of metropolitan postcolonial literary studies" (13).[2] This chapter will insert Palestinian literature firmly within the framework of postcolonial critique and analysis by insisting on the long shadow of the British Empire in the region, and the current imperial regime imposed by Israel and the United States; I do not want to think of Palestine in the ways Bernard claims it is often figured, as "an exception to the postcolonial . . . a holdover of European settler-colonialism, or an unfortunate caveat to the emancipatory power of diaspora" (19–20). Instead, I argue, twenty-first-century Palestine is a unique presence in the field of postcolonial studies, a clear example of a continually occupied space with deep British imperial legacies that is currently propped up by a formerly colonized and oppressed people with the sustaining help of the world's primary global superpower.

This example of "contemporary colonialism," to borrow again Seamus Deane's phrase from chapter 2,[3] is made sense of via the Palestinian novel and its focus on crime, which is the literary form most suited to negotiating the Palestinian situation (Ṭāhā ix). In addition, a focus on Anglophone literature highlights the colonial handover from the British to the Americans: Anglophone writing "will seemingly always be tethered to the legacies of the instrumental roles played by the British Empire and the US in shaping the history and today's circumstances of the Israeli-Palestinian" (Ebileeni

639). In the twentieth century, the novel became a dominant form of Arab writing, and because it as a form is "[preoccupied] with ordinary, everyday, lived experience, it is the form best suited to capture the social imaginary of a whole historical period" (Abu-Manneh 2). The novel, Abu-Manneh continues, can act as "a product of a society in revolt against colonial conquest and expropriation" (19)—in other words, the Palestinian novel can offer up a form of resistance to ongoing imperial regimes, working to enact a type of change in the material reality of many Palestinians.[4]

With the novel situated as a key literary tactic of Palestinian cultural resistance, one might think that the Anglophone Palestinian novel writes towards a clear sense of catharsis, goal, or achievable teleology. Indeed, Bernard Bergonzi writes of the novel that "an expectation of sequaciousness and inevitable forward movement is set up in the reader" (28), which would serve the political goals of the aesthetic object well. This desire for "inevitable forward movement," or a clearly tracked telos (what David Scott calls "that old consoling sense of temporal *concordance*" [*Omens*, 6]), can be difficult to find in Palestinian novels, mirroring the scattered nature of Palestine itself. The occupied territories are not a contiguous space, and the widespread Palestinian diaspora means that it can be more difficult for national imagination to coalesce around a single identifiable geographical understanding. Mourid Barghouti writes of the Palestinian narrator, "He is the one who cannot tell his story in a continuous narrative and lives hours in every moment.... His memory resists ordering" (3-4). This focus on "contingency, chance *peripeteia*, and catastrophe" (David Scott, *Omens*, 2) sets the stage for a focus on tragedy, which as a form "questions ... the view of human history as moving teleologically and transparently toward a determinate end, or as governed by a sovereign and omnisciently rational agent" (David Scott, *Conscripts*, 12). Like in Nairobi, the novels discussed in this chapter challenge any sort of "continuous narrative" or rational teleology—instead, due to Palestinian histories of colonialism and urban space, these narratives are often reliant on the tropes of tragedy, where men and women are asked to "act in a world in which values are unstable and ambiguous" (*Conscripts*, 13). Though Aristotle set up tragedy as the literary form "specifically ... organized in such a way ... to produce a distinctive effect: catharsis" (*Conscripts*, 153), the postcolonial novels of Palestine complicate the option of catharsis in favor of more peripatetic or contingent articulations of criminal cities and crime.

Because of this lack of a clear and trackable geographical space and historical timeline, I argue, much Anglophone Palestinian literature cobbles together disparate and wide-ranging experiences of crime, exile, migration, travel, and absence to present to an English-speaking audience a comprehensible, identifiable whole. Kfir Cohen Lustig writes, "Palestinian novels written in English can be said to be written mostly for the world literary market rather than Palestinians living in Palestine" (240). One of the ways this manifests in reality is through a clear and tangible emphasis on Palestinian displacement and exile; Ghalayini writes, "Absence *generally* is one of the defining features of Palestinian fiction" (xi), and Maurice Ebileeni argues, "It is important to recognize that the ongoing displacement of Palestinians has created diverse geographical, cultural and social settings for the proliferation of their narrative on a global scale" (629). This repeated emphasis on absence, exile, and a multitude of settings helps to emphasize the destruction of the cities of Palestine, the reality of many twenty-first-century Palestinians, and an ongoing attempt on the part of the writers for some kind of catharsis or meaning-making to come of centuries of imperialism, displacement, and catastrophe.

Mourid Barghouti's *I Saw Ramallah* depicts clearly the mourning and melancholia so many feel for a Palestine that is no more. Barghouti, who was studying in Cairo in 1967 during the Six Day War, learned of the fall of Ramallah from the radio: "And from here, from Voice of the Arabs radio station, Ahmad Sa'id tells me that Ramallah is no longer mine and that I will not return to it. The city has fallen.... Displacement is like death" (3). In the 1990s, he is allowed to return to the West Bank after years of forced exile, and he writes of the moment he steps back into Palestine: "And now I pass from my exile to their . . . homeland? My homeland? The West Bank and Gaza? The Occupied Territories? The Areas? Judea and Samari? The Autonomous Government? Israel? Palestine? Is there any other country in the world that so perplexes you with its names? Last time I was clear and things were clear. Now I am ambiguous and vague. Everything is ambiguous and vague" (13). This sense of ambiguity, of a sense of stopped time, of no clearly identifiable goals, means that catharsis, which is necessarily dependent on a type of teleology, can be difficult to achieve in the Palestinian space. Raja Shehadah writes, "I had perceived my life as an ongoing narrative organically linked to the forward march of the Palestinian people toward liberation and freedom from the yoke of occupation. But now I knew this was nothing but a grand delusion" (123). The lack of a "forward march" is linked to how the ravages of imperialism have created the noncontiguous nature of the Palestinian territories, the decentralized Palestinian diaspora, and the difficulty of travel and mobility within Palestine. This lack in turn means that Palestinian literature and novels often force a kind of teleology or momentum to achieve catharsis for readers and characters. Maurice Ebileeni writes that Palestinian diasporas are often presented "as a static outcome of a historical injustice that needs to be undone in order for coming generations to be allowed to move on" (629); the past is articulated as having a direct bearing on the present and future. Catharsis in Palestinian criminal cities and novels must be achieved by looking to the past in search of reparations, and to envision a more just future.

"SCATTERED COMMUNITIES": TWENTIETH-CENTURY HISTORY AND PALESTINE

If we are to trace what imperialism and colonialism have done to Palestine, it is best to sketch out clear historical data. The British Empire took over from the Ottomans in 1920 with the Mandate for Palestine; the terms of this agreement had been agreed upon between French diplomat Francois Georges-Picot and British diplomat Mark Sykes in 1916 when the two split up the Levant between their respective countries in the event of an Allied victory in World War I. Britain desired control of what was then called Palestine (contemporary Israel and the occupied territories) in part because of the commitments made in the Balfour Declaration of 1917, which promised a "national home for the Jewish people" in what we would today call Israel. Early twentieth-century Zionist movements had considered various places for a Jewish state, ranging from South America to eastern Africa. However, with the firm commitment of the British to facilitating Zionist goals in Palestine, the state of Israel was officially created in 1948, with the subsequent Nakba (catastrophe) and creation of millions of Arab refugees and exiles,[5] a situation of exile that persists today.

Twentieth-century Zionism and its creation of the state of Israel can be understood partially as a permutation of Western colonialism. In *The Question of Palestine*, Edward Said notes, "Palestine had always played a special role in the imagination and in the political will of the West, which is where by common agreement modern Zionism also originated" (9). Said goes on to observe of the racial politics of Zionism, Israel, and Palestine, "The Zionist fuses with the White European against the colored Oriental, whose principal political claim seems only to be quantitative (his brute numbers) and otherwise lacking in quality; and the Zionist also—because he 'understands the Eastern mind from within'—represents the Arab, speaks for him, explains him to the European" (28). Zionism, Said concludes, "not only accepted the generic racial concepts of European culture, it also banked on the fact that Palestine was actually peopled not by an advanced but by a backward people, over which it *ought* to be dominant" (81–82). Joe Cleary agrees with Said's assessment of Zionists positioning themselves as a sort of colonial mediator, writing, "Early Zionist leaders deliberately courted first Ottoman and then British imperial support by arguing that a Jewish state in Palestine would serve Western imperial interests in the region" (5). Anna Ball argues that if we are to understand the British Mandate as replacing the Ottoman Empire, then we can also understand Zionism as "a new form of colonialism that replaced the British mandate" (4), and Bernard Regan urges us to keep in mind "the central role that imperialist interests played in shaping the development of British policy in Palestine, and which culminated in the establishment of the Israeli state in 1948" (1).

There is certainly a long chain of imperialism in Palestine, reaching back many centuries, and the indigenous Arab population has been subjected to many injustices from the Ottomans to the British to the Israelis. That said, the current Israeli occupation is not a simple "switch and replace" with earlier British imperialism. The creation of Israel was greatly assisted by the United States, who viewed a Jewish state in the Middle East as a bulwark against the Soviet Union and a key front in the Cold War. It is unlikely that Israel could sustain its occupying force without continual and sustained material support from the United States and, to a lesser extent, other Western powers; in other words, Israel is not a powerful, centralized national empire in the vein of the Ottomans and the British. What exists now in Palestine is a multinational matrix that repeats imperial injustices of the past—what Derek Gregory calls "the colonial present." Gregory argues "the capacities that inhere in the colonial past are routinely reaffirmed and reactivated in the colonial present" (7); what is slightly different from empires of old is the international coalition that "reaffirms and reactivates" such colonial capacities.

It is important to note that the establishment of the state of Israel, as tied up in colonial logics as that establishment was, was still tied inextricably to the legacies of the Holocaust; the state's establishment in 1948 was a mere three years after the genocide of six million European Jews. Yet, mass murder of a population does not give that population carte blanche to enact ethnic cleansing on another group of people; as Edward Said notes in *The Question of Palestine*, it is a "complex irony" that "the classic victims of years of anti-Semitic persecution and the Holocaust have in their new nation become the victimizers of another people, who have become, therefore, the victims of the victims" (xxi). Joe Cleary agrees, arguing, "A persecuted people that flees genocide in one place and is received, whether voluntarily or not, into the homeland of another does not have the right to displace its host community and to establish its own state on its territory" (37). Israel's founding and the ensuing Nakba of the Arab population is a complicated colonial story, but it is one in which a people who had a multitude of crimes committed against them turned around and enacted crimes on a population of people who just happened to be living in a desired space.

For that is what began in the 1940s in earnest and persists through to today: a crime, specifically a crime against humanity, and even more specifically, ethnic cleansing. Ilan Pappé, in his groundbreaking work *The Ethnic Cleansing of Palestine*, refers to the forced killings, exiles, and destructions of 1948 and after as ethnic cleansing, and even more tangibly refers to these campaigns as a "crime" multiple times in the preface to that same book, and even multiple times on the same page:

- It "was a clear-cut case of an ethnic cleansing operation, regarded under international law today as a crime against humanity" (xiii).
- "One such crime has been erased almost totally from the global public memory: the dispossession of the Palestinians in 1948 by Israel. This, the most formative event in the modern history of the land of Palestine, has ever since been systematically denied, and is still today not recognised as an historical fact, let alone acknowledged as a crime that needs to be confronted politically as well as morally" (xiii).
- "Ethnic cleansing is a crime against humanity, and the people who perpetrate it today are considered criminals to be brought before special tribunals" (xiii).

Mourid Barghouti concurs that the Nakba and events after constitutes a crime, writing further, "The Occupation forced us to remain with the old.

That is its crime. It did not deprive us of the clay ovens of yesterday, but of the mystery of what we would invent tomorrow" (69).

What this means is that, in some ways, Palestinians both in Palestine and those exiled from the land, are unable to claim the future for themselves, to look forward to a sense of relief. It is difficult to move forward; there is no immediately identifiable or clear-cut pathway to a catharsis or healing. There are only limited ways to take ownership or lay claim to their own land, their own cities, their own narrative. Raja Shehadah says that one of the ultimate tragedies of Palestine is that it "has been constantly reinvented, with devastating consequences to its original inhabitants. Whether it was the cartographers preparing maps or travelers describing the landscape in the extensive travel literature, what mattered was not the land and its inhabitants as they actually were, but the confirmation of the viewer's or reader's religious or political beliefs" (xiv). There is little space for Palestinians to take ownership of their own narrative; instead, because "the aim of the Zionist project has always been to construct and then defend a 'white' (Western) fortress in a 'black' (Arab) world" (Pappé 253), what exists now in twenty-first-century Palestine is another case of contemporary colonialism, of British legacies intertwining with racist ethnic cleansing interlocking with American foreign policy goals and global proxy conflicts.

One of the most palpable effects of the Occupation has been the control of space and cities, and what that means for Palestinian mobility for those who live in the Occupied Territories. Neve Gordon touches on the issue of limited or impossible mobility for Palestinians in an anecdote about learning to drive in Israel and Palestine in the 1980s. He is telling this story to a class of undergraduates at a university in Israel, and, as he tells it, "It took me a moment before I understood why my story about a few relatively inconsequential incidents at a high school located outside Beer-Sheva had such an effect" among the class (25). "One of my anecdotes," he continues, "was about my classmates who lived in the Jewish settlements located in the northern tip of the Sinai Peninsula" (26). Gordon's classmates did not spend much time thinking about the geopolitical developments happening around them, but "a particular issue that did occupy us . . . was learning to drive," as Gordon puts it (26), and specifically learning to drive in the nearby Palestinian town of Rafah. "My students," Gordon writes, "found this story incomprehensible" (26).

How could this be, Gordon wonders—a simple story about learning to drive being coded as "incomprehensible" by his students? He gradually realizes that "within the current context of the Israeli-Palestinian conflict this act is unfathomable. No taxis from the Occupied Territories are allowed to enter Israel and, even if they had somehow managed to obtain an entry permit, Israeli Jews would be afraid to use them" (26). This spatial segregation, even as the two communities are occupying practically interstitial land, means that "Palestinians from the West Bank are also confined to their villages and towns; however, within this region, Jews, and particularly Jewish settlers, are allowed to travel as they please" (26). As Henri Lefebvre puts it, "We are confronted not by one social space but by many . . . *Social spaces interpenetrate one another and/or superimpose themselves upon one another*" (86, italics original). The social space of Palestine is redolent with political, historical, cultural, and religious meanings, and loaded with different signifiers and meanings for those forced to traverse it in difficult and burdensome ways. Mourid Barghouti laments, "Israel will not let us have sovereignty even over transport. It still controls everything" (141). The difficulty of travel means that Palestine functions essentially as "a system of Palestinian archipelagoes—islands held apart from each other and the wider world—isolated by an elaborate system of infrastructural networks, checkpoints, barriers, and outright closures" (Salamanca 25). Add to this observation the fact that space, as Joseph R. Farag has noted, is a particularly charged concept in Palestine due to the nature of the occupation and the Palestinians being a stateless people, and it becomes clear that space and movement through it is one of the most important elements to parse in both this country and this literature. It is extremely difficult to move *within* Palestine; on the other hand, diasporic movement *out of* Palestine can be comparably easy for those with privilege and access.

Themes of mobility become especially important when considered in the context of Palestinian cities. Zionism modeled its cities in what would eventually become Israel on "European urban ideals," constructed with the goal of "changing the face of the land" (Albert 437). For this type of city planning to take root, Zionism and the Occupation had to engage in what Nurhan Abujidi refers to as "urbicide," or "the killing of cities or the destruction of the urban" (23); Stephen Graham says the objective of this form of murder is to "deny the Palestinian people their collective, individual, and cultural rights to the city-based modernity long enjoyed by the Israelis" (642). Of course, this is at least partly because any dense population of the oppressed represents a threat; as anyone who has seen *The Battle of Algiers* knows, cities represent excellent places for resistors to colonial rule to lose themselves in the crowd, become anonymous, and continue their work pushing back against imperial rule.

As Israel continues to build settlements, criminal cities in their own rights that borrow from the American and European molds like Americanesque "white flight" patterns and "fortification behind protective walls" (Weizman 10), the concurrent effect on Palestinian urban life has been devastating. According to Derek Gregory, "Palestinian towns and cities . . . have been smashed by Israeli missiles and bombs, by tanks and armored bulldozers. The objective is to suppress what Henri Lefebvre called 'the right to the city' through a campaign of coerced de-modernization" (131). Mourid Barghouti articulates this loss by writing, "Our hatred of the Occupation is essentially because it arrests the growth of our cities, of our societies, of our lives. It hinders their natural development" (117). The criminal cities of Israel and of settlement push into what are *perceived* as the criminal cities of Palestine; it is necessary, however, to flip the representational script and point out that Palestinian urban life is not inherently criminal, and that the crime being committed is the one of Israeli-led ethnic cleansing, urbicide, and forced exile.

Though many actions undertaken by the state of Israel and its agents are violent, unjust, and criminal when viewed through a human rights standpoint, they are often not held to account in Israel/Palestine itself; indeed, the scales seem heavily weighted the other way, toward treating Palestinians as criminals. Neve Gordon, when writing about extrajudicial killings carried out by IDF soldiers, articulates this in terms of the value of human life: "The fact that not one Israeli soldier has been tried for these killings," he writes, "and that they are part of an overt policy suggests that some of the occupied inhabitants have been reduced to what the Italian political philosopher Giorgio Agamben has called *homo sacer,* people who can be killed without it being considered a crime" (37). This is in line with Achille Mbembe's theory of necropolitics, which states in part that the idea that "the ultimate expression of sovereignty resides, to a large degree, in the power and the capacity to dictate who may live and who must die" (11). "The most accomplished form of necropower," he writes, "is the contemporary colonial occupation of Palestine" (27). Israel's criminal actions are rarely held to account; this is part of the power of using crime in Palestinian literature, to highlight how these frameworks are used to advantage certain populations and disadvantage others, which almost always fall along racial and ethnic lines.[6]

In light of these narratives about crime—who commits it and who benefits from it—catharsis could serve several useful functions, from providing a cultural outlet for spreading the word about injustice to changing the international narrative about the colonial situation of Palestine to creating the conditions for a collective push for material support and solidarity. Yet, the decentralized nature of the Palestinian community, both inside and outside of the Occupied Territories, makes it hard to formulate the teleology or narrative on which catharsis depends. According to Joe Cleary, "The crux of the problem for Palestinians, however, is that the oppressive conditions that generate a distinctive sense of Palestinian national consciousness among these scattered communities are not necessarily those that allow for the translation of that consciousness into a collective project of state formation. Where a subject people live in a contiguous national territory controlled by a foreign occupier, national consciousness can be directed towards expelling the occupier and building an independent state on that territory" (186). Keeping in mind that "in this context [of Zionism], space becomes paramount, because it provides a concrete, achievable goal" (Abujidi 53), it becomes evident that space, and particularly cities and urban life, hold the key to any kind of aesthetic literary Palestinian catharsis; the need to reclaim space, to form a continuous narrative on the ground, translates into cathartic and continual narrative on the page. Hala Alyan's *Salt Houses* utilizes Palestinian narratives of urban life, diaspora, exile, the Nakba, intercity travel, and displacement to underscore the difficulties of catharsis, utilizing crime and injustice as ways to frame her story.

"A WOUND NEVER COMPLETELY SCABBED OVER": HALA ALYAN'S *SALT HOUSES*

Hala Alyan's 2017 novel *Salt Houses* traces the history of the Yacoub family over four generations, told in a series of vignettes by rotating members of the family. The Yacoubs, displaced from Jaffa in the Nakba, land first in Nablus, then spread from there to Jordan, Kuwait City, Beirut, Paris, and Boston as the years go on. This city-based diaspora considers several different kinds of urban life, from ancient cities like Nablus to twentieth-century creations like Kuwait City to Western spaces like Paris and Boston. As each generation migrates to somewhere new and forms their own lives in the diaspora, they are haunted by the events of 1967, when Mustafa Yacoub, a young man in the second generation of this narrative, was accused of some nebulous crime by the Israelis, thrown into jail, and killed; the family never knows the exact details, and the lack of concrete information haunts them over the decades. This yawning vacuum shapes everyone's lives for generations to come, the creation and deployment of the concept of crime against Mustafa affecting the family for years in a kind of domino effect. This is, of course, in light of the multiple crimes carried out against the Palestinian people that the Yacoubs witness from the Nakba of 1947 to a return to Palestine in 2014; the immense scale of these crimes against humanity highlights the heartbreaking nature of Mustafa's arrest and murder.

The Yacoubs, though forced into exile and generations of displacement, are a comparably well-off and privileged family: their main mobility concerns are less about restricted movement within Palestine than about forced movement out of it. The matriarch, Salma, thinks to herself, "Widad and Alia and Mustafa [her children], they might have known gunfire and war, but they were protected from it with the armor of wealth. It is what separates them from the refugees in the camps dotting the outskirts of Nablus" (11). Ilana Masad in the *Los Angeles Review of Books* writes that the Yacoubs "are not the refugees or working poor that we often imagine when we think of the uprooted; these are people who may have left land behind but whose bank accounts are not depleted. This makes a great difference in the way her [Alyan's] story can move forward as well as which parts of the tale she chooses to tell." This ability for the narrative to "move forward"—that is, explore various cities over multiple time periods, tracking the reaction of each new generation to the events of the past along the way—allows the Yacoub family to work through and negotiate their pain and trauma along the way to catharsis, options that would look very different if this story was told by a family who had lived for generations in the same refugee camp in Jordan or Lebanon. Alyan is able to play with how crime is constructed and narrativized in order to point the reader's attention to injustices in the contemporary colonialism in the criminal cities of Palestine.

Readers do not encounter the Yacoub family before or during the Nakba. The first vignette, told by Salma, takes place in 1963 in the West Bank city of Nablus, which, as we have already seen, holds great resonance both for the British Empire and for Palestine and Arab nationalism. The family fled from Jaffa to Nablus after the Nakba, when the West Bank was occupied by Jordan rather than Israel. Nevertheless, Salma's children have still had run-ins with the occupying Israeli forces in this city of Arab nationalism, as when her son Mustafa and his friend Atef "were arrested at a demonstration in Jerusalem. In another time, their offense might have earned them a fine, merely a court-issued warning. Instead, both Atef and Mustafa were kept in the penitentiary for four nights" (18). Salma's understanding that the Israelis have constructed the concept of crime arbitrarily in ways that benefit them—she notes that the punishment for their "crime" changes on the needs of the occupiers—underscores how crime is utilized to prop up the regime of the colonizers, to re-create colonial conditions earlier established by the Ottomans and the British.

This first brush with the law represents an initial rupture in the Yacoub family. Mustafa's sister, Alia, marries Atef, and the three of them remain very close throughout their young adulthood in Nablus. However, Mustafa notices a slight cooling on Alia's part after he and Atef are arrested for the first time, and chalks it up to her exclusion from their involvement in the Palestinian independence movement: "He knows she resents it," he thinks, "the exclusions, being left in the dark, kept away from a part of her brother's and her husband's lives. Especially after the prison" (29). The "crime" the two have committed, and their subsequent punishment for it, looms large over the family, and particularly within the Mustafa/Atef/Alia generation, demonstrating that crime, as defined and determined by those with power, has the ability to highlight existing tensions—among genders, among family members, among generations—helping to "divide and conquer" the colonized, that old imperial technique.

Though Mustafa and Atef return home after their first arrest and imprisonment, they are not so lucky the second time. Almost immediately after the start of the 1967 Six Day War, Mustafa and Atef "had been arrested soon after the Israeli invasion of Nablus, the fifth day of the war, and swept up along with dozens of their neighbors, men from the mosque, cousins. The charges were spurious and arbitrary: organizing protests, pamphlet distribution, inciting violence. *Planning infiltration* was the charge for him and Mustafa" (79). The two young men appear to have committed no real crime; they attend services at a mosque known for political rhetoric and organizing, but there is no evidence that there is justification in detaining them. Atef is eventually freed, but "they never found out how [Mustafa] had died, just that he had, somewhere in an Israeli prison" (66). Mustafa's declaration by the Israeli state as a *homo sacer* erases the crime of the Israelis and forces instead the figure of the Palestinian criminal into the forefront; the necropower of the Israeli state, and the lack of any attempt to hold their soldiers responsible for the crime of Mustafa's death, highlight the colonial nature of the Israeli occupation of Palestine. Atef, predictably and tragically, blames himself for his friend's death, and his resulting trauma and what seems to be PTSD make it difficult for him to move on, to accept personal changes in his life and political changes in the life of his country. Without the ability to come to terms with what has happened, he is unable to achieve any kind of catharsis; the cathartic possibilities of crime are not available to him, as he seems stuck in the moment in which the crime occurred. The contingency, the chance, of being in a particular place at a particular time plots out the rest of his life as a type of tragedy, though one that cannot provide the "distinctive effect" (David Scott, *Conscripts*, 153) of catharsis.

"'It's like a shadow life,' Atef once tried to explain to the doctor. 'Like there's another me, and that me is still stuck, like a skipping record'" (79). That version of Atef seems to be left behind in Nablus, even after he and Alia relocate to Kuwait City (another place once formerly under the rule of the British Empire). Alia despises Kuwait, wishing to move to Amman, where they know many members of the Palestinian exiled community. Atef, however, accepts a position at the university in Kuwait, essentially consigning him and his family to permanent residence; it is strongly implied that Atef would find it too painful to move to Jordan, with all the attendant memories that being among the diasporic Nabulsis would dredge up. His attempt to move on, to leave the past behind, paradoxically leaves him stuck in the past, unable to shake his "shadow life," or his past self that still yearns to be with Mustafa.

Compare this to Alia, his wife, who is notorious for her rage and her ability to deploy it with only the slightest provocation. Yelling at her youngest daughter, Souad, for coming home after curfew, she views her rage as a kind of release: "There is immense relief in yelling" (142), she thinks. "Her entire life," she muses, "she has been denied a good fight" (144). Alia's anger and her need to find an outlet for it have their roots in the disappearance of Mustafa and the subsequent transformation of her husband; she wants to yell, she has immense anger at the arbitrary nature of the crime and the unjust nature of Mustafa's death, but she has nowhere for that anger to go, and it finds inappropriate targets that do very little for helping Alia achieve a well-adjusted and healthy catharsis.

Part of the rage Alia experiences has to do with how much she hates Kuwait, the new home to where she has been forced to flee after the Israelis occupied her home of Nablus.[7] The movement the Yacoub family is allowed between cities is in stark contrast to how movement is restricted back in the Palestinian territories; the way the Yacoub family moves to many different cities but consistently thinks of Palestine reflects what Steven Salaita says is "a recent trend in Palestinian literature: writing rooted in diasporic countries but focused in theme and content on Palestine" (46). This type of movement, *among* countries rather than the limited and difficult attempts at mobility *within* Palestine itself, highlights how "diasporic space haunts the (post)colonial Palestinian imagination. Millions of Palestinians have endured conditions of displacement, refugeeism, migration and exile as a result of Palestine's traumatic colonial history, and those within the Palestinian diaspora testify to the simultaneously spatial and political dispossession of their nation" (Ball 131). Alia's forced diaspora makes her absolutely miserable. Though she cannot return to Palestine under any circumstances, she longs to move to the closest analogue, Amman, pleading with her husband, "Instead of staying in Kuwait's wasteland, the endless afternoons of television and heat, let them go to Amman, the coffee shops and vendors hawking fruit, neighborhoods filled with old friends" (59). Alia despises the recent creation of Kuwait, hates its gleaming and (to her) artificial nature; she remembers her older sister, Widad, telling her "stories about the Bedouin, how a mere thirty, forty years ago, none of this had existed, none of the villa compounds or courtyards or even the pearl-hued mosques" (74). Hearing these stories, "Alia feels a pang of sorrow for the older generation, the men and women who still remember the desert before all the construction" (74). The newness of Kuwait is an affront to her; she wishes to go somewhere with what she views as a past, a history, something to root herself in to work through her pain over Mustafa and their exile.

Atef feels extremely differently; he adores the newness of Kuwait. He tries to imagine the development of the city in his mind: "In Atef's imaginary photographs, the transformation is astonishing. In the beginning, a stark desert, the landscape sparsely decorate with industrial buildings and compounds. And then, *whoosh*, years pass and things begin to crop up—restaurants, Indian, Pakistani, Lebanese, with bright signs; the newer mosques; the billboards cautiously advertising toothpaste and banks; and slowly, the cranes and concrete pillars, dunes of sand turned into construction sites" (85). What Alia views as falseness, as loss, Atef sees as exciting, as an opportunity for a new start. He loves going to the market, "a place where nobody wanted anything from him except coins" (85). He revels in the transactional nature of the place, eschewing Alia's vision of Amman and the tight-knit community that awaits them there; going back, inserting himself back into his past, would force him to encounter daily the wound of Mustafa's death, and the related notions of crime, culpability, and loss of land that go along with the murder. Atef is comfortable in Kuwait because of its dissimilarities to Palestine, and this particular urban space seemingly fits his needs well, though in the long run, it simply allows him to hide from the past without ever really or fully confronting it.[8]

Near the end of Alia and Atef's lives, Alia gets her wish and they move to Amman. Alia soon falls ill, and continues to decline with what the book suggests is Alzheimer's. As Atef reflects back on their lives, and the many cities they have lived in and homes they have had, he realizes he still has no concrete grasp on the past: "The houses float up to his mind's eye like jinn, past lovers. The sloping roof of his mother's hut, the marbled tiles in Salma's kitchen, the small house he shared with Alia in Nablus. The Kuwait home. The Beirut apartments. This house, here in Amman, for Alia, some old, vanished house in Jaffa. They glitter whitely in his mind, like structures made of salt, before a tidal wave comes and sweeps them away" (273). The unreal nature of these homes for Atef is in direct contrast to how Alyan wrote her novel. In an interview with Amy Shearn, Alyan says, "I made a point of not writing about any cities that I haven't physically walked around myself. In the course of writing this book, I tried to pay extra attention to things like sounds and smells, to how it felt to navigate streets at different times of day." The way Alyan clearly grounds her writing in material reality, compared to Atef's refusal to fully confront the same, indicates the lack of catharsis in Atef's life; still in the past, still thinking about Mustafa and his murder, still stuck in colonial logics of crime, he can only view his houses as salt that can so easily be swept away. Though he moves with ease among international cities, he cannot put himself on the ground in Palestine. The way crime has functioned in his life—even though it has played such a central role—has not offered any catharsis.

Most of the novel takes place in these diasporic cities, but the final vignette, told by Manar of the fourth generation, sees her go back to Palestine, and Jaffa in particular, to discover her roots and her heritage. A child of exile and the diaspora who has moved among Europe, America, and the Middle East her whole life, she encounters the infamous difficulty of mobility in Palestine, calling the West Bank separation wall "a menace, always jolting her freshly when it appears" (282). She is fully aware her travel is easier than it is for most people of Palestinian heritage, because she has an American passport: "*The passport is my key,*" she writes to her brother at one point (282), highlighting the import and power of the American Empire. Though Manar is aware of the difficulties of movement for the average Palestinian, she is still one degree removed from that, with her lifetime of travel among different cities and her passport issued by one of the countries helping to prop up the Israeli occupation. She is as removed from the physical reality of Palestine as Atef, in a different way but ultimately with the same root causes. Her grandmother's generation saw the transition from the Ottomans to the British, her parents' the British to the Israeli, and now she is part of a colonial matrix of Israel and the United States.

When Manar is in Palestine, she realizes that "Palestine was something raw in the family, a wound never completely scabbed over" (281). The loss of Mustafa so many years ago telescopes out to be about so much more: the loss of home, the forced exile, the rupture of family and community. The unrepaired nature of these traumas, the lack of reparation for the crimes, means that no one in the family has been able to experience catharsis for their troubles; though Mustafa was murdered for his supposed crimes, no one has held Israel or its soldiers to account for the crimes committed against the Palestinians. Cathartic crime is not held out as an option; rather, the crimes in the novel spool out unreparated and, to a large extent, unacknowledged.

Manar comforts herself in this moment by trying to think of history as a cycle. "It fascinates Manar," Alyan writes, "not just history in general, with its empires, collapse, and revivals, but also the faint, persistent echoes that seem to travel through the millennia. Land eaten and reshuffled, homes taken—daughters and sons speaking enemy languages, forgetting their own—the belief that we are owed something by the cosmos" (293). Though this seems to help Manar, personally, process what her family has been through, no one else seems to be able to find this level of comfort, nor are they able to revisit Palestine and encounter the land in the way she is, either. Communal catharsis is not possible for the Yacoubs, at least in this moment.

Some kind of catharsis through crime might seem to be possible for the reader, however, someone who can view the story of the Yacoubs from the outside as a consistent whole, rather than the characters who live fragmented and individual lives, scattered through several global cities. Alyan tells Amy Shearn, "I kept telling myself I was just writing a series of stories, only to discover it was a coherent narrative by the end." On the other hand, the Yacoubs, with such physical distance between them, seem unable to knit their experiences together and instead live in loosely connected short stories; Alyan, however, takes these disjointed vignettes and weaves them together to make a whole. Individual Yacoub family members are a kind of stand-in for the "scattered" nature of the Palestinian people themselves; without any kind of cohesive goal, space, or location to coalesce around, "the freedom and autonomy of the private individual can now be achieved irrespective of the freedom of the Palestinian people" (Cohen Lustig 227). The focus, especially in an Anglophone novel geared toward Western readers,[9] shifts to the liberal Western individual and eventually nuclear family, rather than any kind of communal or organized anticolonial resistance; this means that though individual catharsis for characters or readers might be possible, the sheer difficulty of organizing a clear community narrative in a diasporic, neoliberal world makes catharsis for Palestinians who have suffered nearly unimaginable crimes to be practically impossible. The lack of a focal point or inability to focus on a specific city in *Salt Houses* reflects the difficult nature of Palestinian political goals; what should justice look like? How do we envision it, in an age of diaspora, limited mobility within Palestine, lack of reparation for the past, and continuing colonial crime against an oppressed population? Does the nation-state formulation make any sense? Is such a goal achievable, or desirable? What is possible, what is the goal, what could lead to catharsis? *Salt Houses* offers a solution for Manar, a young twenty-first-century American woman of Palestinian descent; it is, however, silent on what wide-ranging liberation for Palestine might look like.

The difficulty of catharsis, especially as related to crime, in the Palestinian context is closely related to mobility. Keeping in mind that "mobility seems self-evidently central to Western modernity" (Cresswell 15), and that "modern metropolitan cultures privilege their own mobility" (Gregory 257), what does this look like when one of Israel's key tactics of control is to keep

Palestinians locked in particular spaces, cutting them off from modernity's emphasis on mobility? Relatedly, what does it mean when mobility is *forced*, as in the case of the Yacoub family? Mourid Barghouti writes of a trip he took with other members of his family to Switzerland, in which they gave their passports to a policeman and he saw "an amazing sight: in his hands were passports from all over the world—Jordan, Syria, the United States, Algeria, Britain, and even Belize—and the names in all of them showed that their holders were from one family: all Barghoutis" (139). What this policeman may have viewed as cosmopolitanism or global sophistication was, in fact, evidence of a family forced into exile and displacement; what are we to do when this is not desired, what kinds of goals are achievable when one nation is scattered without full consent from the Middle East to Europe to Central America and beyond? If, in light of this diaspora, oppression continues in Israel with the help of the United States,[10] and "Gaza and the West Bank—the tattered remnants of Palestine—are placed under erasure within the dominant American and Israeli imaginaries" (Gregory 140), what space is there to imagine something new?

Hannah Arendt wrote over half a century ago in *The Origins of Totalitarianism* that "the solution of the Jewish question [the creation of the state of Israel] merely produced a new category of refugees, the Arabs" (290), further noting, "The Rights of Man, supposedly inalienable, proved to be unenforceable . . . whenever people appeared who were no longer citizens of any sovereign state" (293). Nurhan Abujidi underscores Arendt's point, noting "The Nakba of 1948 and the Naksah of 1967 generated the largest and longest-lasting refugee problems in the world" (47). Does a nation-state formation for Palestine make any sense? Is this an outmoded political goal? What would need to be reparated before such a thing could even be thought, or before new imaginaries for the future could begin to take shape?

Mourid Barghouti laments his own people's treatment of Palestinian refugees, grieving, "How can we explain today, now that we have grown older and wiser, that we on the West Bank treated our people as refugees? Yes, our own people, banished by Israel from their coastal cities and villages in 1948, our people who had to move from one part of the homeland to another and came to live in our cities and towns, we called them refugees! We called them immigrants! Who can apologize to them? Who can apologize to us? Who can explain this great confusion to whom?" (41). As Barghouti goes on to say, "Do I have a problem with '67? Yes, I have a problem. The defeat of

June is not over" (174). Beyond the scattered and decentralized nature of the Palestinian community, it's difficult to conceive of a common political goal, as Edward Said noted in 1979: "The present time impresses upon the Arab world a need to ask *what sort of liberation* it struggles for (or even if liberation is what is being struggled for) as well as what Arabs are to do when they are 'liberated'" (186). There is no catharsis; the crime, the tragedy, the narrative, is still ongoing, in both the literature and the politics.

Part of the blame can be placed back in earlier colonial logics, and these logics have created even further problems. With the Nakba and the creation of the Arab refugee crisis, a commensurate crisis of mobility assembled; these "colonial legacies of fragmented sovereignty and borders have left a highly variegated terrain of social protection and vulnerability," Mimi Sheller writes (xi). Though the Nakba is the most immediate causes of these issues of mobility and exile, the crimes visited upon the Palestinian people have deeper roots, back in at least the early twentieth century with, most notably, Sykes-Picot. The catastrophes created by Sykes-Picot had ramifications beyond Palestine, helping to create one of the most visible catastrophes of the twenty-first century. Shashi Tharoor writes, "The Sykes-Picot Agreement of 1916, by which the British and the French agreed to carve up the former Ottoman territories between themselves and which set the boundaries between independent Syria and Iraq, is another relic of colonial history that haunts us today. For when ISIS ('Daesh') advanced ruthlessly in those countries, it railed against the iniquities of that Anglo-French agreement and avowed its determination to reverse the Sykes-Picot legacy—making the imperial era compellingly current once more" (288). Sykes-Picot and the British Empire, such destructive forces in Palestine, are also closely linked to the contemporary refugee crisis and its connections to ISIS. In the brief coda, we will keep a focus on international forced mobility, and what one of the most pressing political issues of the first decades of the twenty-first century has to do with cathartic crime.

CODA

EXIT WEST, BREXIT, AND MIGRATION

In 2014 the Islamic State of Syria and Iraq (ISIS)[1] published a video titled "The End of Sykes-Picot" on one of its propaganda websites. This video, which also serves as the group's announcement of its goal to build and sustain an Islamic empire known as the Caliphate in the Levant, shows group members destroying—literally bulldozing—what they view as the artificial border between Iraq (a British colony under Sykes-Picot) and Syria (delegated to the French under the same agreement). By identifying Sykes-Picot (1916) as a pivotal moment in the history of the Levant, ISIS is holding Western imperialists of a century ago responsible for much, if not all, of the tumult and political instability present in the Arab and Muslim world, even as ISIS pursued imperialist goals of its own via the dream of the Caliphate.[2]

Western powers drawing lines in the sand and creating nations out of basically thin air is hardly a new criticism, but it is remarkable that Sykes-Picot has taken on such power in ISIS mythology. Because ISIS and its associated terror is such a large part of the twenty-first century's "refugee crisis," as it has been termed by the Western media,[3] it's notable that the terror group has identified Sykes-Picot, which created nations and national identity where there once were neither of these things, as the key motivator for their own grievances and future goals. Sykes-Picot made "Iraqis" and "Syrians" where once there were villages, tribes, and other non-national forms of belonging. ISIS would like to return to a notion of pan-Muslim unity (though through a twisted, violent, massively destructive lens, of course, which simultaneously flattens out many of the rivalries and tensions that existed in the area prior to 1916); along the way and in pursuit of this goal, they have made many people stateless, refugees, migrants with no nation-state to call their own. Hannah Arendt correctly identified that the formation of Israel, an after-effect of Sykes-Picot, "merely produced a new category of refugees, the Arabs," and that this phenomenon was "then repeated in India on a larger scale involving many millions of people" (290). If Sykes-Picot and then the Nakba were the initial dominos that led to the current refugee crisis in the Middle East, Partition and its forced movements did the same for the rise of contemporary Hindu fundamentalism and its associated narrow definitions of who is a citizen of India, events which have led to bloodshed and forced movements of their own. All these events were constructed by the British Empire, and all have meant that in the twenty-first century our refugee discourses are still reliant on centuries-old European notions of the nation-state, as well as constituted by the crimes of colonialism.

Claire Gallien has pointed out that "the term 'refugee' is an occidental construction used to refer negatively to a person who has lost the protection of his/her own country and been forced into border-crossing" (739). While this is true, I use "refugee" as my chosen term in this coda because it is so popularly accepted, and because it is a word Mohsin Hamid's *Exit West* (2017), the core text of this coda, uses frequently, along with "migrant." It also translates across time and space relatively well, which is important as we have seen the (tenuously based) fears of crime refugees engender elsewhere in this book, most notably with the *Makwerekwere* in *Welcome to Our Hillbrow* and the Partition narratives in *Sacred Games*. Even if the imperially defined nation-state is losing the relevance it once had, it is undeniable that membership in a nation-state, or citizenship, is a key requirement of twenty-first-century society, and those without power who are most (involuntarily) mobile are those who are most at risk of being punished for trumped-up criminal charges, being labeled criminals for existing in the wrong place, or being scapegoated for the crimes of others.[4]

Refugees are, generally, extremely mobile—they must move from place to place, whether because of economic necessity, political instability, forced exile, or the threat of violence. Upon arrival in new places, their presence is often criminalized ("illegal aliens"), or they find themselves at the center of an irrational hysteria about crimes being committed on the "host country's" soil. (See former President Trump's invented panics about "angel families," drug smuggling, and his infamous campaign announcement about Mexican immigrants: "They're bringing drugs. They're bringing crime. They're rapists. And some, I assume, are good people.") This makes a city-centric text about refugees a salient end to a book that has been concerned above all with crime in the city, and secondarily with mobility. Tim Creswell writes, "The slippery and intangible nature of mobility makes it an elusive object of study. Yet study it we must for mobility is central to what it is to be human. It is a fundamental geographical fact of existence and, as such, provides a rich terrain from which narratives—and, indeed, ideologies—can be, and have been, constructed" (1). Mobility, and its entanglement with discourses of crime and Enlightenment rationality, forms the backbone of a number of narratives and ideologies explored within the contemporary novel.

So what narratives and ideologies have been constructed out of forced mobility and its association with crime? This coda will look at *Exit West* as an early example of a transnational novel concerned with the contemporary refugee crisis (beginning in roughly 2015). Hamid's novel, notably, is heavily focused on cities, from the unnamed home city in the Middle East or South Asia to a tent city in Greece to London to a new city north of San Francisco. *Exit West* is not primarily concerned with nations, as many refugee narratives are; it is concerned with cities, and what happens in them in an age of refuge-seeking, criminal panics, and migration. These "criminal cities" of empire, scattered across the globe, provide rich sites for explorations of cathartic crime in Hamid's novel, focused as they are on issues of religious extremism, hostility to refugees, economic inequality, and histories of settler colonialism.

Exit West, published in 2017, is the first major Anglophone novel to take on the contemporary migrant and refugee crisis, making it a work of the moment that Alexandra Alter of the *New York Times* calls "ominously relevant." Jia Tolentino, who calls the work "instantly canonical" in the *New Yorker*, says that the novel "rewrites the world as a place thoroughly, gorgeously, and permanently overrun by refugees and migrants." Michiko Kakutani writes that the world in *Exit West* "is, in many respects, an extrapolation of the world we live in now, with wars like the one in Syria turning cities into war zones; with political crises, warp-speed technological changes, and growing tensions between nativists and migrants threatening to upend millions of lives." According to *Slate*'s Isaac Chotiner, the novel is "eerily in tune with these bleak times," while Viet Thanh Nguyen writes that *Exit West* is the latest entry in Hamid's oeuvre that asks the reader to think about how "East and West inevitably meet as a consequence of complicated histories of colonization and globalization." *Exit West*, with its ability to tap into a global contemporary humanitarian concern, works as a fictional exploration of how contemporary issues might link up with past imperial legacies.

Exit West is first and foremost the story of Nadia and Saeed, two lovers in an unnamed country—Chotiner thinks Pakistan, while I suspect a speculative future Jordan[5]—whose lives are upended when their country, long a haven for refugees from other surrounding countries, erupts in a civil war of its own, making the city of both their births too dangerous for continued habitation. A far-right fundamentalist religious group strongly reminiscent of ISIS soon makes the city, already dangerous, practically uninhabitable. Nadia and Saeed manage to escape through magical realist doors, which are scattered through the city seemingly at random to allow people to escape to various points in the Western world, encountering various forms of "natives"[6] in their respective landing places.

Nadia and Saeed first land in Mykonos, Greece, alongside several other refugees from around the world. Their first place of refuge on a Greek isle mirrors our own world's realities, as many rafts of desperate humans wash up on Greek and Italian shores from the Middle East and North Africa (of course, many also drown en route). However, Nadia and Saeed's travels sharply differ from the experiences of refugees in our own world, in that they are able to simply step through doors to reach their destinations. This reliance on magical realism erases the hard work of travel and forced mobility that so many refugees are forced to go through; it takes away the opportunity for catharsis, both for the characters and for the reader, due to the "blink and you'll miss it" structure of the travel. By being in one place one second and a totally different place the next, and not experiencing or depicting the dangerous overland and sea journeys so many refugees are forced to take, *Exit West* evades the harder mobility-related questions about what being a refugee entails; Saeed and Nadia move through the process too quickly to fully process what has happened, and the (likely) Western reader is not asked to confront some of the more disturbing scenarios that occur when "exiting west."

That said, their time on the ground is not easy, and soon their experience in the refugee camp city becomes a limbo. With Saeed and Nadia's funds running low, and no apparent forward momentum in their lives, they decide to find a way to a new door, to a new place. After locating one in Mykonos, they emerge in a sleek, ultramodern bedroom, which they first take to be a hotel, but later realize is an enormous vacant home in Kensington and Chelsea,[7] a wealthy part of London.[8] The two almost immediately get to work "transforming this narrow bedroom, at least partially, temporarily, into a home" (124), putting into praxis Homi Bhabha's call for a postcolonial "poetics of relocation and reinscription" (323). They are to begin the next stage of their lives in a London forced to reconcile with its imperial past coming home to roost in the form of refugees from all over the empire—Nadia and Saeed's particular neighborhood is mostly populated by Nigerians—which leads to the kind of welcome one might expect from the native Britons. The police are called on the refugee settlement, and uneasiness surrounds the neighborhood as the refugees' presence continues to be criminalized; this continues until the authorities cut the power in Kensington and Chelsea, a clear signal to the refugees that they are not wanted or considered to be part of the life of the city.

Once the electricity is cut, the London of *Exit West* alludes to Fanon's colonial city, a schematic that was dissected in this book's introduction. The "native" parts of the city continue to have sufficient light, while in places where refugees and migrants congregate, it remains very dark.[9] Though "in the odd building here and there . . . an enterprising migrant had rigged together a connection to a still-active high-voltage line" (145), the Manichean structure largely holds throughout the city, leading to a binary structure of "dark London" and "light London." Saeed and Nadia's ruminations on the subject echo Fanon's formulation: "From dark London, Saeed and Nadia wondered what life must be like in light London, where they imagined people dined in elegant restaurants and rode in shiny black cabs, or at least went to work in offices and shops and were free to journey about as they pleased. In dark London, rubbish accrued, uncollected, and underground stations were sealed" (146). Compare this to Fanon's colonizer's city, which "is a sector built to last, all stone and steel. It's a sector of lights and paved roads, where the trash cans constantly overflow with strange and wonderful garbage, undreamed-of leftovers" (4). By contrast, the "native" quarters, or the colonized section of the city, "is a disreputable place inhabited by disreputable people.... It's a world with no space, people are piled on top of one another, the shacks squeezed tightly together" (4). This original Fanonian criminal city has never been reparated, though it has been flipped or twisted in a way: now the British "natives" live in the light, while the more recent postcolonial arrivals, some in neighborhoods understood to be very wealthy, live in the dark. The lack of infrastructural upkeep speaks to how the refugees have been treated since arrival in Britain; their very presence is criminalized, and they are not allowed to take part in the life of the city. They are constantly set apart, made to be Other. Even more alarmingly, soon Saeed and Nadia and their fellow refugees must deal with what is called a "nativist mob" (134), who carry out hate crimes and violent attacks in a manner familiar to anyone who watched the run-up and aftermath of Brexit.

The mob claims that it wishes to "reclaim Britain for Britain" (135), rhetoric similar to the Brexit campaigners' "Take Back Control," Donald Trump's "Make American Great Again," or Narendra Modi's pointed comments and legislation indicating India is for Hindus. Nadia and Saeed learn that "military and paramilitary formations had fully mobilized and deployed in the city from all over the country" (161), in both a return to older colonial logics of occupation as well as a frightening foreshadowing of violence ahead. These troops perform an "operation to clear the migrant ghetto" (162), which, predictably, ends in much violence and death, though Nadia and Saeed are able to remain safe.

After the government-sponsored pogrom, peace uneasily returns to the city, but the migrants are forced into "the formerly protected greenbelt around London," where "a ring of new cities was being built, cities that would be able to accommodate more people than London itself" (169). They are no longer on the metaphorical outskirts of city life, but literally and physically on the margins, removed from the central location of Kensington and Chelsea. Saeed and Nadia find themselves here, working on infrastructural projects—Saeed on a road crew, Nadia lays pipe—but they remained largely unhappy in London, partly due to their circumstances but also because their relationship is crumbling. The two decide to go through the doors one more time and end up in a new city north of San Francisco, called Marin (after the wealthy county that exists in our present), that is almost entirely populated by migrants and refugees. Marin is marked by "a spirit of at least intermittent optimism that refused entirely to die" (194), due perhaps to its lack of violence, its oceanic views, or "because of the mix of its people" (195), as

Marin is populated by a wide mix of refugees and migrants, as well as lifelong Californians.

Here, at last, Saeed and Nadia are able to attain a measure of happiness, in this formerly exceedingly wealthy suburban area that has transformed into a place "gorgeously and permanently overrun" (Tolentino) by newcomers, upending capitalist logics to institute their own kind of city, idyllic in its own right and built to resist imperial legacies that make places into criminal cities. Marin is a bit like a more successful revisioning of Kensington and Chelsea—a wealthy, white area that is inhabited and transformed by postcolonial refugees and migrants. There is even an attempt at a rebuke to the settler colonialism that has scarred so many North American cities; though most "natives . . . [had] died out or been exterminated long ago" (197), there is a space for remaining Native Americans in Marin, who tell tales that "felt appropriate to this time of migration, and gave listeners much-needed sustenance" (197). Marin seems to be an attempt at creating a new kind of city out of imperial flows—there are Black Americans, Native Americans, and newer postcolonial migrants—but one that resists imperial logics, one that tries to upend the narratives of crime that have marked so many colonial and postcolonial cities.

Saeed and Nadia each eventually find a form of catharsis and peace—Nadia in Marin, Saeed by moving back to the city of their birth—but neither are able to attain it in London, the place where this empire and this study both began. Perhaps this is because, in large part, Britain has not been able to move on from its own "postcolonial melancholia," as Paul Gilroy terms the country's inability to come to terms with the end of empire. Danny Dorling and Sally Tomlinson link Brexit, the logics of which are clearly visible in *Exit West*, with Britain's imaginings of its past imperial glories, calling the event "the end of Empire," and noting, "In the near future the EU referendum will become widely recognised and understood as part of the last vestiges of empire working their way out of the British psyche" (3). That may be, but even if the British Empire is entering its "last gasp" stage, I am not optimistic about its chances for being completely over; we only have to witness the wreckage and crimes it has left in its wake, from Saeed and Nadia's unnamed city of origin to the cities tracked in this study, among many others. Even if the British Empire, or a less-formal version of empire like that identified by Michael Hardt and Antonio Negri is no more, logics of empire live on in rhetorics of crime, as well as material and imaginative concepts of mobility, not least in the forced migration of many who do not wish to leave their cities of origin and in the criminalization of their presence once they have reached the former seat of empire, these criminal cities.[10] Mohsin Hamid believes that "migration is a fundamental human right," according to his article in the *Guardian* of the same name, but what about people who don't *want* to migrate? Saeed ends up returning to the unnamed city of his birth, indicating he did not have a strong desire to go anywhere to begin with but rather was forced to move. What happens to people like him, who would rather live lives in the places of their birth?

Mimi Sheller insists that we all have a right to *im*mobility, and correspondingly, points out that "mobility may not always be a form of freedom. It can also be a coercion" (18). Being driven out of their home city wasn't pleasant for our protagonists, and there's no indication that they wanted to be driven out of London by accusations of criminality, either. But *Exit West* is an Anglophone novel of bourgeois liberalism, aimed squarely at a Western-educated, relatively affluent, likely white audience. This is an audience that *prizes* mobility, that thinks of it, in large part, as a good thing. But by suggesting mobility as a solution, and an individual solution at that, *Exit West* fails to provide a vision for wide or systemic change (not to mention that it makes mobility and migration seem incredibly easy and instantaneous via the magical realist doors). Its reliance on the notion of progress as dependent on the West (just keep going farther west until you get a great life!) is itself reliant on mobility-based teleologies; there's no emphasis on original community. Instead, the idea seems to be to just on pushing through until you find the right option for you, personally. Then, and only then, are you able to undergo catharsis out of constructions of crime.

So what's a better solution? How can we slow down these Enlightenment narratives of movement or of the harmfulness of the "criminal" Other? It's difficult to answer this question, as we are living in a globalized system rather than a colonial/postcolonial binary; it's harder to figure out what to combat when you have multiple variables instead of just "colonizers versus colonized." We live among the legacies of colonialism every day, negotiating them constantly from all directions. But one thing we *can* do is to continue to draw attention to these rhetorics, what they spring from, and how they can be combated in various settings and examples from around the world.

In the 1980s and 1990s, Americans became absolutely obsessed with crime; Ronald Reagan whipped up racist fears of "welfare queens," Bill

Clinton signed into law the infamous 1994 Crime Bill, broken-windows policing spread from city to city, shows like *Law & Order* surged in popularity. This was all happening even as crime rates were plummeting, and in retrospect, it is much more widely understood that panic over crime was actually an ostensibly colorblind way of expressing racism. We are, of course, swimming in a bigger pond than just the Anglophone postcolony; Foucault observed a similar paradox in eighteenth-century France, that there was a "very widespread belief in a constant and dangerous rise in crime" (76) that belied the actual facts. That belief, Foucault theorized, was part of a massive cultural "switchpoint" that shifted how we think about crime for centuries to come. It's indisputable that what gets declared a crime is about power and control, as in the case of the 1994 Crime Bill or Foucault's poor Damiens the would-be regicide[11]; or, even more relevantly, Narendra Modi's emphasis on declaring Muslim citizens of India to be criminals, or a 2019 extradition bill that led to widespread rebellions in Hong Kong. We see such contours in non-Anglophone texts like Roberto Bolaño's *2666*, on femicides along the Mexican/United States border, or in the recent boom in Korean crime fiction as well. We even see a real-world example directly linked to the refugee "crisis" discussed in this coda, in that movements of postcolonial refugees into Europe and concurrent claims of "crime" have reignited the far right, particularly in Hungary, which seems in turn to be inspiring American fascistic movements with a new vigor. Claims of crime hold a unique ability to whip up populations, to unearth imperial formations, to unleash our worst selves.

However, depictions of crime can also be used to *subvert* power, but to be most effective, that crime has to be utilized to seek systemic change against empire and its legacies. A revolution is no substitute for individual catharsis, which is one of the reasons why *Exit West* falls flat; Saeed and Nadia's resistance to being labeled criminals, their movements, remain resolutely individual, with no larger attempts being made to reform the system under which they suffer. They rely on each other and then solely on themselves instead of building a resilient community; in many ways, however, this can be seen to be the point of the novel. Because we are still living in the wreckage of colonialism and its Enlightenment heritage, what might be seen as flaws in contemporary novels—the lack of resolution or closure—are actually reflections or negotiations of what is messy, complicated, and unfinished about the colonial project. We remain atomized, individualized, cut off from larger communal spaces.

I think this tension gets to the heart of why we as people like talking about crime so much, particularly when it is presented in novelistic or narrative form. All stories are crime stories for many reasons: we love transgression, romance, danger, the opportunity to process our emotions through someone else's stories. As Bertolt Brecht has pointed out, "It is enjoyable just to see people *act*, to witness actions with actual consequences that are attainable straightaway" (92). But we continue to yearn for something more than just individual release, or solo reading; at the heart of it, we know that capitalism and imperialism are unjust, and we crave rebellion against those things. Some of the most powerful stories of cathartic crime let us imagine that rebellion, and then motivate us to enact it in hopefully communal form. Crime in literature has more meaning than we give it credit for; it plays a more substantial role than entertaining us on the beach or on an airplane. It represents a significant societal, collective grasping for catharsis and change in a rough-edged and unstable "post"-colonial world that isn't all that postcolonial after all.

I want to return here to David Scott's observation in *Conscripts of Modernity*, that "anticolonial stories about past, present, and future have typically been emplotted in a distinctive narrative form, one with a distinctive storypotential: that of *Romance* (7)." This form, Scott holds, has "largely depended on a certain (utopian) horizon toward which the emancipationist history is imagined to be moving" (8). Historically, Scott holds, that made sense, but with major shifts in late twentieth and early twenty-first centuries, there is "doubt about the continued critical salience of this narrative form and its underlying mythos. Indeed," Scott continues, "my wager in this book is that the problem about postcolonial futures—how we go about reimagining what we might become of what we have so far made—cannot be recast without recasting the problem about colonial pasts" (8). If a strictly teleological time frame no longer makes sense, when it comes to narratives about crime or about mobility, perhaps the novel is our best option, as it can "[recast] the problem about colonial pasts," even if it does not always choose to do so. The novel's ability to explore multiple temporalities is well suited for a contemporary era where colonialism has become more diffuse, where we must look to the past for a thoroughgoing sense of catharsis about the present.

Hannah Arendt was right when she wrote, "The best criterion by which to decide whether someone has been forced outside the pale of the law is to ask if he would benefit by committing a crime" (286); Mimi Sheller insists on the need for mobility justice, which she writes "requires more sustained attention to aspects of colonial history and an understanding of the historical formation of contemporary forms and patterns of global im/mobilities" (21). We need to pair these understandings together, to reach the root of *why* people are outside the pale of the law, realizing that this story is intimately connected to forward-oriented narratives of catharsis, imperial travel, Enlightenment teleology, Western progress, and so on, especially in an era where once widely accepted notions are beginning to break down (the idea of the nation-state; the importance of the eradication of fascism!). The primacy of mobility was integral to the development of Western imperialism; according to Sheller, "the sea-faring discovery, exploration, and exploitation of the New World for 'primitive accumulation,' the 'spirit of capitalism' associated with modern northwestern European Protestant cultures, and the American ideology of manifest destiny and the opening of the frontier are just a few of the cultural touchstones which define the West as mobile and expansionist" (41). This led to a number of colonial crimes; how do we begin to undo the damage, to rely less on these criminal teleologies and narratives? How do we recast the past to imagine a better future?

The novel form has traditionally been part and parcel of this teleological apparatus. George Lukács theorized over a century ago,

> Thus the fundamental form-determining intention of the novel is objectivised as the psychology of the novel's heroes: they are seekers. The simple fact of seeking implies that neither the goals nor the way leading to them can be directly given, or else that, if they are given in a psychologically direct and solid manner, this is not evidence of really existent relations or ethical necessities but only of a psychological fact to which nothing in the world of objects or norms need necessarily correspond. To put it another way, this 'givenness' may be crime or madness; the boundaries which separate crime from acclaimed heroism and madness from life-mastering wisdom are tentative, purely psychological ones, although at the end, when the aberration makes itself terribly manifest and clear, there is no longer any confusion. (60–61)

If the novel's heroes are seekers, tracing their journeys and mobilities along narratives of crime, then so are the novel's readers, the community created in the imaginative, novelistic city. The contemporary postcolonial urban novel, playing with that desire for "that old consoling sense of temporal *concordance*" (David Scott, *Omens*, 6) uses the mechanism of cathartic crime to try to capture this desire for a straightforward psychological and physical journey through the city and the novel, replacing it with either frustrated resolutions or with glimpses of what the future might hold. Because we are living in an unfinished colonial project, I hold that crime as a central narrative trope wants to draw readers' attention to what is still a world of ongoing negotiations rather than closures or resolutions. It is my hope that *Criminal Cities* can lead readers to imagining better futures out of colonial entanglements, where we can seek a more ethical world.

NOTES

PREFACE

1. In 2021, Buckhead attempted to secede from the city of Atlanta to form its own municipality; the push for incorporation is driven largely, again, by rhetorics of a "crime surge" with little to no basis in reality. As of the time of writing, the attempt was blocked by the Georgia state legislature initially, but may reappear in subsequent legislative sessions.
2. Another package of measures passed again in May 2022.

INTRODUCTION

1. See pages 130, 289, and 475 for representative samples.
2. Lukács was inspired to write "by the outbreak of the First World War" (11) and "in a mood of permanent despair over the state of the world" (12). While he was writing over one hundred years ago, the corollaries to our present day—not least including a global pandemic!—resonate in the early twenty-first century as well.
3. Lukács is writing in the 1920s, when the novel's claim to be "the representative art-form of our age" was stronger. Though the novel has declined in cultural centrality, I argue that its narrative conventions still have a strong grasp on the ways we (often subconsciously) pattern the world. It is possible film or social media will surpass the novel's grasp in time, but the reach and influence of the novel's form is still a central part of our aesthetic, political, and social experiences of the world.

4. I am borrowing a bit here from Frank Kermode's *The Sense of an Ending: Studies in the Theory of Fiction*, which argues that novels help readers map out a pattern for their lives, and that this pattern has a clear narrative logic. Ato Quayson wonders if "our current historical configuration contributes to the 'sense of an ending'" (2), pointing to events like September 11 and the rise of ISIS as moments that may "have been harnessed to forms of delirious sovereignty" (2), disrupting the conventional narrative of the postcolonial novel.
5. For more on how this looks in the detective story specifically, rather than my work on crime *in* literature, Eyal Segal has published "Closure in Detective Fiction" in *Poetics Today* 31.2 (2010): 153–215.
6. There were, of course, several precedents to an early modern conception of crime, not least Roman law and various other forms of criminal codes found in non-Western societies. But in the context of this study of the postcolonial Anglophone novel, the clearest umbrella definition is that which may be found above.
7. For a fascinating look at crime discourse in nineteenth-century Europe, read Marie-Christine Leps's *Apprehending the Criminal: The Production of Deviance in Nineteenth-Century Discourse* (Duke UP, 1992).
8. Jean and John L. Comaroff expand on this, writing that people in the twenty-first century are anxious about crime to an extent that does not line up with the facts: "even where criminality appears, in measurable terms, *not* to threaten major social and material disruption or to endanger life and limb, mass anxiety about it so rife," they write; "the phenomenology of fear is . . . so strikingly, so demonstrably, *dis*proportionate to risk" (xi–xii). They attribute this to a number of causes, notably contemporary governments "outsourcing . . . many of their functions" and "the growing difficulty . . . of discerning the lines that once were held to set apart the key domains of liberal-modern social order" (x). This is also due, I think, to what Yumna Siddiqi has called "the anxieties of empire" in the book of the same name. Siddiqi writes that empire's "anxieties about its own security" are often "expressed in the fiction of intrigue" (1), a similar note to my study on what crime is expressing in postcolonial literature.
9. It's always been the case, of course, that different people view actions differently based on their subject position and cultural contexts; my point is that the postcolonial and, to some extent, neoliberal world of the twenty-first century has provided a forum to more expressly air and articulate these feelings.
10. American audiences might also be familiar with this nexus through understandings of 1970s and 1980s New York, specifically the way in which fear of crime was weaponized by capitalists, police unions, and other reactionary forces to "clean up" the city and make it "safe" for tourism: see especially the election of Mayor Rudolph Giuliani and the "Welcome to Fear City" campaign.

11. I am also indebted here to Kwame Anthony Appiah's 1991 essay, "Is the Post- in Postmodernism the Post- in Postcolonial?"
12. Young is in turn following Paul Gilroy and Achille Mbembe.
13. For example, arrests of people without homes skyrocketed in Atlanta during the lead-up to the 2019 Super Bowl, mimicking an earlier pattern with the 1996 Olympics where the city tried to make itself more "palatable" to tourists (thanks to Dori Coblentz for this insight).

1. "THE PHENOMENON OF WALKING"

1. Though less expressly indebted, *Saturday* is also reminiscent of that other great modernist epic of twenty-four hours in the city, James Joyce's *Ulysses*.
2. As Perowne can see the BT Tower from his window (2), easily within his sight would be the Gherkin/St. Mary Axe; this detail is important to note for the *NW* section of this chapter.
3. See Groes, "Modernist Consciousness," and Brouillete, *Creative Economy*.
4. Of course, it's very good no one was hurt and that the plane crash was due to a boring mechanical failure!
5. This is another point of comparison between *Saturday* and *Mrs. Dalloway*, as the prime minister attends Clarissa Dalloway's party.
6. Worthy of note, too, that so many of the issues here are later relied upon in Brexit rhetoric, from the cuts to the NHS to the sense that "elites" like Perowne are discriminating against "common men" like Baxter.
7. Leah views Shar's scam as sad and desperate rather than a crime; I am using "crime" here in the way indicated in the introduction, as an action that is against the (imperially negotiated and constructed) law.
8. The first time readers meet Nathan Bogle in person, he is illicitly selling Oyster cards (for travel on London public transportation) on a bus.
9. This property crime (stealing) is, it is strongly implied, made necessary by the lack of "legitimate" employment in the neighborhood.
10. In *Unseasonable Youth*, Jed Esty similarly ties arrested adolescence to resistance of progressive logics of imperialism and capitalism, albeit in a modernist age. Like the recitation of "Dover Beach" in *Saturday*, *NW* contains some rich linkages between the age of high imperialism and the twenty-first century.
11. Interestingly, Natalie is something like a far more successful version of Leah's husband, Michel. While Natalie embodies the successful "pull yourself up by your bootstraps" narrative, Michel desperately wants to be a part of that story, but seems unable to be. He spends much of his day attempting to trade stocks

on the internet, interpellating himself into the neoliberal narrative of the importance of entrepreneurship, but he is unsuccessful, setting up Leah's life for further contrast with Natalie's.

12. In a way, Felix's murder is somewhat similar to Septimus Smith's in *Mrs. Dalloway*; none of the other characters really know him, but his death has ripple effects throughout the narrative

13. Interestingly, Frank's anger reads in context as directed more at the email account than at the implications of his wife being registered on a sex website. He asks her, "What is this? 'KeishaNW@gmail.com' What the fuck is this? Fiction? ... Who *are* you?" (353–54). Natalie not only has registered under the childhood name she has attempted to leave behind by renaming herself "Natalie," but has firmly aligned herself with the neighborhood of her childhood to which she has only recently returned, rendering her fictional to her husband.

14. While I postulated earlier that "Natalie" acts as a renaming for professional reasons in a white society, it seems worth considering that Keisha takes on the name "Natalie" because it sounds like "Nathan" and allows her to share Nathan Bogle's initials. There is no indication anywhere in the novel that she has named herself after a family member, or a beloved author, or an admired schoolmate, or anything like that; we have no context at all for why Keisha chose "Natalie," beyond the possibility that Nathan and Natalie may be somehow parallel or linked.

15. One of the people involved in the stabbing had a scar; Nathan has a scar. Nathan desperately wants to leave the surrounding area, and we know Nathan lives on the fringes of society and is sometimes involved in violent acts. That's about the sum of it.

16. "A firm punch came to his side. Punch? The pain sliced to the left, deep and down. Warm liquid reversed up his throat. Over his lips. Yet it couldn't be oblivion as long as he could name it, and with this in mind he said aloud what had been done to him, what was being done to him, he tried to say it, he said nothing" (198).

17. The mugging calls to mind Stuart Hall et al.'s observation that "mugging" is often perceived as a "black crime," and that a late twentieth-century panic over mugging has direct links to the Windrush Generation, which Natalie and Nathan would both be direct descendants of, as well as longer capitalist and colonialist associations. Hall et al. ask readers to "*go behind* the criminal acts to the conditions which are producing black crime as one of their effects" (389, italics original), which is what this chapter attempts to do, in part, in light of ideas about cathartic crime.

18. The Gherkin is quite a new building, especially when considered in the context of St. Paul's. Completed in 2003 and opened in 2004, it replaced the Baltic Exchange, which was irreparably damaged by a Provisional IRA bomb. As I noted previously, Henry Perowne would have also been able to see this building from his window. Jane M. Jacobs points out that, by targeting this building, "the IRA was not simply attacking the symbolic heart of empire, it was also attacking the precariously placed Britain of New Europe" (64), with all the neoliberal financial implications of the EU common market and free trade.
19. Nathan understands this on a level that suggests he doesn't accept the narrative in the way Natalie does here; perhaps this is why he feels trapped in the life that he lives.

2. "CRIME IS CRIME IS CRIME"

1. Chuckie's name, amusingly, is pronounced like "tiocfaidh ár lá," or "our day will come," a phrase commonly used among Irish republicans.
2. As of May 2022, this autocorrect no longer seems to be happening, but I have screenshots!
3. The efficacy and continuing legal status of the Good Friday Agreement has recently been called into question by Brexit, with the potential for a "hard border" being reestablished between the Republic, which remains in the EU, and the North, which has Brexited along with the rest of the United Kingdom.
4. The importance of vehicles and mobility is brought up in other contexts too: for instance, in the car repair shop where maybe-boyfriend works, one day a Bentley Blower race car is brought in and the parts distributed among those who work there. Bentleys traditionally bear an insignia of a Union Jack flag, and maybe-boyfriend comes under suspicion merely for receiving a part that has the flag on it, as it is the flag of the community "over the water" and not his (we can assume) Catholic republican community.

3. WHITENESS, HISTORICAL FICTION, AND AUSTRALIAN CITIES

1. *The Nightingale*, a 2019 film directed by Jennifer Kent, is another example of a contemporary cultural artifact that takes as its subject matter the experience of the Irish "criminal" transported to Australia.

2. This is a novel Graham Huggan says "operates as a foundational Australian victim narrative" (52).
3. Readers attracted to this topic may also be interested in Ruby Langford Ginibi's *Haunted by the Past* (1999). Ginibi, an Aboriginal woman, wrote a memoir about her son Nobby's entanglements with the law and what his story can tell us about the struggles the Aboriginal community faces in contemporary Australia.
4. Mudrooroo also "started a short series of stories in 1990 with 'Westralian Lead,' featuring Detective Inspector Watson Holmes Jackamara of the Black Cockatoo Dreaming who, as well as having a challenging name, is a determined, self-aware indigenous man, sorting out confusions and crimes that result largely from incomer oppression" (Knight, "Postcolonial Crime Novel," 173). I'm not sure what the dig about the inspector's "challenging name" is meant to signify, but Mudrooroo's work on crime in literature is notable.
5. A good complementary account of how this happened in the United States may be found in Noel Ignatiev's *How the Irish Became White* (1995).
6. There are a few places in other settler colonial nations where this also happened; for instance, once again, my state of Georgia in the United States was founded as a penal colony. But Australia was the most large-scale undertaking of this venture, and the fact that its first permanent white settlers were convicts from Britain and Ireland is notable.
7. Of course, many transported criminals were murderers, rapists, and other violent criminals (not that these crimes justified transportation), but in the literary imagination (especially the white Australian literary imagination), transportees are typically figured as having committed low-level, "understandable" crimes.
8. There is a material connection here to how, in the American context, "poor whites" were often pitted against enslaved and then free Black people and encouraged to understand themselves as in alliance with white elites, coalescing around a racial, rather than economic, form of solidarity.
9. Perhaps the most baldly named entry in this genre is Gail Jones's *Sorry* (2007).
10. Remarkably, Grenville writes, seemingly without self-awareness, of her hope that Solomon Wiseman was Jewish. In *Searching for the Secret River*, she records that she was disappointed when she learns he was not, and recounts her Aboriginal friend Melissa's observation that this was something Grenville was hoping for because "that would make him [and by extension, Grenville] just that much less white" (73). Grenville's hopes for some element of a marginalized, non-white identity are an articulation of white privilege if there ever was one.

11. There are six of these moves: settler nativism, fantasizing adoption, colonial equivocation, conscientization, at risk-ing/asterisking Indigenous peoples, and re-occupation and urban homesteading (Tucker and Yang 4).

4. "SHOT THROUGH WITH CRIME"

1. Lin holds a forged New Zealand passport and tells everyone he meets he is from New Zealand so as to avoid anyone's connecting the dots with his previous life.
2. To his vague credit, Lin does realize later that this man's "education was a post-colonial parallel to my own" (430), at least acknowledging a history of imperialism in some way; yet he still does not seem to understand power differentials or recognize that an Indian experience cannot be framed entirely through his own Western history and understanding.
3. A word about terminology: both Umrigar and Chandra, as well as much of the secondary literature I cite, refer regularly to the city as "Bombay." To avoid confusion when quoting, I refer to the city as "Bombay" throughout as well.
4. The word "Bombay" is likely a corruption of the Portuguese for "good harbor" (*Bom Bahia*).
5. According to Stuti Khanna, Bombay is not "an 'authentic,' indigenous, pre-colonial city like old Delhi or Varanasi or Calcutta or Mysore, but a fundamentally self-conscious, artificial, urban creation from the start, down to the very land on which most of stands" (31).
6. Kanchan Jyoti concurs, saying the British "intensified the growing inter-communal rivalry by its divisive policies. Its intent was to curb the growing political consciousness of the people" (232).
7. Tharoor also points out that British Orientalists portrayed Indian civilization as "essentially Hindu," which excluded Muslims and other minorities "from the essential national narrative" and "helped give birth in the twentieth [century] to the two-nation theory that eventually divided the country" (132–33).
8. The rhetoric of the group also, similar to that of many right-wing movements, capitalizes on the fear of crime to shore up their electoral holdings, even though many leaders of the group have criminal records themselves.
9. This is obviously an incredibly vexed term, but I am using "neoliberalism" to refer to a kind of capitalism that operates without much regulation or oversight; this economic model often leads to huge inequality in income, much poverty, and lack of formal social welfare or safety nets.
10. Rashmi Varma refers to the riots as "acts of genocide carried out against a minority community" (*Postcolonial City*, 131).

11. As Bill Ashcroft points out, this focus on travel and mobility as linked to capitalist ideas of production and forward movement is itself linked to Bombay's creation by the British Empire; Bombay, even more so than other British colonial cities, attracted a lot of travel from the rural hinterlands to the newly created city, helping to foreground a kind of "mobility in the postcolonial city [that] is the sign of a larger global movement set in motion by colonialism" (500).
12. Characters also continually think about the 1992–93 riots and bombings, pointing to the way these events still loom very large in collective memory.
13. Adish performs a similar maneuver on a smaller scale in *The World We Found*.
14. Manu argues with Ganesh's gang, telling them that "capitalism would collapse because of its internal contradictions, that the march of history was inevitable, and that they were an ignorant lot who didn't and couldn't see the forces working under the surface of events" (680). However, Manu's predictions about the future collapse of capitalism ultimately turn out to be well-founded. His theories about the progressive nature of history leading to a collapse, not to mention his scolding that the observers "couldn't see the forces working under the surface of events," utilizes the same logic as the novel and its plot points.
15. Notice the similarity between this and Klein's notion of "the shock doctrine": "Believers in the shock doctrine are convinced that only a great rupture— a flood, a war, a terrorist attack—can generate the kind of vast, clean canvases they crave. It is in these malleable moments, when we are psychologically unmoored and physically uprooted, that these artists of the real plunge in their hands and begin their world of remaking the world" (21).
16. The lack of catharsis in climax happens in multiple registers throughout the novel: Ganesh struggles with impotence, for example, and, as noted before, Sartaj's aunt did not make it to India from Pakistan in the chaos of Partition with the rest of her family, and has been pretending to be a Pakistani Muslim her entire life. When we readers realize who she is, on her deathbed, it is not portrayed in a climactic way, nor does it change anything about the novel. "It is crucial to realise," Anwer writes, "that the 'revelation' that the two women were once members of the same family, although mysteriously dramatic and even sensational, serves no functional purpose in the detective plot" (11).

5. NEOLIBERAL CRIMINALITY

1. Of course, in this context, "decline" has a double meaning: that of "decline in standards," but also, grammatically, "to decline a verb." In the postcolonial context, it also immediately brings to mind Edward Gibbon's *The Decline and Fall of the Roman Empire*.
2. In addition to the apartheid parallels with the zoos, the phenomenon of "animalling," or the pairing of animal familiars with those who have committed crimes, came to prominence in the 1980s, much like the HIV/AIDS crisis and the advent of neoliberalism.
3. Note the heavily city-centric route: she only once notes anything that isn't a city, with "southern Uganda."
4. Though it is not specifically mentioned in this quotation, if one consults a map of Hillbrow, one will see that there is an "Empire Road" just to the north of the designated area. Do with that what you will.
5. I'm playing a little here with the title of Kwame Anthony Appiah's essay "Is the Post- in Postmodernism the Post- in Postcolonial?," though Appiah and I are engaging with different registers of this idea.
6. For what it is worth, Cousin is employed as a policeman, or an agent of an organization that was primarily tasked with maintaining apartheid order and punishing what was and is deemed as "crime."
7. See chapter 2 for more details on this idea in the Northern Irish context.
8. As previously noted, the zoos in *Zoo City* also began to proliferate around the time the HIV/AIDS virus did the same; it bears noting that neoliberal, individual-centric, Reaganesque lack of involvement in curtailing the disease led to its continuing spread. (This perspective on public health has taken on even more resonance as I write during the United States' botched response to the COVID-19 pandemic.)
9. In this, Refilwe's life mimics Mpe's own: Mpe also died of complications from AIDS and had pursued graduate work in Oxford.

6. "THIS LINE CREATED A COUNTRY"

1. I have chosen to style both father and son's names as above, to hew as closely as possible to what both authors typically use; any deviation in such when quoted is as the original author wrote.
2. *Petals of Blood* is the last of his novels to be written first in English.

3. Though "Mau Mau" was the British name for the guerilla fighters, while those who took part preferred "Kenya Land and Freedom Army," I have chosen to use "Mau Mau" for clarity's sake as most of the literature and sources cited in this chapter use that phrase.
4. He was released a year later when Daniel arap Moi replaced Jomo Kenyatta as president of Kenya.
5. The immediate successor to *Petals of Blood*, *Devil on the Cross*, was written while Ngũgĩ was in prison.
6. For example, in Aristotelian catharsis, if you kill the king on stage, this precludes the need to kill the king in real life.
7. Godfrey figures out that Munira set the fire that killed two of the businessmen; he does not understand why, nor does he solve the puzzle that Wanja killed the remaining third with a panga.
8. Mukoma earned his PhD at the University of Wisconsin, and there is, of course, an inevitable "Call me Ishmael" early in the book.
9. O calls the city of his residence "Nairobbery," a pejorative label for the city used by locals and foreigners alike that highlights the city's depiction in popular culture as a place of crime.
10. This scene brings to mind Ngũgĩ's short story "The Martyr," about Mau Mau murders of white Europeans.
11. In Ishmael's words: "The black Schindler, as the media had called him, had saved a few in order to use them as bait and reel in whole villages searching for refuge" (124).
12. This is, unfortunately, as convoluted as it sounds.
13. Note the connection between a "foreign-owned hotel" in Mukoma's fiction and a "foreign-owned brewery" in Ngũgĩ's.
14. Certainly a lot of postcolonial relevance in having Kenya's first post-independence leader hide the bomb that would eventually destroy the city!
15. Though it's not directly addressed in any of the literature discussed in this chapter, it is worth noting that China has recently invested heavily in several railroad projects in Africa—including one that closely mimics the route of the original "Lunatic Express" in Kenya.

7. "HIS MEMORY RESISTS ORDERING"

1. For purposes of this chapter, I will be using the term "Palestine" to refer to the occupied Palestinian territories of the West Bank, East Jerusalem, and the Gaza Strip, though the literature considered in this chapter takes

place overwhelmingly in the West Bank. Though Gaza is commonly referred to as "the world's largest open-air prison," due to Israel's extreme repression of that space, and might seem like a more logical choice for a work based on crime in postcolonial literature, the availability of Anglophone novels set in the West Bank is far greater and as such, this part of Palestine is more representative for my purposes. In addition, travel restrictions imposed on Gazans are highly punitive, and it is difficult to track travel in Gaza, whereas travel is a little more available for residents of the West Bank.

2. This is not to discount what Bernard calls the "towering presence" of Edward Said, whose work has made "the Palestinian situation . . . as visible as it is in postcolonial studies" (19).
3. I use this phrase again to highlight the many connections between Palestine and Northern Ireland; republican/Catholic neighborhoods in cities like Derry and Belfast often identify with Palestine, while unionist/Protestant neighborhoods utilize the iconography of Israel to stake their own claim to land. For an excellent study of this phenomenon, please see Joe Cleary's *Literature, Partition, and the Nation-State*.
4. The novel's ability to change the situation on the ground has a particular resonance in Palestinian history and culture. George Eliot's *Daniel Deronda*, for example, famously swayed many Europeans to the cause of Zionism, causing that settler colonial movement to gain backing and power in a way it had not previously enjoyed.
5. When I say "millions," I mean the number since 1948, not the numbers of refugees created by the initial Nakba. Currently (as of 2022), nearly six million Palestinian refugees are registered with the United Nations.
6. I do not include "religious" here because Palestinian Christians are targeted alongside the Palestinian Muslim majority, as well as other religious minorities.
7. Nablus, remember, is not even the family's ancestral home; that is Jaffa, from which they were driven out in 1947.
8. Compare this to Atef and Alia's youngest daughter, Souad, who wants something totally different from her own experience of urban life. She moves to Paris as a young woman and revels in its European-style close quarters and old-style city planning. She adores "the ability it gives you to walk, to literally put space between your body and distress. In Kuwait, nobody walks anywhere" (165). Her way of dealing with "distress" is unlike her mother's rage or her father's embrace of newness; she enjoys the life of the flaneur, of someone who can explore the modernist city on foot.
9. See my earlier citations of Cohen Lustig's work.

10. Ariel Sharon aligned Israel firmly with America's "War on Terror," using it as a justification to "[launch] its helicopter gunships against Hamas, Islamic Jihad, and the Palestinian Authority in Gaza and the West Bank" (Gregory 110).

CODA

1. Also known as the Islamic State of Iraq and the Levant (ISIL) or by its Arabic acronym DAESH.
2. I first became aware of this video via a December 2018 episode of *The East Is a Podcast*, which presented an interview with journalist Robert Fisk by Vancouver's *Redeye Collective*. You can listen here: https://eastisapodcast.libsyn.com/the-indefatigable-robert-fisk.
3. The "crisis," of course, is that people are being violently pushed out of their homes, not that they are arriving in Europe and North America.
4. I say "those without power who are most (involuntarily) mobile" because of course, many people with a great deal of power are also quite mobile; choosing to travel and to live in several different places is quite different from being forced to.
5. Several characters observe that their country was the first to experience a deluge of migrants and refugees, before the citizens of that country became refugees and migrants themselves due to a military coup in the country. This could happen in Jordan, situated as it is in a volatile geography and with its long-established position as a catching ground for refugees and migrants from all over the Middle East. Additionally, there is resonance in the possibility of the country being Jordan, keeping in mind Arendt's points about Arab refugees cited earlier: many Palestinian refugees after the 1948 creation of the state of Israel found refuge in Jordan ("Saeed" also sounds like "Said," as in Edward Said, whose family was Palestinian). Lastly, at the start of the novel, we learn "their city had yet to experience any major fighting, just some shootings and the odd car bombing" (4), which roughly mirrors the contemporary state of Jordan, and the eventual encroachment of ISIS onto the city would be Amman's absolute worst-case scenario. Of course, if the city is Amman in Jordan, the colonial roots of the violence are very similar to those outlined in the chapter on the West Bank, specifically with regard to Sykes-Picot and the Balfour Declaration.
6. Hamid refers to Westerners, whether in Mykonos, London, or California, as "the natives" throughout, a move Nguyen calls a "postcolonial reverse."

7. Though Kensington and Chelsea is very affluent and "posh," it is also worth noting that Grenfell Towers was located in this neighborhood as well; there are certainly pockets where the narrative of wealth and privilege is interrupted, though Nadia and Saeed seem to be living among fellow refugees in the more stereotypically wealthy areas.
8. Given that the house is empty, the setting seems as though it is a reference to the "absentee landlord" problem London is currently experiencing, where foreign investors buy up homes as investment properties and then let them sit empty for much of the year.
9. Of course, part of the irony here is that the refugees have "taken over" wealthy neighborhoods like Kensington and Chelsea, something that is a particular kind of Briton's worst nightmare and is partially echoed in the foreign investors buying up these properties.
10. Ruvani Ranasinha points out, "In the racialised political discourse of the global North, the term 'migrant' is discursively constituted to suit political agendas that attempt to mask the real cause of economic inequalities by stigmatising and criminalising migration, claiming that migrants are a strain on the economy" (239). Criminalization is often reliant on logics not just of imperialism, but also of capital.
11. A gruesome account of Damiens's 1757 murder at the hands of the French state opens Foucault's *Discipline and Punish*; Damiens's dismemberment, Foucault holds, marked the shift to more modern conceptions of punishment and views on crime.

BIBLIOGRAPHY

Abujidi, Nurhan. *Urbicide in Palestine: Spaces of Oppression and Resilience.* Routledge, 2014.

Abu-Manneh, Bashir. *The Palestinian Novel: From 1948 to Present.* Cambridge UP, 2016.

Affeldt, Stefanie. "The Burden of 'White' Sugar: Producing and Consuming Whiteness in Australia." *Studia Anglica Posnaniensia* 52.4 (2017): 440–66.

Albert, Samuel D. "Egypt and Mandatory Palestine and Iraq." In *Architecture and Urbanism in the British Empire,* edited by G. A. Bremner, pp. 423–55. Oxford UP, 2016.

Alexander, Michelle. *The New Jim Crow: Mass Incarceration in the Age of Colorblindness.* New Press, 2010.

Allen, Theodore W. *The Invention of the White Race.* Vol. 1: *Racial Oppression and Social Control.* Verso, 1994.

Alter, Alexandra. "Global Migration Meets Magic in Mohsin Hamid's Timely Novel." *New York Times,* 7 March 2017.

Alyan, Hala. *Salt Houses.* Mariner Books, 2018.

Anwer, Megha. "Resisting the Event: Aesthetics of the Non-Event in the Contemporary South Asian Novel." *ariel: A Review of International English Literature* 45.4 (2014): 1–30.

Appadurai, Arjun. "Spectral Housing and Urban Cleansing: Notes on Millennial Mumbai." *Public Culture* 12.3 (Fall 2000): 627–51.

Appiah, Kwame Anthony. "Is the Post- in Postmodernism the Post- in Postcolonial?" *Critical Inquiry* 17.2 (Winter 1991): 336–57.

Arata, Stephen. *Fictions of Loss in the Victorian Fin de Siècle.* Cambridge UP, 2010.

Aravamudan, Srinivas. *Enlightenment Orientalism: Resisting the Rise of the Novel.* U of Chicago P, 2011.

Arendt, Hannah. *The Origins of Totalitarianism*. Harcourt, Brace, Jovanovich, 1973.
Aristotle. *Poetics*. Penguin Classics: 1997.
Arnett, James. "Neoliberalism and False Consciousness Before and After Brexit in Zadie Smith's *NW*." *Explicator* 76.1 (2018): 1–7.
Ashcroft, Bill. "Urbanism, Mobility, and Bombay: Reading the Postcolonial City." *Journal of Postcolonial Writing* 47.5 (2011): 497–509.
Ashcroft, Bill, Gareth Griffiths, and Helen Tiffin. *The Empire Writes Back: Theory and Practice in Post-Colonial Literatures*. 2nd ed. Routledge, 2002.
Bahri, Deepika. *Native Intelligence: Aesthetics, Politics, and Postcolonial Literature*. U of Minnesota P, 2003.
Ball, Anna. *Palestinian Literature and Film in Postcolonial Feminist Perspective*. Routledge, 2017.
Banville, John. "A Day in the Life." *New York Review of Books*, 26 May 2005.
Barghouti, Mourid. *I Saw Ramallah*. Anchor Books, 2003.
Barnard, Rita. *Apartheid and Beyond: South African Writers and the Politics of Place*. Oxford UP, 2007.
Beaumont, Alexander. *Contemporary British Fiction and the Cultural Politics of Disenfranchisement*. Palgrave Macmillan, 2015.
Belliappa, Mukund. "Bombay Writing: Are You Experienced?" *Antioch Review* 66.2 (Spring 2008): 345–62.
Berger, John. *Ways of Seeing*. Peter Smith Publications, 1972.
Bergonzi, Bernard. *The Situation of the Novel*. U of Pittsburgh P, 1970.
Bernard, Anna. *Rhetorics of Belonging: Nation, Narration, and Israel/Palestine*. Liverpool UP, 2014.
Beukes, Lauren. *Zoo City*. Angry Robot, 2011.
Bhabha, Homi. *The Location of Culture*. 2nd ed. Routledge Classics, 2004.
Birch, Carol. "*That Deadman Dance* by Kim Scott—Review." *Guardian*, 7 December 2012.
Blomley, Nicholas. "Cuts, Flows, and the Geographies of Property." *Law, Culture, and the Humanities* 7.2 (2010): 203–16.
Boehmer, Elleke, and Dominic Davies, eds. *Planned Violence: Post/Colonial Urban Infrastructure, Literature and Culture*. Palgrave Macmillan, 2018.
Brecht, Bertolt. "On the Popularity of the Crime Novel." Translated by Martin Harvey and Aaron K. Kelly. *Irish Review* 31 (2004): 90–96.
Bremner, Lindsay. "Crime and the Emerging Landscape of Post-Apartheid Johannesburg." In *blank ___: Architecture, Apartheid, and After,* edited by Hilton Judin and Ivan Vladislavić, pp. 48–63. NAi Publishers, 1998.
Brewster, Anne. "Can You Anchor a Shimmering Nation State via Regional Indigenous Roots? Kim Scott Talks to Anne Brewster about *That Deadman Dance*." *Cultural Studies Review* 18.1 (March 2012): 228–46.

Brouillette, Sarah. *Literature and the Creative Economy.* Stanford UP, 2014.

Brown, Jayna. "Celebrating the Abject." *American Book Review* 34.2 (January/February 2013): 7–8.

Brown, Richard. "Politics, the Domestic, and the Uncanny Effects of the Everyday in Ian McEwan's 'Saturday.'" *Critical Survey* 20.1 (2008): 80–93.

Burns, Anna. *Milkman.* Faber and Faber, 2018.

Carey, Peter. *True History of the Kelly Gang: A Novel.* Vintage, 2001.

Carter, Paul. *The Road to Botany Bay.* U of Minnesota P, 1987.

Carter, Stephen R. "Decolonization and Detective Fiction: Ngugi wa Thiong'o's *Petals of Blood*." In *Mysteries of Africa*, edited by Eugene Schleh, pp. 72–91. Bowling Green State U Popular P, 1991.

Chambers, Claire. "Postcolonial *Noir*: Vikram Chandra's 'Kama.'" In *Detective Fiction in a Postcolonial and Transnational World*, edited by Nels Pearson and Marc Singer, pp. 31–46. Ashgate, 2009.

Chambers, Claire, and Graham Huggan. "Reevaluating the Postcolonial City: Production, Reconstruction, Representation." *Interventions: International Journal of Postcolonial Studies* 17.6 (2015): 783–88.

Chandra, Vikram. *Sacred Games.* Harper Perennial, 2007.

Charles, Ron. "*NW* by Zadie Smith—A Brilliant Novel for the Dedicated, Attentive Reader." *Washington Post*, 28 August 2012.

Chotiner, Isaac. "Faceless Masses." *Slate*, 6 March 2017, https://slate.com/culture/2017/03/exit-west-by-mohsin-hamid-reviewed.html.

Christian, Ed, ed. *The Post-Colonial Detective.* Palgrave Macmillan, 2001.

Cleary, Joe. *Literature, Partition, and the Nation-State: Culture and Conflict in Ireland, Israel, and Palestine.* Cambridge UP, 2002.

Clendinnen, Inga. "The History Question: Who Owns the Past?" *Quarterly Essay* 23 (2006): 1–72.

Cohen Lustig, Kfir. *Makers of Worlds, Readers of Signs: Israeli and Palestinian Literature of the Global Contemporary.* Verso, 2019.

Collins, Eleanor. "Poison in the Flour: Kate Grenville's *The Secret River*." In *Lighting Dark Places: Essays on Kate Grenville*, edited by Sue Kossew, pp. 167–78. Rodopi, 2010.

Comaroff, Jean, and John L. "Criminal Obsessions, after Foucault: Postcoloniality, Policing, and the Metaphysics of Disorder." *Critical Inquiry* 30.4 (Summer 2004): 800–824.

———. *The Truth about Crime: Sovereignty, Knowledge, Social Order.* U of Chicago P, 2016.

Conrad, Joseph. *Heart of Darkness.* Edited by Paul B. Armstrong. 5th Norton Critical Edition. W. W. Norton, 2016.

Cooke, Rachel. "NW by Zadie Smith—Review." *Guardian*, 26 August 2012.

Cooper, Frederick. *Colonialism in Question: Theory, Knowledge, History*. U of California P, 2005.

Coundouriotis, Elena. "Memory and the Popular: Rwanda in Mukoma Wa Ngugi's Fiction." *Cambridge Journal of Postcolonial Literary Inquiry* 4.3 (September 2017): 382–97.

Crane, Ralph J. "Out of the Center: Thoughts on the Post-Colonial Literatures of Australia and New Zealand." In *Postcolonial Discourses: An Anthology*, edited by Gregory Castle, pp. 389–98. Wiley, 2001.

Cresswell, Tim. *On the Move: Mobility in the Modern Western World*. Routledge, 2006.

Darling, Danny, and Sally Tomlinson. *Rule Britannia: Brexit and the End of Empire*. Biteback Publishing, 2019.

Davis, Emily S. "Contagion, Cosmopolitanism, and Human Rights in Phaswane Mpe's *Welcome to Our Hillbrow*." *College Literature* 40.3 (Summer 2013): 99–112.

Dawson, Ashley, and Brent Hayes Edwards. "Introduction: Global Cities of the South." *Social Text* 22.4 (Winter 2004): 1–7.

Deane, Seamus. Introduction to *Nationalism, Colonialism, and Literature*, by Terry Eagleton, Fredric Jameson, and Edward W. Said, pp. 3–19. U of Minnesota P, 1990.

DiAngelo, Robin. *White Fragility: Why It's So Hard for White People to Talk about Racism*. Beacon Press, 2018.

Dossal, Mariam. *Imperial Designs and Indian Realities: The Planning of Bombay City, 1845–1875*. Oxford UP, 1991.

duBois, Page. "The Death of Character." *International Journal of the Classical Tradition* 21 (2014): 301–8.

Durkheim, Émile. *The Rules of Sociological Method and Selected Texts on Sociology and Its Method*. Translated by W. D. Halls. Edited by Steven Lukes. Free Press, 1982.

Eagleton, Terry. "In the Gaudy Supermarket." *London Review of Books* 21.10 (13 May 1999).

Eatough, Matthew. "Planning the Future: Scenario Planning, Infrastructural Time, and South African Fiction." *MFS Modern Fiction Studies* 61.4 (Winter 2015): 690–714.

Ebileeni, Maurice. "Breaking the Script: The Generational Conjuncture in the Anglophone Palestinian Novel." *Journal of Postcolonial Writing* 55.5 (2019): 628–41.

Eide, Marian. *Terrible Beauty: The Violent Aesthetic and Twentieth-Century Literature*. U of Virginia P, 2019.

Elkin, Lauren. "'NW' by Zadie Smith: Review." *Daily Beast*, 12 September 2012, www.thedailybeast.com/nw-by-zadie-smith-review.

Elkins, Caroline. *Imperial Reckoning: The Untold Story of Britain's Gulag*. Holt Paperbacks, 2005.

Enright, Anne. "Mind the Gap." *New York Times*, 23 September 2012.

Esty, Jed. *Unseasonable Youth: Modernism, Colonialism, and the Fiction of Development.* Oxford UP, 2013.

Fadem, Maureen Ruprecht. *The Literature of Northern Ireland: Spectral Borderlands.* Palgrave Macmillan, 2015.

Fanon, Frantz. *The Wretched of the Earth.* Translated by Richard Philcox. Grove Press, 2004.

Farag, Joseph R. *Palestinian Literature in Exile: Gender, Aesthetics, and Resistance in the Short Story.* I. B. Tauris, 2016.

Foucault, Michel. *Discipline and Punish: The Birth of the Prison.* Translated by Alan Sheridan. 2nd ed. Vintage Books, 1995.

Franklin, Ruth. "The Identity Crisis of Zadie Smith." *New Republic*, 14 September 2012, https://newrepublic.com/article/107209/reader-keep-up.

Frenkel, Ronit. "South African Literary Cartographies: A Post-transitional Palimpsest." *ariel: A Review of International English Literature* 44.1 (January 2013): 25–44.

Gallagher, Jodi. "'Relaxed and Comfortable': Carey, Grenville, and the Politics of the History Novel." In *Remaking Literary History*, edited by Helen Groth and Paul Sheehan, pp. 233–44. Cambridge Scholars Publishing, 2010.

Gallien, Claire. "Forcing Displacement: The Postcolonial Interventions of Refugee Literature and the Arts." *Journal of Postcolonial Writing* 54.6 (2018): 735–50.

Garner, Dwight. "'Milkman' Slogs through Political and Cultural Tensions in Northern Ireland." *New York Times*, 3 December 2018.

Ghalayini, Basma. Introduction to *Palestine + 100: Stories from a Century after the Nakba*, edited by Basma Ghalayini, pp. vii–xiii. Comma Press, 2019.

Gikandi, Simon. *Ngugi wa Thiong'o*. Cambridge UP, 2000.

Gilroy, Paul. *Postcolonial Melancholia*. Columbia UP, 2005.

Ginibi, Ruby Langford. *Haunted by the Past*. Allen and Unwin, 1999.

Goan, Cathal. "Experiencing the Troubles." In *Remembering the Troubles: Contesting the Recent Past in Northern Ireland*, edited by Jim Smyth, pp. 179–95. U of Notre Dame P, 2017.

Gooder, Haydie, and Jane M. Jacobs. "'On the Border of the Unsayable': The Apology in Postcolonizing Australia." *Interventions: International Journal of Postcolonial Studies* 2.2 (2000): 229–47.

Gopal, Priyamvada. *The Indian English Novel: Nation, History, and Narration.* Oxford UP, 2009.

Gordon, Neve. "From Colonization to Separation: Exploring the Structure of Israel's Occupation." *Third World Quarterly* 29.1 (2008): 25–44.

Graham, Shane. "Memory, Memorialization, and the Transformation of Johannesburg: Ivan Vladislavić's *The Restless Supermarket* and *Propaganda by Monuments*." *MFS Modern Fiction Studies* 53.1 (Spring 2007): 70–97.

Graham, Stephen. "Bulldozers and Bombs: The Latest Palestinian-Israeli Conflict as Asymmetric Urbicide." *Antipode* 34.4 (2002): 642–49.

Green, Michael. "Translating the Nation: From Plaatje to Mpe." *Journal of Southern African Studies* 34.2 (June 2008): 325–42.

Gregory, Derek. *The Colonial Present: Afghanistan, Palestine, Iraq*. Wiley-Blackwell, 2004.

Grenville, Kate. *Searching for the Secret River: The Story behind the Bestselling Novel*. Canongate, 2007.

———. *The Secret River*. Canongate, 2005.

Groes, Sebastian. "Ian McEwan and the Modernist Consciousness of the City in *Saturday*." In *Ian McEwan: Contemporary Critical Perspectives*, 2nd ed., edited by Sebastian Groes, pp. 99–114. Bloomsbury, 2013.

Hadley, Elaine. "On a Darkling Plain: Victorian Liberalism and the Fantasy of Agency." *Victorian Studies* 48.1 (Autumn 2005): 92–102.

Hage, Ghassan. *Against Paranoid Nationalism: Searching for Hope in a Shrinking Society*. Gardners Books, 2003.

Hall, Stuart, Chas Critcher, Tony Jefferson, John Clarke, and Brian Roberts. *Policing the Crisis: Mugging, the State, and Law and Order*. Macmillan, 1978.

Hamid, Mohsin. *Exit West*. Riverhead Books, 2017.

———. "Why Migration Is a Fundamental Human Right." *Guardian*, 21 November 2014.

Hammad, Isabella. *The Parisian*. Grove Press, 2019.

Hansen, Thomas Blom. *The Saffron Wave: Democracy and Hindu Nationalism in Modern India*. Princeton UP, 1999.

———. *Wages of Violence: Naming and Identity in Postcolonial Bombay*. Princeton UP, 2001.

Hardt, Michael, and Antonio Negri. *Empire*. Harvard UP, 2000.

Hart, Ariel. "Voters Reject Transportation Tax." *Atlanta Journal-Constitution*, 1 August 2012.

Heidemann, Birte. *Post-Agreement Northern Irish Literature*. Palgrave Macmillan, 2016.

Herbert, Caroline. "Spectrality and Secularism in Bombay Fiction: Salman Rushdie's *The Moor's Last Sigh* and Vikram Chandra's *Sacred Games*." *Textual Practice* 26.5 (2012): 941–71.

Herrero, Dolores. "Crossing *The Secret River*: From Victim to Perpetrator, or the Silent/Dark Side of the Australian Settlement." *Journal of the Spanish Association of Anglo-American Studies* 36.1 (June 2014): 87–105.

Heywood, Christopher. *A History of South African Literature*. Cambridge UP, 2004.

Hilliard, Molly Clark. "'When Desert Armies Stand Ready to Fight': Re-reading McEwan's *Saturday* and Arnold's 'Dover Beach.'" *Partial Answers: Journal of Literature and The History of Ideas* 6.1 (January 2008): 181–206.

Hoad, Neville. *African Intimacies: Race, Homosexuality, and Globalization.* U of Minnesota P, 2007.

Hodge, Bob, and Vijay Mishra. *Dark Side of the Dream: Australian Literature and the Postcolonial Mind.* Allen and Unwin, 1992.

Horton, Emily. *Contemporary Crisis Fictions: Affect and Ethics in the Modern British Novel.* Palgrave Macmillan, 2014.

Huggan, Graham. *Australian Literature: Postcolonialism, Racism, Transnationalism.* Oxford UP, 2007.

Hughes, Eamonn. "Introduction: Northern Ireland—Border Country." In *Culture and Politics in Northern Ireland, 1960–1990,* edited by Eamonn Hughes, 1–12. Open UP, 1991.

Hughes, Robert. *The Fatal Shore: The Epic of Australia's Founding.* Vintage, 1988.

Hughes-D'Aeth, Tony. "The Case for Kim Scott's *That Deadman Dance.*" *Conversation,* 18 February 2014.

Hunt, Tristram. *Cities of Empire: The British Colonies and the Creation of the Urban World.* Metropolitan Books, 2014.

Ignatiev, Noel. *How the Irish Became White.* Routledge, 1995.

Isegawa, Moses. Introduction to *Petals of Blood,* by Ngũgĩ wa Thiong'o, pp. xi–xix. Penguin Classics, 2005.

Itani, Frances. "Book World: Thrity Umrigar's 'The World We Found.'" *Washington Post,* 9 February 2012.

Jacobs, Jane M. *Edge of Empire: Postcolonialism and the City.* Routledge, 1996.

Jameson, Fredric. Afterword to *Aesthetics and Politics: The Key Texts of the Classic Debate Within German Marxism,* by Theodor Adorno, Walter Benjamin, Ernst Bloch, Bertolt Brecht, and Georg Lukács, pp. 196–213. Verso, 1977.

———. *The Geopolitical Aesthetic: Cinema and Space in the World System.* Indiana UP, 1995.

———. *The Political Unconscious: Narrative as a Socially Symbolic Act.* Cornell UP, 1982.

———. *Raymond Chandler and the Detections of Totality.* Verso, 2016.

Johnson, Colin. "White Forms, Aboriginal Content." In *Aboriginal Writing Today: Papers from the First National Conference of Aboriginal Writers Held in Perth, Western Australia in 1983,* edited by Jack Davis and Bob Hodge, pp. 21–33. Australian Institute of Aboriginal Studies, 1985.

Jyoti, Kanchan. "Impact of Colonial Rule on Urban Life." In *The City in Indian History: Urban Demography, Society, and Politics,* edited by Indu Banga, pp. 207–35. Manohar Publications, 1991.

Kakutani, Michiko. "Review: In 'Exit West,' Mohsin Hamid Mixes Global Trouble with a Bit of Magic." *New York Times*, 27 February 2017.

Kamenju, Grant. "*Petals of Blood* as a Mirror of the African Revolution." In *Marxism and African Literature*, edited by Georg M. Gugelberger, pp. 130–35. Africa World Press, 1985.

Kearney, Richard. "Narrating Pain: The Power of Catharsis." *Paragraph: A Journal of Modern Critical Theory* 30.1 (March 2007): 51–66.

Kelly, Aaron. *The Thriller and Northern Ireland since 1969: Utterly Resigned Terror*. Routledge, 2005.

Keneally, Meg. *Fled*. Arcade, 2019.

Kermode, Frank. *The Sense of an Ending: Studies in the Theory of Fiction*. Oxford UP, 1967.

Khanna, Stuti. *The Contemporary Novel and the City: Re-conceiving National and Narrative Form*. Palgrave Macmillan, 2013.

Kilroy, Claire. "*Milkman* by Anna Burns Review: Creepy Invention at Heart of An Original, Funny Novel." *Guardian*, 31 May 2018.

Kim, Jaecheol. "Cognitive Cartography in the Neocolonial World: Jameson's 'Third-World Literature' and Ngũgĩ's *Petals of Blood*." *Texas Studies in Literature and Language* 55.2 (Summer 2013): 184–206.

Kimani, Peter. *Dance of the Jakaranda*. Akashic Books, 2017.

Klein, Naomi. *The Shock Doctrine: The Rise of Disaster Capitalism*. Picador, 2007.

Knight, Stephen. *Australian Crime Fiction: A 200-Year History*. McFarland, 2018.

———. "Crimes Domestic and Crimes Colonial: The Role of Crime Fiction in Developing Postcolonial Consciousness." In *Postcolonial Postmortems: Crime Fiction from a Transcultural Perspective*, edited by Christine Matzke and Susanne Mühleisen, pp. 17–34. Rodopi, 2006.

———. "The Postcolonial Crime Novel." In *The Cambridge Companion to the Postcolonial Novel*, edited by Ato Quayson, pp. 166–87. Cambridge UP, 2015.

Kossew, Sue. "Recovering the Past: Entangled Histories in Kim Scott's *That Deadman Dance*." In *Decolonizing the Landscape: Indigenous Cultures in Australia*, edited by Beate Neumeier and Kay Schaffer, pp. 169–82. Brill, 2014.

———. "Saying Sorry: The Politics of Apology and Reconciliation in Recent Australian Fiction." *Locating Postcolonial Narrative Genres*, edited by Walter Goebel and Saskia Schabio, pp. 171–83. Routledge, 2013.

Kruger, Loren. "Filming the Edgy City: Cinematic Narrative and Urban Form in Postapartheid Johannesburg." *Research in African Literatures* 37.2 (Summer 2006): 141–63.

Kurtz, J. Roger. *Urban Obsessions, Urban Fears: The Postcolonial Kenyan Novel*. Africa World Press, 1998.

Lazarus, Neil. *The Political Unconscious*. Cambridge UP, 2011.

Lefebvre, Henri. *The Production of Space*. Translated by Donald Nicholson-Smith. Blackwell Publishing, 1991.

Lehner, Stefanie. "Post-Conflict Masculinities: *Filiative* Reconciliation in *Five Minutes of Heaven* and David Park's *The Truth Commissioner*." In *Irish Masculinities: Reflections on Literature and Culture*, edited by Caroline Magennis and Raymond Mullen, pp. 65–76. Irish Academic Press, 2011.

Lenin, Vladimir Il'ich. *Imperialism, The Highest Stage of Capitalism; A Popular Outline*. Foreign Language Press, 1970.

Levay, Matthew. *Violent Minds: Modernism and the Criminal*. Cambridge UP, 2019.

Lindsay, Joan. *Picnic at Hanging Rock*. Penguin, 2017.

Longley, Edna. *The Living Stream: Literature and Revisionism in Ireland*. Bloodaxe Books, 1994.

Lorde, Audre. "The Uses of Anger." *Women's Studies Quarterly* 25.1/2 (Spring–Summer 1997): 278–85.

Lorentzen, Christian. "Why Am I So Fucked Up?" *London Review of Books* 34.21 (8 November 2012): 21–22.

Lukács, Georg. *The Theory of the Novel*. Translated by Anna Bostock. MIT Press, 1971.

Lyden, Jacki. "Searching for Clues in a Dangerous Nairobi." *All Things Considered*, National Public Radio, 13 July 2013.

Mahon, Peter. *Violence, Politics, and Textual Interventions in Northern Ireland*. Palgrave Macmillan, 2010.

Manase, Irikidzayi. "Mapping the City Space in Current Zimbabwean and South African Fiction." *Transformation: Critical Perspectives on Southern Africa* 57 (2005): 88–105.

Marais, Mike, and Carita Backström. "An Interview with Ivan Vladislavić." *English in Africa* 29.2 (October 2002): 119–28.

Marcus, David. "Post-Hysterics: Zadie Smith and the Fiction of Austerity." *Dissent* (Spring 2013): 67–73.

Mars-Jones, Adam. "NW by Zadie Smith—Review." *Guardian*, 31 August 2012.

Martin, Theodore. "The Long Wait: Timely Secrets of the Contemporary Detective Novel." *Novel: A Forum on Fiction* 45.2 (Summer 2012): 165–83.

Marx, John. "What Happened to the Postcolonial Novel: The Urban Longing for Form." *Novel: A Forum on Fiction* 50.3 (2017): 409–25.

Marx, Karl. "The Usefulness of Crime." In *Crime and Capitalism: Readings in Marxist Criminology*, edited by David Greenberg, pp. 52–53. Temple UP, 1992.

Masad, Ilana. "Middle East, Middle Class: Pain and Privilege in Hala Alyan's 'Salt Houses.'" *Los Angeles Review of Books*, 3 May 2017.

Masilela, Ntongela. "Ngugi wa Thiong'o's *Petals of Blood*." *Ufahamu: A Journal of African Studies* 9.2 (1979): 9–28.

Maral, Louise. "Warts and All: On Writing *The Secret River*." Interview with Kate Grenville, University of Sydney, 29 August 2006.

Massey, Doreen. *Space, Place, and Gender*. U of Minnesota P, 1994.

Matzke, Christine, and Susanne Muhleisen, eds. *Postcolonial Postmortems: Crime Fiction from a Transcultural Perspective*. Rodopi, 2006.

Mbembe, Achille. "Aesthetics of Superfluity." In *Johannesburg: The Elusive Metropolis*, edited by Sarah Nuttall and Achille Mbembe, pp. 37–67. Duke UP, 2008.

———. "Necropolitics." Translated by Libby Meintjes. *Public Culture* 15.1 (Winter 2003): 11–40.

———. *On the Postcolony*. U of California P, 2001.

McEwan, Ian. *Saturday*. Jonathan Cape, 2005.

McLeod, John. *Postcolonial London: Rewriting the Metropolis*. Routledge, 2004.

Meier, William, and Ian Campbell Ross. "Editors' Introduction: Irish Crime since 1921." *Eire-Ireland* 49.1–2 (Spring/Summer 2014): 7–21.

Merli, Carol. "National Mythologies and Secret Histories: Faultlines in the Bark Hut in Some Recent Australian Fiction." In *Southern Postcolonialisms: The Global South and the New Literary Representations*, edited by Sumanyu Satpathy, pp. 205–18. Routledge, 2009.

Miller, Laura. "The Salon Interview: Ian McEwan." *Salon*, 9 April 2005, www.salon.com/2005/04/09/mcewan_5/.

Mills, Charles W. *The Racial Contract*. Cornell UP, 1999.

Mishra, Pankaj. "Bombay Noir." *New Yorker*, 15 January 2007.

Mitchell, Kate. "Australia's 'Other' History Wars: Trauma and the Work of Cultural Memory in Kate Grenville's *The Secret River*." In *Neo-Victorian Tropes of Trauma: The Politics of Bearing After-Witness to Nineteenth-Century Suffering*, edited by Marie-Luise Kohlke and Christian Gutleben, pp. 253–82. Brill, 2010.

Morris, Jan, and Simon Winchester. *Stones of Empire: The Buildings of the Raj*. Oxford UP, 1983.

Morrison, Toni. *Playing in the Dark: Whiteness and the Literary Imagination*. Harvard UP, 1992.

Moseley, Merritt. "On the 2018 Man Booker Prize." *Sewanee Review* 127.1 (Winter 2019): 141–55.

Mpe, Phaswane. *Welcome to Our Hillbrow: A Novel of Postapartheid South Africa*. Ohio UP, 2011.

Mudrooroo. *Wild Cat Falling*. Angus and Robertson, 1965.

Mukherjee, Upamanyu Pablo. *Crime and Empire: The Colony in Nineteenth-Century Fictions of Crime*. Oxford UP, 2003.

Mukoma Wa Ngugi. "Beauty, Mourning, and Melancholy in *Africa39*." *Los Angeles Review of Books*, 9 November 2014.

———. *Black Star Nairobi*. Melville House, 2013.

———. *Nairobi Heat*. Melville House, 2009.

Negash, Ghirmai. Introduction to *Welcome to Our Hillbrow: A Novel of Postapartheid South Africa*, by Phaswane Mpe, pp. xi–xxvii. Ohio UP, 2011.

Neville, Stuart. *The Twelve*. Vintage, 2010.

Ngũgĩ wa Thiong'o. *Petals of Blood*. Heinemann, 1977.

———. "Petals of Love." In *Writers in Politics: Essays*, by Ngũgĩ wa Thiong'o, pp. 94–98. East African Educational Publishers, 1981.

———. *Writing against Neocolonialism*. Vita Books, 1986.

Nguyen, Viet Thanh. "A Refugee Crisis in a World of Open Doors." *New York Times*, 10 March 2017.

Nicol, Bran, Patricia Pullham, and Eugene McNulty, eds. *Crime Culture: Figuring Criminality in Fiction and Film*. Continuum, 2012.

Nkrumah, Kwame. *Neo-Colonialism: The Last Stage of Imperialism*. Panaf, 1965.

Noah, Trevor. *Born a Crime: Stories from a South African Childhood*. Spiegel and Grau, 2016.

Nolan, Marguerite, and Robert Clarke. "Reading *The Secret River*." *Journal of Commonwealth and Postcolonial Studies* 17 (2011): 9–25.

Nuttall, Sarah. "Literary City." In *Johannesburg: The Elusive Metropolis*, edited by Sarah Nuttall and Achille Mbembe, pp. 195–218. Duke UP, 2008.

O'Connell, Mark. "*Milkman* by Anna Burns, Reviewed." *Slate*, 19 December 2018, https://slate.com/culture/2018/12/milkman-booker-prize-novel-review.html.

O'Connor, Joseph. "Public Men and Private Troubles." *Guardian*, 9 February 2008.

Ogude, James A. "Imagining the Oppressed in Conditions of Marginality and Displacement: Ngugi's Portrayal of Heroes, Workers, and Peasants." *Wasafari* 28 (1998): 3–9.

O'Neill, Stephen. "'Throwing Petrol on the Fire': Writing in the Shadow of the Belfast Urban Motorway." In *Planned Violence: Post/Colonial Urban Infrastructure, Literature and Culture*, edited by Elleke Boehmer and Dominic Davies, pp. 177–94. Palgrave Macmillan, 2018.

Oza, Rupal. *The Making of Neoliberal India: Nationalism, Gender, and the Paradoxes of Globalization*. Routledge, 2006.

Page, Benedicte. "Darkness Down Under: Kate Grenville's New Novel Is an Attempt to Understand the Lives of Her Ancestors." *Bookseller*, 4 November 2005, p. 21.

Pahl, Miriam. "Reframing the Nation-State: The Transgression and Redrawing of Borders in African Crime Fiction." *Research in African Literatures* 49.1 (Spring 2018): 84–102.

Pappé, Ilan. *The Ethnic Cleansing of Palestine.* Oneworld Publications, 2006.

Park, David. *The Truth Commissioner.* Bloomsbury, 2008.

Pepper, Andrew. *Unwilling Executioner: Crime Fiction and the State.* Oxford UP, 2016.

Pinto, Sarah. "Emotional Histories and Historical Emotions: Looking at the Past in Historical Novels." *Rethinking History* 14.2 (2010): 189–207.

Prakash, Gyan. *Mumbai Fables: A History of an Enchanted City.* Princeton UP, 2010.

Propst, Lisa, "Information Glut and Conspicuous Silence in Lauren Beukes's *Zoo City.*" *Journal of Postcolonial Writing* 53.4 (11 November 2016): 1–11.

———. "Truth Commissions and Unspoken Narratives in Gillian Slovo's *Red Dust* and David Park's *The Truth Commissioner.*" *Comparatist* 41 (October 2017): 288–308.

Quayson, Ato. "Introduction: Changing Contexts of the Postcolonial Novel." In *The Cambridge Companion to the Postcolonial Novel*, edited by Ato Quayson, pp. 1–14. Cambridge UP, 2016.

Quinn, Justin. "Postcolonial Poetry of Ireland." In *The Cambridge Companion to Postcolonial Poetry*, edited by Jahan Ramazani, pp. 98–109. Cambridge UP, 2017.

Radstone, Susannah. "'The Place Where We Live': Memory, Mirrors, and *The Secret River.*" *Memory Studies* 6.3 (2013): 286–98.

Ranasinha, Ruvani. "'A Shadow Class Condemned to Movement': Literary Urban Imaginings of Illegal Migrant Lives in the Global North." In *Planned Violence: Post/Colonial Urban Infrastructure, Literature and Culture*, edited by Elleke Boehmer and Dominic Davies, pp. 237–53. Palgrave Macmillan, 2018.

Regan, Bernard. *The Balfour Declaration: Empire, the Mandate, and Resistance in Palestine.* Verso, 2017.

Reitz, Caroline. *Detecting the Nation: Fictions of Detection and the Imperial Venture.* Ohio State UP, 2004.

Roberts, Gregory David. *Shantaram.* St. Martin's Griffin, 2005.

Rooney, Brigid. "Kate Grenville as a Public Intellectual." In *Lighting Dark Places: Essays on Kate Grenville*, edited by Sue Kossew, pp. 17–38. Rodopi, 2010.

Root, Christina. "A Melodiousness at Odds with Pessimism: Ian McEwan's *Saturday.*" *Journal of Modern Literature* 35.1 (Fall 2011): 60–78.

Ross, Michael L. "On a Darkling Planet: Ian McEwan's 'Saturday' and the Condition of England." *Twentieth Century Literature* 54.1 (Spring 2008): 75–96.

Roth, Mitchel P. *An Eye for an Eye: A Global History of Crime and Punishment.* Reaktion Books, 2014.

Ruggiero, Vincenzo. *Crime in Literature: Sociology of Deviance and Fiction.* Verso, 2003.

Rushdie, Salman. *Midnight's Children.* Random House, 1981.

———. *The Moor's Last Sigh.* Vintage International, 1995.

Ryle, Martin. "Anosognosia, or the Political Unconscious: Limits of Vision in Ian McEwan's *Saturday*." *Criticism* 52.1 (Winter 2010): 25–40.
Said, Edward W. *Culture and Imperialism*. Vintage Books, 1994.
———. *Orientalism*. Vintage Books, 1979.
———. *The Question of Palestine*. Vintage Books, 1992.
Saint-Amour, Paul K. *Tense Future: Modernism, Total War, Encyclopedic Form*. Oxford UP, 2015.
Salaita, Steven. "Scattered like Seeds: Palestinian Prose Goes Global." *Studies in the Humanities* 30 (2003): 1–14.
Salamanca, Omar Jabary. "Unplug and Play: Manufacturing Collapse in Gaza." *Human Geography* 4.1 (2011): 22–37.
Schmidt, William E. "Racial Roadblock Seen in Atlanta Transit System." *New York Times*, 22 July 1987.
Schwarz, Bill. "Britain, America, and Europe." In *British Cultural Studies: Geography, Nationality, and Identity*, edited by David Morley and Kevin Robins, pp. 157–69. Oxford UP, 2001.
Scott, David. *Conscripts of Modernity: The Tragedy of Colonial Enlightenment*. Duke UP, 2004.
———. *Omens of Adversity: Tragedy, Time, Memory, Justice*. Duke UP, 2014.
Scott, Kim. *That Deadman Dance*. Picador, 2010.
Shearn, Amy. "How to Recreate Palestine: Researching *Salt Houses*." *JSTOR Daily*, 6 July 2017.
Shehadeh, Raja. *Palestinian Walks: Forays into a Vanishing Landscape*. Scribner, 2007.
Sheller, Mimi. *Mobility Justice: The Politics of Movement in an Age of Extremes*. Verso, 2018.
Shirlow, Peter. "Belfast: The 'Post-Conflict' City." *Space and Polity* 10.2 (August 2006): 99–107.
Siddiqi, Yumna. *Anxieties of Empire and the Fiction of Intrigue*. Columbia UP, 2008.
Smith, Zadie. *NW*. Random House, 2012.
Soja, Edward W. *The Geography of Modernization in Kenya: A Spatial Analysis of Social, Economic, and Political Change*. Syracuse UP, 1968.
———. *Postmodern Geographies: The Reassertion of Space in Critical Social Theory*. Verso, 1989.
———. *Seeking Spatial Justice*. U of Minnesota P, 2010.
Spence, Lester K. *Knocking the Hustle: Against the Neoliberal Turn in Black Politics*. Punctum Books, 2015.
Spivak, Gayatri Chakravorty. *A Critique of Postcolonial Reason: Towards a History of the Vanishing Present*. Harvard UP, 1999.
St. John, Pete. "The Fields of Athenry." 1979.

Staniforth, M. J. "Depicting the Colonial Home: Representations of the Domestic in Kate Grenville's *The Secret River* and *Sarah Thornhill*." *Journal of the Association for the Study of Australian Literature* 13.2 (2013): 1–12.

Ṭāhā, Ibrāhīm. *The Palestinian Novel: A Communication Study*. Routledge, 2010.

Tharoor, Shashi. *An Era of Darkness: The British Empire in India*. Aleph, 2016.

Thatcher, Margaret. "Press Conference Ending Visit to Saudi Arabia (IRA Hunger Strikes)." 21 April 1981. *Margaret Thatcher Foundation*, https://www.margaretthatcher.org/document/104501.

———. "Speech in Belfast." 5 March 1981. *Margaret Thatcher Foundation*, https://www.margaretthatcher.org/document/104589.

———. "Speech to Conservative Women's Congress." Conservative Women's Congress, 24 May 1978, Central Hall, Westminster, London.

Thompson, Jon. *Fiction, Crime, and Empire: Clues to Modernity and Postmodernism*. U of Illinois P, 1993.

Tickell, Alex. "Writing the City and Indian English Fiction: Planning, Violence, and Aesthetics." In *Planned Violence: Post/Colonial Urban Infrastructure, Literature and Culture*, edited by Elleke Boehmer and Dominic Davies, pp. 195–211. Palgrave Macmillan, 2018.

Toal, Catherine. "*Milkman* by Anna Burns: Putting Ardoyne on the Literary Map." *Irish Times*, 16 October 2018.

Tolentino, Jia. "A Novel about Refugees That Feels Instantly Canonical." *New Yorker*, 10 March 2017.

Tonkin, Boyd. "NW, by Zadie Smith." *Independent*, 30 August 2012.

Tuck, Eve, and K. Wayne Yang. "Decolonization Is Not a Metaphor." *Decolonization: Indigeneity, Education & Society* 1.1 (2012): 1–40.

U2. "Van Diemen's Land." *Rattle and Hum*, Sun Studio, 1988.

Umrigar, Thrity. *The World We Found*. Harper Perennial, 2012.

United Nations. "2018 Revision of World Urbanization Prospects." May 2018. https://www.un.org/development/desa/publications.

Uraizee, Joya F. "'Flowers in All Their Colours': *Natios* and Communities in Ngugi wa Thiong'o's *Petals of Blood*." *International Fiction Review* 31 (2004): 27–38.

Varma, Rashmi. "The Gleam and the Darkness: Representations of the City in the Postcolonial Novel." In *The Cambridge Companion to the Postcolonial Novel*, edited by Ato Quayson, 188–207. Cambridge UP, 2015.

———. *The Postcolonial City and Its Subjects: London, Nairobi, Bombay*. Routledge, 2012.

———. "Provincializing the Global City: From Bombay to Mumbai." *Social Text* 22.4 (Winter 2004): 65–89.

Vladislavić, Ivan. *The Restless Supermarket*. And Other Stories, 2014.

Wallace, Elizabeth Kowaleski. "Postcolonial Melancholia in Ian McEwan's *Saturday*." *Studies in the Novel* 39.4 (Winter 2007): 465–80.

Watt, Ian. *Rise of the Novel: Studies in Defoe, Richardson, and Fielding.* U of California P, 1957.

Weizman, Eyal. *Hollow Land: Israel's Architecture of Occupation.* Verso, 2007.

Welsh, David. *The Rise and Fall of Apartheid.* U of Virginia P, 2009.

Williams, Raymond. *The Country and the City.* Oxford UP, 1973.

Wilson, Robert McLiam. *Eureka Street: A Novel of Ireland like No Other.* Arcade Publishing, 1996.

Wolfe, Patrick. "Settler Colonialism and the Elimination of the Native." *Journal of Genocide Research* 8.4 (2006): 387–409.

Wright, Laura. "Inventing Tradition and Colonizing the Plans: Ngugi wa Thiong'o's *Petals of Blood* and Zakes Mda's *The Heart of Redness*." In *Environment at the Margins: Literary and Environmental Studies in Africa,* edited by Byron Caminero-Santangelo and Garth Myers, pp. 235–56. Ohio UP, 2011.

Young, Robert J. C. "Postcolonial Remains." *New Literary History* 43.1 (Winter 2012): 19–42.

INDEX

Aboriginal peoples: crimes done to, 75, 76, 97; marginalization of, 75, 76–77, 79; novel form and Aboriginal writers, 93–94; "Stolen Generations" period, 97. *See also* Australia; *Secret River, The* (Grenville); *That Deadman Dance* (Scott)

Abujidi, Nurhan, 197

Abu-Manneh, Bashir, 181

Agamben, Giorgio, 188

Albany, Australia: as criminal city, 15–16, 74, 92, 93; origins of, 91. See also *That Deadman Dance* (Scott)

Alexander, Michelle, *The New Jim Crow*, 14, 135

Alter, Alexandra, 201

Alyan, Hala. See *Salt Houses* (Alyan)

ancient Greek world: catharsis in, 3–4; totality of world in, 4, 101. *See also* Aristotle

animal familiars in Beukes's *Zoo City*, 131–33, 135–36, 219n2

anticolonialism: catharsis sought by anticolonial theorists, 4; in Irish folklore, 73, 74; renaming of Bombay to Mumbai and, 105; Scott on difference between anticolonialism and postcolonialism, 167; Scott on plot structure of anticolonial stories, 208; Scott on revolution of, 157–58; as stage of struggle in Kenya, 157, 175

Anwer, Megha, 121, 218n16

apartheid: Africans defined as temporary sojourners in city, 128; analogy to zoos, 219n2; crime of, 126, 129; criminal city created by, 127–28; domestic imperialism of, 127–28; end of, 124–26, 129; legacy of, 127–30, 134–36, 142–44; miscegenation as crime under Immorality Act (1927), 128; purpose of, 127, 128. *See also* Johannesburg

Appadurai, Arjun, 105, 112

Appiah, Kwame Anthony, 213n11, 219n5

Arata, Stephen, *Fictions of Loss in the Victorian Fin de Siècle: Identity and Empire*, 14

Aravamudan, Srinivas, 12

Arendt, Hannah, *The Origins of Totalitarianism*, 197, 200, 208, 222n5

Aristotle: *Poetics*, 3; on tragedy and catharsis, 3, 5, 60, 121, 181, 220n6
Arnett, James, 44
Arnold, Matthew, "Dover Beach," 31, 32, 213n10
Ashcroft, Bill, 75, 218n11
Atlanta: arrests triggered by Super Bowl (2019) and Olympics (1996) tourism, 213n13; Buckhead seeking to secede from, 211n1; legacy of racism in contemporary city, viii–ix; as postcolonial city, viii; public transportation (MARTA) in, vii–viii, x; racism and crime in, vii–ix; transformation into multiethnic city, viii, ix
audience. *See* readers
Australia, 15–16, 73–97; British penal colonies established in, 73–74, 77, 215n1 (chap. 3), 216n6; cathartic crime in historical novels of, 75–76, 80, 83, 88, 89–90, 96–97; convicted whites becoming colonizers who murder and displace indigenous peoples, 75, 77, 78; crime defined in, 80; crimes done to Aboriginal peoples in, 75–78, 97; criminal cities in, 15–16, 74, 78, 80, 83, 86, 90, 92, 93; double guilt in criminal founding of, 75; early settlers' need to cooperate with indigenous peoples, 91–92; highest city-based population in today's world, 79; Irish criminals transported to Australia, 77, 215n1 (chap. 3); literary culture compared to contemporary American fiction, 75; literary whiteness and white fragility in, 80; marginalization of Aboriginal Australians, 75, 76–77, 79; need to break free from colonial history to achieve catharsis, 15, 77, 78, 80; original crimes committed in imperial center by those expelled to, 75, 78, 216n6; purification of Britain by expelling criminals to, 78; racial contract in, 79–80, 90–91, 93; reversal of fortunes for poor white colonizers in, 78; Roberts's *Shantaram* equating Australians with the British, 99; sense of victimhood of white settlers in, 77–78; urban planning in, 78–79, 91, 94; whiteness and white privilege in, 76, 77–80, 216n8. *See also* Albany, Australia; *Secret River, The* (Grenville); Sydney; *That Deadman Dance* (Scott)

Bahri, Deepika, 52–53
Balfour Declaration (1917), 177, 178, 183, 222n5
Ball, Anna, 184
Bandung movement, 105; post-Bandung world's collapse of anticolonial hopes, 107, 113
Banville, John, 26
Barghouti, Mourid, *I Saw Ramallah*, 16, 181, 182, 185–88, 197
Barnard, Rita, 127
Barthes, Roland, 5
Beaumont, Alexander, 32, 34
Belfast, 15, 48–72; bustling city and tourist life of today, 49–50, 52, 62; as capital of Northern Ireland, 51–52; cathartic crime not possible in novels of, 51, 52, 54–55, 72;

colonial roots of crime in, 52–53; as criminal city, 50, 52, 54, 57, 60; gentrification in, 49, 52, 65; geography and mapping of interest to writers in, 50, 59, 62; global capitalism of, 62, 64–65; imperial favoritism of Protestants over Catholics in, 15, 51–52; incomprehensible violence in, 54; literary trope used to represent the Troubles in, 59; meaning of crimes in, 50–51; neocolonialism in, 52, 62, 65, 67; neoliberalism in, 52, 62, 65; religious division in, 59; seemingly incomprehensible violence in, 48–49; stereotyping of, 69. See also *Milkman* (Burns); Troubles, the; *Truth Commissioner, The* (Park); *Twelve, The* (Neville)

Belliappa, Mukund, 116, 119

Berger, John, 46

Bergonzi, Bernard, 181

Bernard, Anna, 180, 221n2

Beukes, Lauren. See *Zoo City* (Beukes)

Beveridge Report (Britain, 1942), 21

Bhabha, Homi, 203

Birch, Carol, 93

Black Star Nairobi (Mukoma), 16, 154, 166–76; African American detective working with Kenyan detective, 166–67, 170–71; bombing of American-owned hotel linked to murder, 171; compared to Ngũgĩ's *Petals of Blood*, 171, 174; continuing from *Nairobi Heat,* 170; criminal city of Nairobi in, 173; critical reception of, 172; impossibility of closure in, 175; interethnic violence and tribal tensions in 1980s and 1990s, 172; international crimescape in, 172; International Democracy and Economic Security Council as villain in, 173–75; legacies of colonialism in, 172, 175; neocolonialism in, 166; politics of disillusionment and, 174; set in lead-up to both Kenyan and American elections of 2007/8, 171, 172

Blair, Tony, 29–30

Blomley, Nicholas, 85

Boehmer, Elleke, 17

Bolaño, Roberto, 26n6, 207

Bombay/Mumbai, 1, 98–123; British creation of city in late eighteenth century, 102, 217n5, 218n11; British pitting Hindus and Muslims against each other, 102–3, 113, 217n6; cathartic crime not possible in, 103, 105–7, 114, 122; colonial legacy of, 11, 102–3, 105–7, 112–14, 122; cosmopolitanism of, 100, 104, 115, 122; as criminal city, 101, 114, 117, 118, 123; economic liberalization and globalization of, 105–7, 109, 111; Hindu/Muslim riots (1992–93), 100, 104, 218n12; imperial inflection of city constructed in English model, 102; Indian pride rising in, 100; neoliberal economics mirroring logics of colonial rule in, 105–6, 115, 119; Partition's effects on, 103, 117, 200; political crime in, 105, 117; in precolonial era, 101–2; promise and betrayals of Independence in, 103; romanticism and beauty of, 98, 99; Rushdie's novels set in criminal underworld of, 6; Shivaji statue replacing King Edward VII statue, 106–7, 114; Shiv Sena

Bombay/Mumbai (*continued*)
(right-wing Hindu nationalist political party), 100, 103–4, 106, 112, 114, 116, 122; significance of renaming to Mumbai, 100–101, 104–7, 117, 122; temporal concordance missing in, 101, 121; as Urbs Prima in India, 103; use of "Bombay" as name throughout the book, 217n3; in Westerner's experience in Roberts's *Shantaram*, 98–99. See also *Sacred Games* (Chandra); *World We Found, The* (Umrigar)

Brecht, Bertolt, 60, 208

Bremner, Lindsay, 130

Brexit, 53, 204, 205, 213n6, 215n3

British East India Company, 102

British Empire: emigration as solution to British poverty and urban overcrowding, 82; as focus of study, 15, 205; purification of Britain by expelling criminals to Australia, 78; white Britons' anxiety and melancholia about loss of, 29, 104, 205. *See also* colonialism; imperialism, history of; *specific countries and cities*

Brouillette, Sarah, 26–27, 32

Brown, Jayna, 134

Brown, Richard, 32

Bryant, Mary (Australian folk hero), 76

Burns, Anna. See *Milkman* (Burns)

capitalism: in Beukes's *Zoo City*, 134; capitalist imperialism, 66; continuing imperial and racial capitalism in postcolonial cities, 6; creating "shock therapy" in vulnerable places, 14; disaster capitalism, 14; global capitalism in Neville's *The Twelve*, 62, 64–65; in Grenville's *The Secret River*, 83–84; injustice of, 208; Marxist view of crime as necessary for, 8; mobility and, 209, 218n11; neoliberal capitalism, 10, 14, 38, 62, 105; in Neville's *The Twelve*, former IRA members turned into capitalist investors, 61–62; novel as cultural artifact of, 13; postmodern, 36–37; racial, 2, 6, 12, 83–84; railways and, 155

Carey, Peter, *True History of the Kelly Gang*, 77

Carter, Stephen R., "Decolonization and Detective Fiction: Ngugi wa Thiong'o's *Petals of Blood*," 160, 165

catharsis: Aristotle on, 3, 5, 60, 121, 181, 220n6; change from ancient Greek to present-day conception of, 3–4; from crime in literature, 13, 17, 208; denial of, and empire's continuation, 47; hope for future catharsis, 166, 210; Lukács on, 3–4, 89; in postcolonial urban world, 4, 17; in Thatcher's London, 23; as top-down tool, 3; truth as, 47. *See also specific authors and titles*

cathartic crime, 2–3; in Australian historical novels, 75–76, 80, 83, 88, 89–90, 96–97; in Belfast novels, 51, 52, 54–55, 72; in Bombay/Mumbai novels, 103, 105–7, 114, 122; collective political work in response to, 6–7; as fantasy outcomes for urban anxiety, 7; as impetus for social change to systemic injustice and oppression, 3–4, 96–97, 208; in Johannesburg novels, 51, 68, 70–71, 128, 131, 141, 148; in Kenyan novels, 163–64, 166, 167; in London novels, 23, 34–35, 44–46, 47; in Palestinian novels, 181–83, 186, 189, 195, 198, 201; rebellion and, 208; as way to confront colonial legacies, 6, 97, 175. *See also specific authors and titles*

Chabon, Michael, 120

Chambers, Claire, 10

Chandra, Vikram. See *Sacred Games* (Chandra)

Charles, Ron, 36

Chestnut, J. David, vii

Chotiner, Isaac, 202

Christian, Ed, *The Post-Colonial Detective* (ed.), 14, 160

citizenship's importance in twenty-first century, 176, 200

city, the: crime as collective social negotiation of, 9; as dangerous and inhabited by criminals, 8; division between natives and migrants, 10, 203–4; division into valuable vs. disposable people, 22–23; population growth projected for 2050, 11; as quintessential space of modernity and colonialism, 4; reorganization in daily urban lives, 11; as setting of crime fiction, 14. *See also* criminal city; postcolonial cities; *specific cities by name*

Clancy, Tom, *Patriot Games*, 13

Clarke, John, 22

Clarke, Marcus, *For the Term of His Natural Life*, 74

Clarke, Robert, 82–83

class: in Bombay, 105, 108, 119; Brexit and, 213n6; crime in Britain associated with, 22; experience of crime differentiated by, 3, 66; in Johannesburg of Beukes's *Zoo City*, 132, 134–35; privilege and power from social rise in Grenville's *The Secret River*, 83–86; sentencing and punishment determined by, 75; stereotyping of criminality in crime in literature and, 8. *See also* readers

Cleary, Joe, 62, 184, 185, 189, 221n3

Clendinnen, Inga, 88

Clinton, Bill, 206–7

closure. *See* catharsis

Collins, Eleanor, 88

Collins, Wilkie, *The Moonstone*, 13

colonialism: anticolonialism, 157–58, 167, 208; contemporary, 53, 180–81, 186, 190, 221n3; crime's roots in, 5, 52–53, 92, 95, 99, 107, 112–14, 117, 127, 191, 209; differentiation of terminology from "neocolonialism" and "postcoloniality," 11–12, 167; forced migration to colonies as solution to English poverty and urban overcrowding, 82, 206; globalized system vs. colonial/postcolonial binary, 206; legacies of, 6, 11, 12, 26–27, 38, 61–62, 64, 76–77, 79, 102–3, 105–6, 107, 112–14, 122, 127, 142, 143, 148, 152, 153, 157, 164–65, 172, 175–76, 178, 184, 195, 198, 205–7; metaphor of decolonization, 81, 87; mobility set in motion by, 218n11; as structure not an event, 79, 97

Comaroff, Jean and John L., 9, 131, 212n8

communism: loss of relevance in India, 108, 110–11, 114; US support for Israel in Cold War and, 184. *See also* Marxism

communitarianism: hope for, in Australia, 97; individualism and capitalism in India vs., 105; in McEwan's *Saturday*, 34; in Mpe's *Welcome to Our Hillbrow*, 147

Conrad, Joseph, *Heart of Darkness*, 174

Conservative Women's Conference (London, 1978), 20–21

Cooke, Rachel, 45

Cooper, Frederick, 22

cosmopolitanism: of Bombay, 100, 104, 115, 122; cathartic social cohesion and, 7; of Johannesburg, 132–33, 147; of Palestinians in diaspora, 197

Coundouriotis, Eleni, 172

Craigavon, Lord, 52

Crane, Ralph J., 75

Creswell, Tim, 201

crime: American obsession of 1980s and 1990s with, 206–7, 212n10; in Atlanta, vii–viii, ix; central importance in twenty-first century globalization, 9; colonial roots of, 5, 52–53, 92, 95, 99, 107, 112–14, 117, 127, 191, 209; as constituent of novel form, 13; crimes against humanity, 185, 190; criminal as scapegoat, 9; defined, 8, 80, 212n6; Durkheim on, 9; evolution of concept of, 5, 7–8; hate crimes, 3, 204; international crimescape, 171–72; Marxist understanding of, 8–9; mobility associated with, 23, 113, 153, 154, 168, 201; in modern state system, 8; as political manifestation, 9, 57, 63–65, 69, 97, 99, 207; in postcolonial urban novels, ix, 5–7, 10, 17, 99, 210; right-wing and reactionary rhetorics using for apocalyptic visions, 11; social boundaries crossed by, 9; subversion of power by, 207; unfounded belief in increase of, 206–7; war crimes, 28, 179. *See also* cathartic crime; crime in literature; criminal city; fearmongering about crime; murder; violence; *specific authors and titles*

Crime Bill (1994), 207

crime fiction: Brecht on, 60; Burns's *Milkman*'s relationship to, 58, 60; distinguished from crime in fiction, 14, 100; in Kenya, 156; in Korea, 207; links to colonialism and its aftermath, 156–57; in Northern Ireland, 55; often first voice to respond to postcolonial situation, 99–100. *See also* detective novels

crime in literature: anxieties and fears of changes in urban environments linked with, 2, 212n8; catharsis from, 13, 17, 208; crime fiction distinguished from crime in fiction, 14, 100; as form of collective unconscious, 2, 208; as outlet for colonial tensions, 10; postmodern fiction's relationship to crime depictions, 13, 208; racial and class stereotyping of criminality and, 8; as social and political critique, 15, 208; solving the crime giving closure

to narrative, 5, 7, 12, 122, 165. *See also specific authors and titles*
criminal city: Albany as, 15–16, 74, 92, 93; Belfast as, 50, 52, 54, 57, 60; Bombay as, 101, 114, 117, 118, 123; created by apartheid, 127–28; Johannesburg as, 128, 132, 138–39, 145, 146, 150; London as, 22, 23, 25, 27, 30, 32, 35, 41, 42, 44, 46, 83; multiple definitions of, 10; Nairobi as, 152, 154, 156, 165, 170, 173, 176, 220n9; Palestinian criminal cities, 179, 181, 190; Sydney as, 15–16, 74, 83, 86, 90; transnational imperialism and, 169–70, 175, 176
Critcher, Chas, 22

Daniel arap Moi, 157, 167, 220n4
Davies, Dominic, 17
Davis, Emily S., 144
Deane, Seamus, 53, 180
Derry Girls (Irish sitcom), 72
detective novels, 212n5; extreme violence examined in, 171; linked with imperial ventures and anxieties, 14; of Ngũgĩ and Mukoma, 156, 160, 171; in postcolonial settings, 14. *See also* crime fiction
DiAngelo, Robin, 80, 81
divide-and-rule policy of the British: in Africa, 153, 156, 169; in India, 102–3, 113; in Palestine, 178; similar approach taken by Israelis to Palestinians, 191
Dorling, Danny, 205
Dossal, Mariam, 102
Du Bois, W. E. B., viii, 5

Durant, Will, 103
Durkheim, Émile, 9

Eagleton, Terry, "In the Gaudy Supermarket," 11
Eatough, Matthew, 134, 135–36
Ebileeni, Maurice, 183
Eide, Marian, 6–7
Eliot, Charles Norton Edgecumbe, 151
Eliot, George, *Daniel Deronda*, 221n4
Elkin, Lauren, 37–38, 45
Elkins, Caroline, 155
Enlightenment, 8, 12, 39, 76, 93, 100, 201, 206, 207, 209
Enright, Anne, 37
Erskine, George, 155
Esty, Jed, *Unseasonable Youth*, 213n10
ethnic cleansing: of Hindu/Muslim riots (Bombay, 1992–93), 104, 110; of Palestine, 178, 179, 185, 188
Eureka Street (Wilson), 48–49, 51, 59; compared to Neville's *The Twelve*, 66; sameness on both sides of political divide in, 54–55, 66
exclusion through race, 97, 217n7; Aboriginal peoples, 75, 76–77, 79; in Hamid's *Exit West*, 204. *See also* Other, the; racism
Exit West (Hamid), 16, 200–205, 222n6; binary split of city between natives and migrants, 203–4; catharsis in, 202, 205–6, 207; cathartic crime in, 201; contemporary refugee crisis in, 201; criminal cities in, 201; criminalized presence of refugees in London in, 203–4; critical reception of, 201–2; globalization in, 202; government-sponsored

Exit West (Hamid) *(continued)* pogrom in, 204; hate crimes in, 204; individualism stressed over communalism in, 207; intended audience of affluent, educated white readers, 206; legacies of colonialism in, 202; London as original source of empire unable to move on from "postcolonial melancholia," 205; marginalization of Saeed and Nadia to outskirts of London, 204; Marin in California, as home to both refugees and lifelong Californians in, 204–5; migration as fundamental human right, 206; Nadia and Saeed as refugees moving repeatedly through magical realism, 202–3, 206; refugees as "Other" in, 204; West seen as progressive option, 206

Fadem, Maureen E. Ruprecht, 53
Fanon, Frantz, 4, 203–4; *The Wretched of the Earth*, 10, 164
Farag, Joseph R., 187
fearmongering about crime: capitalist projects relying on, 14; in New York City of 1970s and 1980s, 212n10; privatized travel in reaction to, 23; racialized nature of, 22; refugee crisis and, 207; Thatcher's speech and, 20–21; Trump's remarks on immigrants and, 201; unfounded belief in increase of crime, 206–7, 212n8
Field Day group (Northern Ireland), 53
Foucault, Michel, 9; *Discipline and Punish*, 207, 223n11

France: imperial legacies of, 169–70, 183, 198; unfounded eighteenth-century belief in rise of crime in, 207
Franklin, Ruth, 36, 45
Frenkel, Ronit, 140

Gallagher, Jodi, 89
Gallien, Claire, 200
Gandhi, Mahatma, 102
Garner, Dwight, 56
Gates, Henry Louis, viii
gender. *See* masculinity; sexual harassment of women
gentrification: Belfast and, 49, 52, 65; London and, 10, 35, 40
Georgia: as English penal colony, ix, 216n6. *See also* Atlanta
Ghalayini, Basma, 178, 182
Gibbon, Edward, *The Decline and Fall of the Roman Empire*, 219n1
Gikandi, Simon, 159
Gilroy, Paul, 205, 213n12
Ginibi, Ruby Langford, 216n3
globalization, 9, 105–7, 109, 111, 202, 206
Goan, Cathal, 72
Good Friday Agreement (Northern Ireland, 1998), 48–49, 52, 53, 60, 64, 71, 215n3
Gopal, Priyamvada, 103
Gordon, Neve, 186–88
Graham, Shane, 141
Graham, Stephen, 187
Gregory, Derek, 184, 188
Grenville, Kate. *See Secret River, The* (Grenville)
Griffiths, Gareth, 75

Hadley, Elaine, 32
Hage, Ghassan, 96–97
Hall, Stuart, et al., *Policing the Crisis: Mugging, the State, and Law and Order*, 22
Hamas, 222n10
Hamid, Mohsin. See *Exit West* (Hamid)
Hammad, Isabella, *The Parisian*, 16, 177–78
Hansen, Thomas Blom: *The Saffron Wave: Democracy and Hindu Nationalism in Modern India*, 100, 111; *Wages of Violence: Naming and Identity in Postcolonial Bombay*, 104–5
Hardt, Michael, 169–70, 172, 175, 205
hate crimes, 3, 204
Heidemann, Birte, 66
Herbert, Caroline, 107, 117, 123
Herrero, Dolores, 87
Heywood, Christopher, 126–27
Hilliard, Molly Clark, 32
HIV/AIDS, 137, 148, 219n8
Hoad, Neville, 132, 147
Hobbes, Thomas, *Leviathan*, 8
Hodge, Bob, 75
Holocaust, 185
home invasion in McEwan's *Saturday*, 15, 28–29, 31
Hong Kong extradition bill (2019), 207
hooks, bell, viii
Hornby, William, 102
Horton, Emily, 31, 32
Huggan, Graham, 10, 216n2
Hughes, Eamonn, 59
Hughes-D'Aeth, Tony, 91–92, 95
Hungary, fear of immigrants in, 207
Hunt, Tristram, 102

imaginaries: in Park's *The Truth Commissioner*, 67, 69; Shiv Sena's appeal to social imaginaries in India, 104; spatial order of imperial imaginings, 10
immigration. See refugees and immigrants
imperialism, history of: artificial borders, creation of, 11, 198, 199; continuation of, 47; injustice in, 208; Iraq invasion (2003) as one last gasp for British imperial glory, 25; in Neville's *The Twelve*, 62, 66, 67; novel as cultural artifact of, 13–14; racism linked to, 42; in Smith's *NW*, 23, 42. See also colonialism
India. See Bombay/Mumbai; *Sacred Games* (Chandra); *World We Found, The* (Umrigar)
individualism: as Enlightenment concept, 8; in Hamid's *Exit West*, 207; in McEwan's *Saturday*, 27–28, 32, 34; neoliberalism and, 105, 129, 147; in novels, 13
inequality: among cities, 12; gender inequality, 57–60; neoliberal inequality, 111, 112, 115, 129, 130, 138. See also class; exclusion through race; racism
international humanitarian organizations, 169–70, 173–74
IRA. See Belfast; Northern Ireland; *Twelve, The* (Neville)
Iraq invasion (2003), 15, 23–26, 28, 30
Ireland: Catholic sufferings in, 77; criminals transported to Australia, 74, 77, 215n1 (chap. 3); Great Famine (1840s), 73–74; independence from United Kingdom, 52;

Ireland (*continued*)
    Irish immigrants inscribed into whiteness in new countries, 77, 216n5; partition from North Ireland (1921), 51–52
I Saw Ramallah (Barghouti), 16, 181, 182, 185–88, 197
ISIS, 198, 212n4, 222n1, 222n5; "The End of Sykes-Picot" (video), 199; imperialist goals of creating Caliphate, 199–200
Israel: as contemporary colonial power in Palestine, 180–81; criminal cities of, 188; establishment of state of (1948), 178, 183, 184; Israeli-only roads constructed, 180; legacies of Holocaust and, 185; as outpost of Western hegemony, 179; settlements, construction of, 179, 186, 188; US support for, 178, 180, 184, 222n10; Western economic model adopted in, 179; Western urban model adopted in, 187. See also *Salt Houses* (Alyan); Zionist movements

Jacobs, Jane M., 20, 79, 215n18; *Edge of Empire: Postcolonialism and the City*, 9–10
Jameson, Fredric, 2, 4–5; *Aesthetics and Politics*, 154; on closure in narrative, 122; on collective political work in response to cathartic crime, 6–7; on historical fiction, 74; on political interpretation of literary texts, 9; *The Political Unconscious*, 6–7, 9; *Raymond Chandler and the Detections of Totality*, 5, 46

Jefferson, Tony, 22
Jim Crow, ix, 14
Johannesburg, 16, 124–50; cathartic crime in, 51, 68, 70–71, 128, 131, 141, 148; comparison of Hillbrow to London's East End, 130; cosmopolitanism of, 132–33, 147; crime supplanting racism in, 128–29, 131; as criminal city, 128, 132, 138–39, 145, 146, 150; demographic changes in 1990s, 129; emotional catharsis in, 126; end of apartheid in, 124–26, 129; Hillbrow neighborhood as focus of texts, 130; as largest city in South Africa, 127; legacies of imperialism and apartheid, 127–30; limited integration in white neighborhoods in, 129, 130; neoliberal inequality in, 129, 130, 138; neoliberal system of criminality in, 126, 128–31, 134, 135, 138, 143, 146–48; racism with veneer of colorblind oppression, 126, 128–29; reconciliation in, 148; systemic injustices going undetected in, 139; as unimaginable and unmanageable city, 130; white flight, 129, 130, 132. See also apartheid; *Welcome to Our Hillbrow* (Mpe); *Zoo City* (Beukes)
Johnson, Colin. See Mudrooroo
Jordan, 202, 222n5
Joyce, James: "The Dead," 34; *Ulysses*, 30, 213n1
Jyoti, Kanchan, 217n6

Kakutani, Michiko, 201–2
Kearney, Richard, 6, 47

Kelly, Aaron, 58, 62
Kelly, Ned (Australian folk hero), 77
Keneally, Meg, *Fled*, 76–77
Kenya, 16, 151–76; brutality of British imperialism in, 155–56; colonial legacies in, 153, 157, 164–65; colonial racial hierarchy in, 153, 155; creation by British colonialism, 151; formalization of British rule as East Africa Protectorate, 154; interethnic violence and tribal tensions in (1980s and 1990s), 167, 172; Mau Mau guerrilla war in, 154–55, 220n3, 220n10; neocolonialism in, 155, 157–58, 163–66, 168, 169, 175; novels emphasizing city life in, 156; railways in, 151–52, 155–56, 159, 176, 220n15; Western continuing interference in, 157; white minority presence in, 154. *See also* Mukoma Wa Ngugi; Nairobi; Ngũgĩ wa Thiong'o
Kermode, Frank, 212n4
Keynesian economics, 21
Khanna, Stuti, 217n5
Kilroy, Claire, 57, 59
Kim, Jaecheol, 161
Kimani, Peter, *Dance of the Jakaranda*, 152, 176
King George Town. *See* Albany, Australia
Klein, Naomi, 105; *The Shock Doctrine*, 14, 111, 218n15
Knight, Stephen, 99, 156
Kowaleski Wallace, Elizabeth, 26, 32–33
Kruger, Loren, 127, 129–30, 146
Kurtz, J. Roger, 156, 160, 166
Kuwait. See *Salt Houses* (Alyan)

Lazarus, Neil, 164
Lefebvre, Henri, 16, 187, 188
Lehner, Stephanie, 71
Lenin, Vladimir, 155
Levay, Matthew, *Violent Minds: Modernism and the Criminal*, 15
Lindsay, Joan, *Picnic at Hanging Rock*, 16, 76
literary detectives. *See* detective novels
London, 15, 19–47; "absentee landlord" problem in, 223nn8–9; British attitude on urban social danger, 21; cathartic crime in, 23, 34–35, 44–46, 47; crime associated with race, class, immigration, and imperialism in, 22; as criminal city, 22, 23, 25, 27, 30, 32, 35, 41, 42, 44, 46, 83; division into valuable vs. disposable people, 22; as fractured city, 22–23; gentrification of northwest section, 35, 40; impact of British Empire on, 11, 15, 205; Met as formalized police in, 22; neoliberalism of, 20–21, 25, 35; of Woolf's *Mrs. Dalloway* compared to McEwan's *Saturday*, 24–25, 30, 32. *See also* Brexit; *NW* (Smith); *Saturday* (McEwan)
Longley, Edna, 53
Lorde, Audre, 89
Lorentzen, Christian, 36, 44
Lukács, Georg, 3–4, 89, 92–93, 101, 209, 211nn2–3
Lustig, Kfir Cohen, 182

MacLaverty, Bernard, 59
Mahon, Peter, 54, 57, 66, 72, 74
Manase, Irikidzayi, 128, 144

Marcus, David, 36, 43, 45
Mars-Jones, Adam, 36, 38
MARTA (Metropolitan Atlanta Rapid Transit Authority). *See* public transportation
Martin, Theodore, 120
Marxism: on crime, 8–9; historical view of, 101, 114; Mukoma as Marxist, 172; Ngũgĩ as Marxist, 154, 157, 159, 161, 165, 172
Masad, Ilana, 190
masculinity: male gaze of Northern Irish writers, 59; restored masculine pride in India after colonial history of emasculation, 119; Shiv Sena's appeal to in India, 104, 117; unwanted sexual attention from men, 59–60
Massey, Doreen, 17
Matzke, Christine, *Postcolonial Postmortems: Crime Fiction from a Transcultural Perspective* (ed., with Muhleisen), 14
Mau Mau guerilla war, 154–55, 220n3, 220n10
Mbembe, Achille, 188, 213n12; *On the Postcolony*, 155, 158
McDermid, Val, 55
McEwan, Ian. *See Saturday* (McEwan)
McNulty, Eugene, *Crime Culture: Figuring Criminality in Fiction and Film* (ed. with Nicol and Pullham), 14
Meier, William, 55
migration. *See* refugees and immigrants
Milkman (Burns), 15, 51, 55–61, 67; background menace creating suspended animation in, 56–57; cathartic crime not possible in, 51, 56, 58, 60; crime fiction genre and, 58; critical reception of, 56, 57; disengagement of middle sister from violent conflict, 56–58; gender-based violence in, 55–61, 71; gender inequality in, 59; human essentialism in, 57; maybe-boyfriend of middle sister as Milkman's target, 57–58; middle sister's relationship with Milkman and sexual harassment/stalking, 55–61; Milkman only named character, 55–56; Milkman shot and killed by state forces, 60; mobility and transportation in, 56, 58–60, 215n4; no community support to stop violence in, 71; pervasive urban crime and violence in, 57; political nature of crime in, 57; publication decades after the Troubles, 60; sectarian warfare between two communities, 55; universal applicability of, 60–61; unspecified city in, 55, 57
Miller, Laura, 26
Mills, Charles W., 79
Mishra, Pankaj, 121
Mishra, Vijay, 75
Mitchell, Kate, 88
mobility: in Australian historical novels, 76; British crackdown in colonial Kenya on, 155; British expulsion of criminals to Australia and, 78; in Burns's *Milkman*, 56, 58–60, 215n4; capitalism linked to, 209, 218n11; central to Western modernity, 196; colonialism setting in motion, 209, 218n11; comparison of mobility of those with and

without power, 206, 222n4; crime associated with, 23, 113, 153, 154, 168, 201; international travel in Mukoma's novels, 170; in Kenya, 151, 161–63, 170, 175; in McEwan's *Saturday*, 20, 46; in Ngũgĩ's *Petals of Blood*, 161–63, 170; Palestinians, restrictions on, 178, 179–80, 186–87, 193, 195–97; politics and, 23; in postcolonial urban novels, ix, 13; right to immobility, 206; Sheller on need for mobility justice, 208–9; in Smith's *NW*, 19–20, 36, 37–39, 43, 46, 213n8; in Thatcher's London, 23. See also refugees and immigrants; *specific authors and titles*

modernity: city epitomizing, 4, 8, 105; mobility central to, 196; novel as text of, 12–13, 211n3; Palestinians locked out of, 187, 197

Modi, Narendra, 204, 207

Morris, Jan, 114

Moseley, Merritt, 56

Mpe, Phaswane. See *Welcome to Our Hillbrow* (Mpe)

Mrs. Dalloway (Woolf): compared to McEwan's *Saturday*, 24–25, 30, 32, 213n5; compared to Smith's *NW*, 214n12

Mudrooroo (Colin Johnson): detective series by, 216n4; on novel form as problem for Aboriginal writers, 93–94; *Wild Cat Falling*, 16, 76

Muhleisen, Susanne, *Postcolonial Postmortems: Crime Fiction from a Transcultural Perspective* (ed., with Matzke), 14

Mukherjee, Upamanyu Pablo, *Crime and Empire: The Colony in Nineteenth-Century Fictions of Crime*, 14

Mukoma Wa Ngugi, 16; on colonial legacies in Nairobi, 153, 172, 175; compared to his father, Ngũgĩ wa Thiong'o, 167, 170, 174, 175; denial of postcolonial catharsis in, 153, 167; European influences on novels of, 156; mapping together crime, travel, and imperial legacies, 154; Marxist-like approach of, 154. See also *Black Star Nairobi* (Mukoma); *Nairobi Heat* (Mukoma)

Mumbai. See Bombay/Mumbai

murder: in Beukes's *Zoo City*, 136–39; in Mukoma's *Nairobi Heat* and *Black Star Nairobi*, 168–69, 171; in Ngũgĩ's *Petals of Blood*, 158–59, 164–65; in Park's *The Truth Commissioner*, 67, 70; in Smith's *NW*, 19–20, 41, 42, 44, 46; unexplained death while in Israeli jail in Alyan's *Salt Houses*, 190, 192, 195

Nairobi, 16, 151–76; British brutality in, 155; colonial legacies overlaid with African stylings, 156, 171; creation by British colonialism, 151; as criminal city, 152, 154, 156, 165, 170, 173, 176, 220n9; international crime in, 171–72; novel as European import to, 156; as postcolonial city, 156; railway creation of modern city of, 151, 156; travel and crime as parallel tropes in literature of, 153; violence of twenty-first century in, 171, 175. See also Mukoma Wa Ngugi; Ngũgĩ wa Thiong'o

Nairobi Heat (Mukoma), 16, 154, 166–76; African American detective working with Kenyan detective, 166, 168; compared to Ngũgĩ's *Petals of Blood*, 170; criminal city of Nairobi in, 170; expanding upon themes of crime, transportation, and colonial legacies in Mukoma's father's work, 168; impossibility of closure in, 170; links to Mau Mau uprising, 168; murder occurring in Wisconsin leading to Nairobi, 168; neocolonialism in, 166, 168, 169; Never Again Foundation operating as money-making shell, 173; remnants of colonialism to be ferreted out, 168; revenge killing of white settler (Lord Thompson) signaling end of an era, 169; Rwandan genocide in, 167–70; transnational imperialism in, 169–70; understanding oppression and how to deal with it, 169

necropolitics, 188, 192

Negash, Ghirmai, 142

Negri, Antonio, 169–70, 172, 175, 205

neocolonialism: in Belfast, 52, 62, 66, 67; differentiation of terminology from "colonialism" and "postcoloniality," 11–12, 167; in Kenya, 155, 157–58, 163–66, 168, 169, 175; Ngũgĩ on dangers of, 157, 163–66, 175; Nkrumah on, 157

neo-imperialism in McEwan's *Saturday*, 23, 32, 35

neoliberalism: of Belfast, 52, 62, 65; of Bombay, 105–6, 109, 111, 113–14, 118–19; definition of, 217n9; growth in reaction to communism's collapse, 114; individualism and, 105, 129; inequality resulting from, 111, 112, 115, 129, 130, 138; of Johannesburg, 126, 128–31, 134, 135, 138, 143, 146–48; of London, 20–21, 25, 35; policy trinity of, 111; Thatcher and, 23, 27. *See also* capitalism; *specific authors and titles*

Neville, Stuart. See *Twelve, The* (Neville)

New York City, fear of crime in 1970s and 1980s in, 212n10

Ngũgĩ wa Thiong'o, 16, 153–57; on colonial legacies, 153, 157, 164–65; compared to his son, Mukoma, 167; on crime in postcolonial Kenya, 154; on dangers of neocolonialism, 157, 163–66, 175; denial of postcolonial catharsis in, 153, 163–65; *Devil on the Cross*, 220n5; European influences on novels of, 156; in exile, 159; imprisonment of, 157, 159, 220n4; mapping together crime, travel, and imperial legacies, 154; "The Martyr" (short story), 220n10; as Marxist, 154, 159, 161, 165; name change of, 166; native languages and village life as main focuses of, 153–54, 166; politics of disillusionment and, 171; on post–World War II Kenya consisting of three stages, 157, 175; praising his son, Mukoma, for writing detective novel, 171; *Writing against Neocolonialism*, 157, 175. *See also Petals of Blood* (Ngũgĩ)

Nguyen, Viet Thanh, 202

Nicol, Bran, *Crime Culture: Figuring Criminality in Fiction and Film* (ed. with Pullham and McNulty), 14
Nkrumah, Kwame, 157
Noah, Trevor, *Born a Crime: Stories from a South African Childhood*, 127–28
Nolan, Marguerite, 82–83
Northern Ireland: Brexit opposition in, 53; continuing as part of United Kingdom, 52–53; Craigavon declaring a Protestant state in, 52; crime fiction's popularity in, 55; geography of interest to writers in, 59; imperial settlement by English and Scottish immigrants, 51; lack of engagement with past foreclosing possibility of catharsis in future, 71–72; Palestine analogy to, 221n3; partition of Ireland creating, 51–52; Protestants retaining economic and social power in, 53; sameness on both sides of political divide in, 54–55, 66. *See also* Belfast; Troubles, the
novels: Aboriginal writers and novel form, 93–94; as Arab writing's dominant form, 181; closure in, 5, 7, 12, 122, 165, 170, 175; as European import to Nairobi, 156; exploration of multiple temporalities in, 208; forward movement of, 181, 182, 209; Lukács on novel form, 4, 92–93, 209, 211n3; realist fiction, 159, 171; shift away from central epiphanic episode in, 121; stream-of-consciousness style in, 36, 38; as successors to epics, 101; teleological role of, 7, 12, 208; as texts of modernity, 12–13, 211n3; world-making and structure of, 4, 5, 17. *See also* postcolonialism
Nuttall, Sarah, 142
NW (Smith), 15, 19–20, 35–47; bildungsroman in, 36; cartographies of characters in, 37, 39, 41–43; cathartic crime's failure in, 35, 44–46; centrality of NW to its residents while central London is nowhere for them, 37–38, 42; chronicle of Natalie's and Nathan's nighttime walk in, 36, 41–43; compared to McEwan's *Saturday*, 35–38, 45, 46; compared to Woolf's *Mrs. Dalloway*, 214n12; crime occurring after travel in, 23; critical reception of, 36, 45, 46; Felix's murder as center of narrative in, 41, 42, 44, 46; fragmented story told in fragments in, 36, 37; Frank's (Natalie/Keisha's husband) reaction to Natalie's registration on sex website, 41, 214n13; gentrification in, 35, 40; immigrants in, 36, 38; Keisha's name change to Natalie, 35, 40, 42, 214n14; Leah's story showing allegiance to place, 38–40; legacies of imperialism in, 38, 213n10; living outside of traditional teleology and London's postmodern age as a crime, 39; London as criminal city in, 35, 41, 42, 44, 46; Michel's (Leah's husband) as unsuccessful entrepreneur in, 44, 213–14n11; mobility in, 19–20, 36, 37–39, 43, 46, 213n8; mugging of Felix prior to his murder, 42, 214n17; multicultural perspectives of characters in, 35;

NW (Smith) *(continued)*
    Natalie/Keisha's experience of space compared to Leah's, 40, 41–43; Nathan reported by Leah and Natalie to police as suspect for Felix's murder, 45–46, 214n15; Nathan's story providing key to later plot, 43, 215n19; passage of time in, 38–41; plot's location in NW as nowhere area of London, 37, 41; postmodern capitalism in, 36–37; racism in, 38, 42, 44, 46; stream-of-consciousness style in, 36, 38; third-person narration in, 36

Obama, Barack, 171
O'Connell, Mark, 60
O'Connor, Joseph, 71
Ogude, James A., 163
O'Neill, Stephen, 68
Orientalism, 98, 100, 217n7
Other, the: crime creating panic about, 17, 22; fear of and antagonism to, 17, 47, 79, 206; in Hamid's *Exit West*, 204; in Johannesburg society, 129, 130; in Kimani's *Dance of the Jakaranda*, 153; in McEwan's *Saturday*, 29, 33; in Mpe's *Welcome to Our Hillbrow*, 144; xenophobia in India, 104, 110, 111–12. *See also* exclusion through race; subaltern populations
Oza, Rupal, 111, 118–19

Palestine, 16, 177–98; ambiguity of Palestinians, 182; Anglophone literary and cultural understanding of crime in, 179; Anglophone novels' focus on West Bank, 221n1; Balfour Declaration (1917), 177, 178, 183; British Mandate, 177–78, 183; catharsis (unattainable) sought in novels of, 181–83, 186, 189, 195, 198; constant reinvention of, 186; contemporary colonialism in, 180–81, 186, 190, 221n3; contrast of low-level Palestinian crimes vs. British and Israeli war crimes, 179; crime in novels of, 188; criminal cities in, 179, 181, 190; displacement and exile of Palestinians, 180, 182, 183, 221n5; ethnic cleansing in, 178, 179, 185, 188; extrajudicial killings in, 188, 190, 192, 195; Israeli occupation, 178–79; legacies of colonialism in, 178, 184, 195, 198; locked out of modernity, 187, 197; mobility restrictions on Palestinians, 178, 179–80, 186–87, 193, 195–97; multiple social spaces in, 187; Nablus in West Bank, 177–78, 190–91; Nakba (1948) exiling of Palestinians, 180, 183, 185–86, 189–90, 197–98, 200; Northern Ireland analogy to, 221n3; novel offering a form of resistance to ongoing imperial regimes, 181; Ottoman rule, end of, 177, 183; scattered nature of novels paralleling scattered nature of Palestine and its diaspora, 181, 182, 187, 189, 196; Sykes-Picot Agreement (1916), 178, 183, 198–200, 222n5; tragedy tropes in Palestinian writing, 181; unique and underrepresented in postcolonial discourse, 180; use of term

"Palestine," 220–21n1. See also *Exit West* (Hamid); *I Saw Ramallah* (Barghouti); *Salt Houses* (Alyan)

Pappé, Ilan, *The Ethnic Cleansing of Palestine*, 185

Park, David. See *Truth Commissioner, The* (Park)

Paterson, Glenn, 59

Peel, Robert, 92

penal colonies during British Empire: Australia, 73–74, 77, 215n1 (chap. 3), 216n6; Georgia, ix, 216n6

Pepper, Andrew, 8, 139; *Unwilling Executioner: Crime Fiction and the State*, 15

Petals of Blood (Ngũgĩ), 153, 158–66; capitalism in, 163; cathartic crime not part of, 163–64, 166; compared to Mukoma's *Black Star Nairobi*, 171, 174; compared to Mukoma's *Nairobi Heat*, 170; crime-driven narrative of murder of three Kenyan businessmen, 158–59, 164–65; critical reception of, 159, 160, 163–65; evaluated as detective novel, 160; on failings of newly independent Kenyan government, 158–60; Godrey as unsuccessful detective, 160–61, 164–65, 220n7; hope for future catharsis in, 166; Ilmorog and Nairobi's relationship as central to, 158, 161–63; imperial legacies in Kenya in, 158–59, 164–65; linkage to Yeats's "The Second Coming," 166; marginalized workers in, 163; Mau Mau rebellion as historical background to, 158; mobility and Trans-Africa highway in, 161–63, 170; moving away from anticolonial narrative form, 167; neocolonialism in, 163–66, 175; political catharsis in, 160, 163, 166; socialist realism in, 163–64

place, affection for, 17, 38–40, 44–45, 122, 146, 194

political conditions: cathartic crime as impetus for social change to, 3–4, 96–97, 208; crime as political manifestation, 9, 53–54, 105, 117; mobility and, 23; violent aesthetic challenging, 6. See also neoliberalism

postcolonial cities: Belfast as, 52–53; cathartic crime in, 10; continuing imperial and racial oppression in, 6, 10; crime in, as trope in contemporary novels, 1; defined by crime, 1; meaning of "postcolonial," 11; as palimpsest, 6, 105–6, 115; spatial order of imperial imaginings in, 10; trying to make sense of crime of colonialism, 5

postcolonialism: cathartic crime in postcolonial urban novels, 6–7, 10, 17, 210; crime resonating with past crimes of colonialism, 5, 99; differentiation of terminology from "colonialism" and "neocolonialism," 11–12, 167; international humanitarian organizations manifesting power in, 170; lingering effects of, ix, 5; Scott on, 208; underrepresentation of Palestine in postcolonial novels, 180. See also postcolonial cities

postmodernism, 13, 36, 39, 141

Prakash, Gyan, 102, 106–7, 122

Propst, Lisa, 71, 132, 138
public transportation: in Burns's *Milkman*, 59; city not planned for use of, 17; improvement in twenty-first century, x; MARTA in Atlanta, vii–viii, x; reduced public funding for, 23; in Smith's *NW*, 37, 38
Pullham, Patricia, *Crime Culture: Figuring Criminality in Fiction and Film* (ed. with Nicol and McNulty), 14

Quayson, Ato, 212n4
Quinn, Justin, 53

racial capitalism, 2, 6, 12, 83–84
racism: in Atlanta, vii–ix; in Australia, 79; in conviction and sentencing, 14, 46, 97; criminality as replacement for, in Beukes's *Zoo City*, 133–36, 138; fearmongering and, 21; in India, 110–11; Kenya, colonial racial hierarchy in, 153, 155; racial contract to ensure "white" individuals keep power, 79–80, 90–91, 93; in Smith's *NW*, 38, 42, 44, 46; stereotyping of criminality and, 8, 97, 207. *See also* apartheid
Radstone, Susannah, 81
railways. *See* transport
Ranasinha, Ruvani, 223n10
Raspail, Jean, *The Camp of the Saints*, 7
readers: Alyan's *Salt Houses* intended for Western audience, 196; Beukes urging to become detectives, 139; Bobby's dance not understood by white audience of Scott's *That Deadman Dance*, 94–95; Grenville's assumption that readers are white, 87, 88; Hamid's *Exit West* intended for affluent, educated white audience, 206; Mpe's *Welcome to Our Hillbrow* drawing reader in through use of second-person narration, 140, 141, 146, 148; viewing texts through sedimented reading habits, 2
Reagan, Ronald, 206
rebellion, 207–8. *See also* Mau Mau guerilla war; Troubles, the
refugees and immigrants: in Chandra's *Sacred Games*, 117, 200; contemporary refugee crisis, 201, 207; criminalizing, 22, 201, 223n10; fears of Londoners, 15, 21, 223n9; in Johannesburg, 130, 143–44; migration as fundamental human right, 206; mobility of, 200–201; in Mpe's *Welcome to Our Hillbrow*, 143–44, 200; nativism and far-right movements in reaction to, 17, 104, 202, 204, 207; Palestinians in exile, 180, 182, 183, 221n5; resettlement in Atlanta area, ix; in Smith's *NW*, 36, 38; use of term "refugee," 200. *See also Salt Houses* (Alyan)
Regan, Bernard, 184
Reitz, Caroline, *Detecting the Nation: Fictions of Detection and the Imperial Venture*, 13
religion in India: colonial legacy pitting Hindus and Muslims against each other, 102–3, 113; Hindu-based citizenship and, 100, 204, 207; Hindu/Muslim riots (1992–93), 100, 104, 218n12; linkage between

anti-communism and Islamophobia, 111; Partition's hardening of Hindu/Muslim binary, 103, 200

religion in Northern Ireland: Craigavon declaring a Protestant state, 52; imperial favoritism of Protestants over Catholics in, 15, 51–52; Protestants retaining economic and social power, 53; religious division in Belfast, 59; sectarian warfare between two communities in Burns's *Milkman*, 55

Rhys, Jean, *Wide Sargasso Sea*, 6

Roberts, Brian, 22

Roberts, Gregory David, *Shantaram*, 16, 98–99

Roman law, 212n6

Rooney, Patrick, 50, 62

Root, Christina, 34

Ross, Ian Campbell, 55

Ross, Michael L., 32

Ruggiero, Vincenzo, *Crime in Literature: Sociology of Deviance and Fiction*, 15

Rushdie, Salman: *Midnight's Children*, 1, 6, 103; *The Moor's Last Sigh*, 6

Rwandan genocide, 167–70

Ryle, Martin, 31–32

Sacred Games (Chandra), 16, 101, 115–23; anti-cathartic conclusion to the crime, 119–20, 122, 218n16; Bollywood film industry in, 119, 123; bombing apocalypse planned, 118, 120; corruption of postcolonial state in, 107–8, 117; criminal city in, 117–18, 123; criminal underworld flourishing in Bombay, 115–17; critical reception of, 107, 116–17, 120–21; detective fiction's mold rejected in, 123; Hindu organization's (Kalki Sena) plan to purge city of "other" foreign elements, 116; imperial and postcolonial crimes recounted in, 116–17; legacy of colonial crimes in, 107, 117; neoliberal economy in, 117–19; Qu'ran used to play into Muslim stereotyping, 116; Sartaj Singh, Sikh police inspector, in negotiation with Hindu gangster, Gaitonde, 115; Sikh woman (mother of Sartaj) driven out of Pakistan by Partition, 117; traffic jam at end accepted as part of city life, 122; worldview that transcends good and evil, 121

Said, Edward, 13, 180, 221n2, 222n5; *Culture and Imperialism*, 10, 13; definition of Orientalism by, 98; *The Question of Palestine*, 183–84, 185; on what liberation looks like for Palestinian community, 198

Saint-Amour, Paul K., 5

Salaita, Steven, 193

Salt Houses (Alyan), 16, 178, 179, 189–98; Alia's dislike of Kuwait and desire to move to Amman, 192, 193; Alia's venting of her rage, 192–93; American passport's power in, 195; Atef and Alia's move to Kuwait, 192–93; Atef's admiration for Kuwait's growth, 193–94; catharsis as impossibility in, 189, 190, 192–96; colonial nature of Israeli occupation in, 192, 195; construction of crime by Israeli occupiers in, 191; contemporary colonialism in, 190,

Salt Houses (Alyan) *(continued)*
221n3; crimes against humanity in, 185, 190; crime's power to divide and conquer the colonized, 191; critical reception of, 190; Manar's story at conclusion about her return to Jaffa, 195, 221n7; mobility concerns of Yacoub family, 190, 195; multigenerational history of displaced Yacoub family, 189–90; Salma's story in Nablus, 190–91; scattered nature of novel mirroring scattered nature of Palestine and its diaspora, 196; Souad's move to Paris and enjoyment of walking, 221n8; story's ability to move forward aided by Yacoubs' family wealth, 190; unexplained death of Mustafa Yacoub while in Israeli jail, 190, 192, 195; Western readers as intended audience for, 196

Saturday (McEwan), 15, 20, 23–35; anxiety over crime in, 28; Blair mistaking Perowne in, 29–30; cathartic crime in, 23, 34–35, 47; climatic scene of Perowne medically treating home invader Baxter, 32–34; communitarianism in, 34; compared to Joyce's "The Dead," 34; compared to Joyce's *Ulysses*, 30, 213n1; compared to Smith's *NW*, 35–38, 45, 46; compared to Woolf's *Mrs. Dalloway*, 24–25, 30, 32, 213n5; crime occurring after travel in, 23; critical reception of, 26–27, 31–32; "Dover Beach" recitation, 31, 32, 213n10; everyday events with larger political meanings in, 30; home invasion in, 15, 28–29, 31; imperial gaze in, 33; imperial legacies critiqued in, 26–27; individualism and privatization of life in, 27–28, 32, 34; insurmountable gulf between classes in, 33; Iraq invasion (2003) in, 24–26, 28, 30; London as criminal city in, 22, 23, 25, 27, 30, 32, 35; McEwan's relationship to his protagonist Perowne, 26–27, 33; mobility in, 20, 46; neo-imperialism of, 23, 32, 35; neoliberal politics of, 26, 30, 32–33, 35; the Other in, 29, 33; Perowne (protagonist) as bland, checked-out neoliberal in, 24, 27; Perowne's view from his window, 25, 213n2, 215n18; twenty-four hour period of plot, 24–25, 34, 46; unreliable and untrustworthy narrator (Perowne) in, 29, 35; utopic vision of city in, 25; war crime (Iraq war) vs. personal criminal encounter, 28

Schmidt, William E., vii

Schwartz, Alexandra, 36

Schwarz, Bill, 41

Scott, David: *Conscripts of Modernity*, 107, 123, 157, 167, 169, 172, 175–76, 192, 208; *Omens of Adversity*, 101, 114, 123, 148, 181, 210

Scott, Kim. See *That Deadman Dance* (Scott)

Secret River, The (Grenville), 16, 74, 80–90; cathartic crime not possible in, 83, 88, 89–90; cohesive society of white settlers in Australia, 83–84; "colonial equivocation" in, 87, 217n11; compared to Scott's *That Deadman Dance*, 92, 96; critical reception of, 80, 82, 87–89, 96; Grenville's assumption that reader will be white, 87, 88; Grenville's desire for reader to empathize with Thornhill, 86; Grenville's personal background as genesis for, 80–81, 216n10; guilt for the past while ignoring complexities of the present, 81, 87, 89–90, 97; hoped-for reconciliation unachievable in, 88–89; impossible task of "double apology" in, 87; interaction of capital and race in, 83–84; metaphor of decolonization and, 81, 87; origins of Sydney in, 82, 86; raid on Aboriginal people for white settlers to acquire more land, 85; Scott commenting on, 96; "settler moves to innocence" signature in, 87; social rise of Thornhill with associated privilege and power, 83–86; "sorry novel" genre of, 82, 88–89, 216n9; white catharsis as goal of, 81, 87, 88; white colonists' unease at benefiting from crimes against Aboriginal peoples, 83–84, 86; white narcissism in, 81, 83, 87, 96; white privilege displayed by Grenville in discussing, 89, 216n10

Segal, Eyal, 212n5

sense of place, 17, 38–40, 44–45, 122, 146, 194

sexual harassment of women, 57–60

Sharon, Ariel, 222n10

Shehadeh, Raja, *Palestinian Walks*, 179–80, 182, 186

Sheller, Mimi, 11, 23, 198, 206, 208–9

shock theory, 14, 111, 218n15

Siddiqi, Yumna, *Anxieties of Empire and the Fiction of Intrigue*, 14, 107, 212n8

Six Day War (Israel), 182, 191

slavery, ix; brutality of British trade in Africa, 155; disparities in crime and sentencing building on, 14; linkage with imperial infrastructure in Africa, 152; Rhys's *Wide Sargasso Sea* raising questions on, 6

Smith, Zadie. *See NW* (Smith)

social programs: British rollback of, 21–22, 33–34, 44, 213n6; neoliberalism's rejection of, 129

Soja, Edward W.: *Postmodern Geographies: The Reassertion of Space in Critical Social Theory*, 11; *Seeking Spatial Justice*, ix, 78, 129

"sorry novel" genre: Grenville's *The Secret River* and, 82, 88–89, 216n9; Scott's *That Deadman Dance* and, 90

South Africa. *See* apartheid; Johannesburg; *Welcome to Our Hillbrow* (Mpe); *Zoo City* (Beukes)

Soviet Union. *See* communism

Spence, Lester K., 146

Spivak, Gayatri Chakravorty, 11–12

statelessness, 176, 187, 197, 200

St. John, Pete, "The Fields of Athenry" (song), 73–74, 77

subaltern populations: cathartic crime in postcolonial novels benefiting, 7; as targets of crime, 3. *See also* Other, the

Sydney: as criminal city, 15–16, 74, 83, 86, 90; origins of, 82, 86; unfinished colonial projects in contemporary city of, 90. *See also Secret River, The* (Grenville)

Sykes-Picot Agreement (1916), 178, 183, 198–200, 222n5

teleology: Burns's *Milkman* and, 56, 58; catharsis and, 60; crime in literature and, 7, 20; Enlightenment roots of teleological thinking, 12, 39, 100, 209; failure of Western teleological thinking, 101, 107, 114, 121, 167, 176, 181, 208; and name change from Bombay to Mumbai, 100–101; novel's role in, 5, 209; Smith's *NW* and, 38, 46

Thackeray, Bal, 103

Tharoor, Shashi, 12, 102, 198, 217n7

Thatcher, Margaret: neoliberalism of, 23, 27; Northern Ireland speeches by, 53–54, 63, 65; on rise in crime linked to loss of family responsibility, 20–23, 35; upwardly mobile aspirations in Thatcherite Britain, 38

That Deadman Dance (Scott), 16, 74, 80, 90–96; Albany as criminal city, 15–16, 74, 92, 93; arrest of Bobby for act of self-defense and tribal honor, 94; Bobby (Aboriginal man) telling story of white invaders, 91; Bobby's dance not understood by white audience, 94–95; cathartic crime possible in, 96–97; compared to Grenville's *The Secret River*, 92, 96; cooperative relationship in early days of colonial settlement, 91–92; crime of colonialism and colonial law of crime in, 92, 95; critical reception of, 95; dialectic and language differences between European and Aboriginal peoples in, 93–94; mourning loss created by historical injustice, 91, 96; not a story of hope, 95–96; purpose of Scott to bring attention to regenerative community work, 95; racial contract's adoption in, 90–91, 93; "sorry novel" genre and, 90; urban growth and concept of private property in, 93–94

Thompson, Jon, *Fiction, Crime, and Empire: Clues to Modernity and Postmodernism*, 13

Tickell, Alex, 102

Tiffin, Helen, 75

Toal, Catherine, 59

Tolentino, Jia, 201

Tomlinson, Sally, 205

Tonkin, Boyd, 36

tragedy, 3, 86, 171, 175, 181, 192

transnational imperialism and criminal city, 169–70, 175, 176

transport: Chinese investment in African railroad projects, 220n15; as colonial priority, 152; forced transportation of convicts to Australia, 74–75; privatization of individual car and driver, 17, 23, 28, 38, 151; railways in Kenya, 151–52, 155–56, 159, 176, 220n15. *See also* mobility; public transportation

Troubles, the (1968-98), 15; Belfast's depiction in literature dealing with, 59, 69; bombing of Baltic Exchange, 215n18; Burns's *Milkman* and, 55–56; colonial roots of, 52, 72; Divis Tower and killing of Patrick Rooney, 50–51; erasure of community memory of, 65–66; Good Friday Agreement (1998), 48–49, 52, 53, 60, 64, 71, 215n3; human essentialism in texts of, 57; lack of closure, 72; male-domination of fiction on, 59–60; problems in novelistic portrayals of, 54–55; reparation moneys invested in Northern Ireland, 62; seeking catharsis from, 66; Wilson's *Eureka Street* set in, 48–49. *See also Truth Commissioner, The* (Park); *Twelve, The* (Neville)

Trump, Donald: inciting nativism, 204; inciting panics against immigrants, 201

Truth Commissioner, The (Park), 15, 51, 67–71; cathartic crime not possible in, 51, 68, 70–71; characterization of the Troubles in, 68; critical reception of, 71; Irish stereotyped as primitive in, 68, 69, 71; mediating on nature of truth, 67; murder of Connor Walshe, investigation of, 67, 70; refusal of Belfast to let go of the past, 70; South African Truth and Reconciliation process training in, 68; Truth Commission's building burning down with all relevant documents, 70–71; Truth Commission's failure to understand roots of crime and violence, 67, 69–71; wish for dead to stay dead, 69–70

Truth Commissions. *See Truth Commissioner, The* (Park)

Tuck, Eve, 77, 81, 87, 88–89

Twelve, The (Neville), 15, 51, 61–67; cathartic crime in, 51, 61, 62, 71; compared to Wilson's *Eureka Street*, 66; continuing imperialism and neocolonialism in, 62, 66, 67; critical reception of, 62; erasure of community memory in, 65–66; failure to link individual actions to a larger cause, 71; Fegan on avenging tour against those who ordered him to kill ghost-victims, 61, 62–64; former IRA members turned into capitalist investors, 61–62; gentrification in, 65; global capitalism in, 62, 64–65; IRA hitman Fegan released from prison and haunted by ghosts of those he killed, 61, 62–65; legacy of colonialism and the Troubles in, 61–62, 64; neoliberalism's desire to forget the Troubles and, 67; political vs. ordinary crime in, 63–65, 69; reinvention of former IRA members in, 61–62, 65

Umrigar, Thirty. *See World We Found, The* (Umrigar)

Unconscious, the, 4–5

United Nations project on urban population in 2050, 11

United States: as contemporary colonial power in Palestine, 180–81, 184; manifest destiny as form of Western imperialism, 209

unjust city design, 12

urban planning: in Australia, 78–79, 91, 94; in Israel, 179, 187; as planned violence, 17, 91, 179, 187

U2, "Van Diemen's Land" (song), 74, 77

Varma, Rashmi, 105, 109, 217n10; *The Postcolonial City and Its Subjects*, 162–63

Victorians, 13, 76

violence: blamed on primitive people in Park's *The Truth Commissioner*, 68, 69, 71; bombing apocalypse planned in Chandra's *Sacred Games*, 118, 120; Eide on violent crime, 6; gender-based violence in Burns's *Milkman*, 55–61, 71; hate crimes, 3, 204; Hindu/Muslim riots (Bombay, 1992–93), 100, 104, 110, 218n12; incomprehensible violence in Belfast, 48–49, 54; Kenya, inter-ethnic violence and tribal tensions in (1980s and 1990s), 167, 172; mugging perceived to be a "black crime," 214n17; revenge killing in Mukoma's *Nairobi Heat*, 169; Rhys's *Wide Sargasso Sea* linking to colonial slavery, 6; sameness on both sides of political divide committing, 54–55, 66; state-instituted, 10; Thatcher's incitement of, 23; Wilson's *Eureka Street* describing bomb explosion, 48–49. *See also* Mau Mau guerilla war; murder; Troubles, the

Vladislavić, Ivan, *The Restless Supermarket*, 124–26, 130, 131, 150

war crimes, 28, 179
War on Terror, 222n10
Watt, Ian, 13
Welcome to Our Hillbrow (Mpe), 16, 126, 130, 131, 140–50; apartheid's legacies in, 142–44; cathartic crime in, 131, 141, 148; compared to Beukes's *Zoo City*, 140, 143, 144–45, 147, 148; consequences of inattention to urban planning, 143; criminal city in, 146, 150; critical reception of, 140, 142, 144, 147; Heaven's presentation as community without prejudices, 145, 147–49; Hillbrow as liveable, companionable neighborhood, 146; immigrants (*Makwerekwere*) blamed for crime and subject to discrimination, 143–44, 200; imperial legacies in, 142, 143, 148; neoliberal system in, 143, 146–48; open cosmopolitanism in, 147; personal catharsis for way to reparate, 150; as post-apartheid map of Hillbrow, 140, 142; postcolonial possibilities in, 150; racialized ideas about crime, 143–44; reconciliation in, 148, 150; Refentše's suicide and its relation to apartheid-era suicides, 144, 145; Refilwe returning to Hillbrow as *Makwerekwere*, 149; Refilwe's exit from Hillbrow to study at Oxford, 145, 148; Refilwe's welcome into Heaven at conclusion, 149; refuting claims of Johannesburg as unmanageable, 146; return to Hillbrow by both Refentše and Refilwe, 145, 148–49; second-person narration drawing reader into, 140, 141, 146, 148

welfare capitalism. *See* social programs
Welsh, David, 128
West Bank. *See* Palestine; *Salt Houses* (Alyan)
white feminism, 76
white supremacy, 23, 216n8; in Australia, 79; racial contract and, 79–80, 90–91, 93. *See also* apartheid; racism
Williams, Raymond, 21, 82
Wilson, Robert McLiam. See *Eureka Street* (Wilson)

Windrush Generation (Caribbean immigrants to Britain), 214n17
Wolfe, Patrick, 79
Woolf, Virginia. See *Mrs. Dalloway* (Woolf)
World We Found, The (Umrigar), 16, 101, 108–15; Adish enabling escape of Nishta from her Muslim husband (Iqbal), 112–13; cathartic crime not possible in, 114; collapse of communist movement in, 108, 111, 114; critical reception of, 107; female college friends' reunion as failure in parallel to original postcolonial failure and socialism's failure, 113–14; Hindu nationalism's rise in, 111; inequality in Indian life in, 111, 112, 115; Iqbal denied catharsis in, 113; legacy of colonial crimes in, 107, 112–14; loss of socialist future in, 112, 114; neoliberal economic policy in, 109, 111, 113, 114, 119; Nishta's marriage to conservative Muslim (Iqbal), 109; protests of late 1970s in Bombay leading to arrest of some characters, 108–9, 112; riots of 1992–93 in Bombay, 109–10, 112, 218n12; shattering of Muslim world in Bombay, 110; transportation cojoined with crime in, 113; transportation linked with catharsis in, 113; xenophobia and racism in, 110–13

Yang, K. Wayne, 77, 81, 87, 88–89
Yeats, William Butler, "The Second Coming" (poem), 166
Young, Robert, ix, 12, 213n12

Zionist movements, 178, 183–84, 187, 221n4
Zoo City (Beukes), 16, 126, 130, 131–39; animal familiars in, 131–33, 135–36, 219n2; capitalist hyperconsumption in, 134; cathartic crime in, 131–33, 139; class in, 132, 134–35; compared to Mpe's *Welcome to Our Hillbrow*, 140, 143, 144–45, 147, 148; criminality replacing racism in, 133–36, 138; critical reception of, 132, 134, 138, 139; Johannesburg as criminal city in, 132, 138–39; language of post-apartheid city remaining same as in apartheid era, 132–33; legacies of apartheid and imperialism in, 134–36; missing person case of Songweza mirroring real-life *muti* murders, 136–37; murderers eluding punishment for their actions, 138–39; neoliberal system in, 134–35, 138; postcolonial possibilities in, 150; readers urged to become detectives in, 139; rejection of city when Zinzi leaves to travel through Africa, 139, 145; science fiction story in dystopic Johannesburg to highlight crime in the real contemporary city, 131, 138; Zinzi December (protagonist) working in black market and internet scams, 131–32, 133–34, 135, 147; Zoo City representing post-apartheid segregated Hillbrow, 132, 133

CULTURAL FRAMES, FRAMING CULTURE

Skimpy Coverage: Sports Illustrated and the Shaping of the Female Athlete
BONNIE M. HAGERMAN

Institutional Character: Collectivity, Agency, and the Modernist Novel
ROBERT HIGNEY

*Walk the Barrio: The Streets of Twenty-First-
Century Transnational Latinx Literature*
CRISTINA RODRIGUEZ

*Fashioning Character: Style, Performance, and Identity
in Contemporary American Literature*
LAUREN S. CARDON

Neoliberal Nonfictions: The Documentary Aesthetic from Joan Didion to Jay-Z
DANIEL WORDEN

Dandyism: Forming Fiction from Modernism to the Present
LEN GUTKIN

Terrible Beauty: The Violent Aesthetic and Twentieth-Century Literature
MARIAN EIDE

Women Writers of the Beat Era: Autobiography and Intertextuality
MARY PANICCIA CARDEN

Stranger America: A Narrative Ethics of Exclusion
JOSH TOTH

Fashion and Fiction: Self-Transformation in Twentieth-Century American Literature
LAUREN S. CARDON

American Road Narratives: Reimagining Mobility in Literature and Film
ANN BRIGHAM

The Arresting Eye: Race and the Anxiety of Detection
JINNY HUH

Failed Frontiersmen: White Men and Myth in the Post-Sixties American Historical Romance
JAMES J. DONAHUE

Composing Cultures: Modernism, American Literary Studies, and the Problem of Culture
ERIC ARONOFF

Quirks of the Quantum: Postmodernism and Contemporary American Fiction
SAMUEL CHASE COALE

Chick Lit and Postfeminism
STEPHANIE HARZEWSKI

American Iconographic: "National Geographic," Global Culture, and the Visual Imagination
STEPHANIE L. HAWKINS

Wanted: The Outlaw in American Visual Culture
RACHEL HALL

Male Armor: The Soldier-Hero in Contemporary American Culture
JON ROBERT ADAMS

African Americans and the Culture of Pain
DEBRA WALKER KING

www.ingramcontent.com/pod-product-compliance
Lightning Source LLC
Chambersburg PA
CBHW031802220426
43662CB00007B/499